PEACE & WAR

THE SCHOOLS HISTORY PROJECT

This project was set up by the Schools Council in 1972. Its main aim was to suggest suitable objectives for History teachers, and to promote the use of appropriate materials and teaching methods for their realisation. This involved a reconsideration of the nature of History and its relevance in secondary schools, the design of a syllabus framework which shows the uses of History in the education of adolescents, and the setting up of appropriate examinations.

Since 1978 the project has been based at Trinity and All Saints' College, Leeds, where it is one of three curriculum development projects run and supported by the Centre for History Education. The project is now self funding and with the advent of the National Curriculum it has expanded its publications to provide courses throughout the Key Stages for pupils aged 5–16. The project provides INSET for all aspects of National Curriculum History.

Series consultants
Tim Lomas
Martin and Jennifer Tucker
Terry Fiehn

Pupils' Book ISBN 0–7195–4977–9
Teachers' Resource Book ISBN 0–7195–4978–7

© Colin Shephard, Andy Reid, Keith Shephard, 1993

First published in 1993
by John Murray (Publishers) Ltd
50 Albemarle Street, London W1X 4BD

Reprinted 1993, 1994, 1995

Typeset by Wearset, Boldon, Tyne & Wear
Printed in Great Britain by Butler & Tanner Ltd, London and Frome

A CIP catalogue record for this book is available from the British Library
ISBN 0–7195–4977–9

S·H·P
THE
SCHOOLS
HISTORY
PROJECT

DISCOVERING THE PAST Y9

PEACE &WAR

Colin Shephard (Director, SHP)
Andy Reid
Keith Shephard

JOHN MURRAY

Contents

N.B. Words in SMALL CAPITALS are explained in the glossary on page 214.

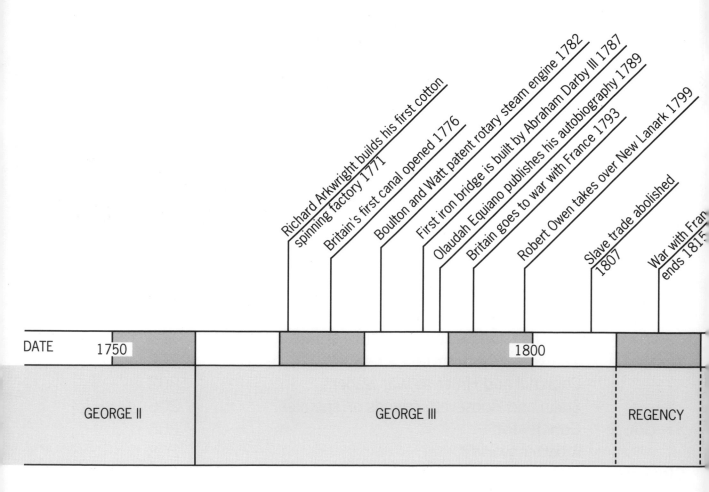

Richard Arkwright builds his first cotton
spinning factory 1771

Britain's first canal opened 1776

Boulton and Watt patent rotary steam engine 1782

First iron bridge is built by Abraham Darby III 1787

Olaudah Equiano publishes his autobiography 1789

Britain goes to war with France 1793

Robert Owen takes over New Lanark 1799

Slave trade abolished
1807

War with Fran
ends 1815

DATE   1750

1800

GEORGE II

GEORGE III

REGENCY

EXPANSION, TRADE & INDUSTRY

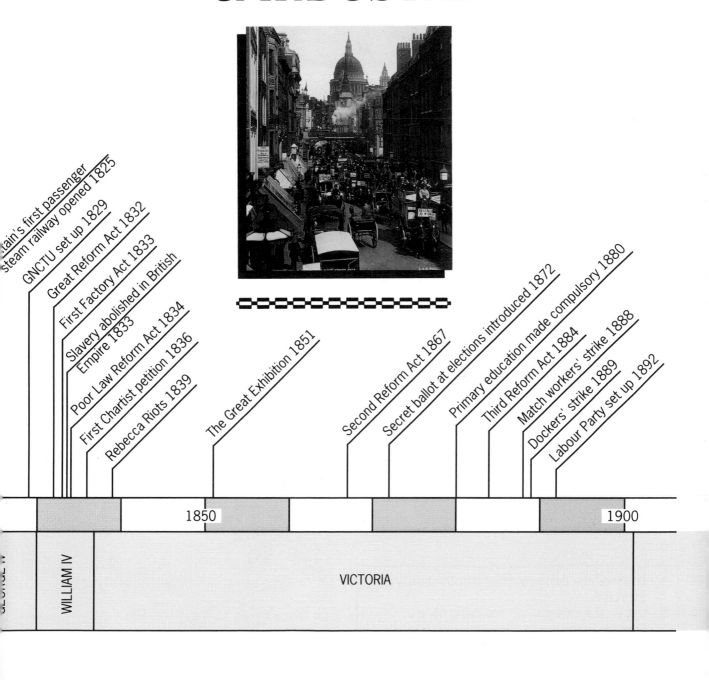

Britain's first passenger steam railway opened 1825

GNCTU set up 1829

Great Reform Act 1832

First Factory Act 1833

Slavery abolished in British Empire 1833

Poor Law Reform Act 1834

First Chartist petition 1836

Rebecca Riots 1839

The Great Exhibition 1851

Second Reform Act 1867

Secret ballot at elections introduced 1872

Primary education made compulsory 1880

Third Reform Act 1884

Match workers' strike 1888

Dockers' strike 1889

Labour Party set up 1892

1850

1900

GEORGE IV

WILLIAM IV

VICTORIA

Britain 1750–1900: what changed?

Population

- **T**OTAL population: about eleven million.
- About 80 per cent of people lived and worked in the countryside.
- Many babies died before their first birthday.
- The annual death rate was 28 deaths per 1000 people.

SOURCE 1 Major cities and industries in 1750

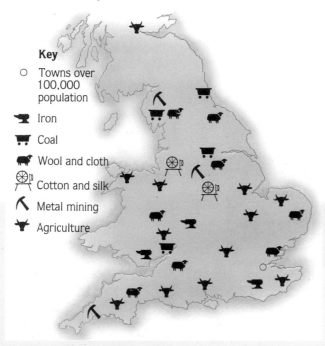

Key

- ○ Towns over 100,000 population
- Iron
- Coal
- Wool and cloth
- Cotton and silk
- Metal mining
- Agriculture

SOURCE 2 A contemporary engraving of Leeds, a market town, in the early eighteenth century

Health and medicine

- People did not know that germs caused disease and could do little to fight diseases like smallpox and diphtheria, which killed many people.
- Only simple operations on patients were possible, because there were no anaesthetics or blood transfusions, and patients often died from infection.

SOURCE 4
Spinning flax at home, an engraving from the 1790s. The woman on the right is reeling the spun thread ready to hand it on to the weaver, who wove it into cloth

Work

- The most important industry was farming – food and wool production in particular.
- All industries were small-scale. Manufacturing was done in people's homes, or in workshops attached to their homes.
- Power to make machines work was provided by water wheels, or by horses, or by human hands or feet.
- Steam power was used to pump water from some mines.

1. Describe the living conditions of the family in Source 4.
2. List all the jobs you can see being done in Sources 3 and 4.

SOURCE 3 An eighteenth-century engraving of a farm yard

Transport

■ Getting around the country was a slow process.
■ People and goods travelled by water if possible – either around the coast or along rivers. Some rivers had been deepened or straightened so boats could use them. The first canal, the Bridgewater Canal, was completed in 1776.
■ Roads were mostly as bad as they had been for centuries, but some were being improved by groups of businessmen called TURNPIKE TRUSTS, who improved a road and then charged people a toll to use it.
■ The journey from London to Edinburgh by boat took a week and by road took ten to twelve days.

SOURCE 6 A turnpike on the outskirts of London in the late eighteenth century

SOURCE 5 A lock on the Regent's Canal in the early nineteenth century

1. Look at Sources 5 and 6. List all the different ways in which horses are being used in these two pictures.

Politics

■ King George II had fewer powers than kings had in the seventeenth century.
■ Parliament made laws for England, Scotland and Wales, but not for Ireland.
■ Only five per cent of the population could vote in elections for the House of Commons. No women were allowed to vote.

Culture

■ Most children in England did not go to school at all and few could read or write.
■ In Scotland all parishes had schools and most people could read and write.
■ There were two universities in England, four in Scotland and one in Ireland.
■ Newspapers, novels and plays were becoming popular.

1. Look at Source 7. Do you think much learning went on in this school? Give reasons for your answer.

SOURCE 7
A nineteenth-century painting of a 'dame school' in the eighteenth century. Children were often sent here to be minded while their parents worked, rather than for an education

1. Divide a page into two, half for 1750 and half for today. Using the different headings on these two pages compare life in 1750 with life today. You can use drawings or writing. You might need to do some research, e.g. for population figures today.
2. Which of the following improvements do you think would be of most benefit for the farmer (Source 3) or the home worker (Source 4) in 1750:
   ■ being able to travel more easily and quickly
   ■ having machines to make work easier
   ■ being allowed to vote in elections?
   Explain your choice.

BRITAIN 1750–1900: WHAT CHANGED?

SOURCE 8 An engraving of Leeds, a factory town, in the mid-nineteenth century

Population

- Total population: about 21 million.
- About 60 per cent of people lived and worked in the countryside.
- Many babies still died in their first year of life, but families were very large.
- The annual death rate was 22 deaths per 1000 people.

Work

- Many people still worked in small workshops, but some industries were now based in factories, where the machines were driven by steam engines.
- The cotton industry was now bigger and more important than the wool industry.
- Since 1750 coal production had tripled, and iron production had increased by ten times.
- Farmers were growing more food than in 1750.
- Common grazing land or waste land in many villages had been successfully turned into land to grow crops.
- New crops and new farming methods were being tried out by farmers all over the country.

Key Towns over
- o 100,000 population
- 🛒 Coal
- Iron
- 🐑 Wool and cloth
- ⚙ Cotton and silk
- 🔨 Metal mining
- 🐂 Agriculture

SOURCE 9 Major cities and industries in 1825

1. Look at Source 10. Can you see:
   - the wheel to drive the machinery
   - the foremen to make sure people work hard?

Health and medicine

- A vaccination had been developed for smallpox, but there were no other vaccinations or drugs because people still did not know that germs caused disease.
- So many people were crowded into towns like Leeds or Glasgow that killer diseases such as cholera, typhoid and tuberculosis spread rapidly because of infected water, dirty living conditions and poor diet.

SOURCE 10 Children working in the winding room of a cotton mill in 1820

SOURCE 11 A farm worker's cottage. The majority of people in Britain still lived in the countryside, in homes like these, in 1825

Transport

■ There were now 20,000 miles of well surfaced turnpike roads.
■ Many canals had been built. A network of waterways linked the most important industrial areas.
■ In mining areas horse-drawn trams and waggons that ran on rails were used.
■ The first steam railway was transporting coal and passengers from Stockton to Darlington.
■ The journey from London to Edinburgh took three to five days by boat and 46 hours by road.

Politics

■ Five per cent of the population could vote in elections for the House of Commons, but women were not allowed to vote.
■ Most of Britain's new growing cities were not allowed to elect their own MPs.
■ Demands for 'parliamentary reform' were made at large meetings. At a political meeting held in Manchester in 1819 to demand reform of Parliament, troops killed eleven people. This event is known as the 'Peterloo Massacre'.

SOURCE 13 A contemporary painting of the opening of the Stockton to Darlington Railway, 1825

Culture

■ Most middle-class and upper-class boys (but not many girls) went to school.
■ Elementary schools in England provided education for the children of the poor if they wanted to attend. Many did not.
■ No new universities had been set up since 1750.
■ There was a new interest in religion, especially among the middle and lower classes.

SOURCE 14 A 'ragged school' in London in the mid-nineteenth century. Ragged schools for the poor were set up by charities in some areas

SOURCE 12 A cartoon called *A Court for King Cholera,* published in the mid-nineteenth century

1. Choose three categories. For each one describe what changed between 1750 and 1825.
2. Of all the six categories, which one saw the most change between 1750 and 1825?
3. In what ways were people's lives getting better? In what ways were they not?

Population

- Total population: about 40 million.
- The population of England had risen at a rapid rate since 1825. In Scotland and Wales population was also rising, but more slowly than in England. The population of Ireland had actually fallen owing to a dreadful famine and the emigration that followed it.
- In England about 75 per cent of people lived in towns. Huge urban areas had developed.
- The annual death rate had fallen to eighteen deaths per 1000 people and the birth rate was now falling as well.

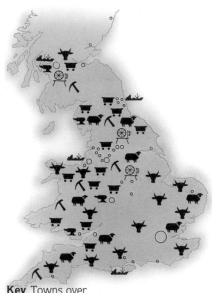

Key Towns over
- o 100,000 population
- 🛒 Coal
- Iron
- 🐑 Wool and cloth
- ⊕ Cotton and silk
- ⋀ Metal mining
- 🐂 Agriculture
- Shipbuilding

SOURCE 15 Major cities and industries in 1900

Health and medicine

- Louis Pasteur had discovered that germs cause diseases. This led to vaccinations being developed for diphtheria and other diseases.
- Anaesthetics and antiseptics were developed, which made more complicated operations possible.
- Local councils began to improve water supplies and sewers to improve the health of people in towns.

SOURCE 18 Working-class housing in Leeds in 1901

Work

- Many farmers now used machines, although the machines were still mostly horse-powered.
- Industry was dominated by coal, iron, steel and textiles (cloth).
- Steam power had been introduced into most industries, even in small factories and workshops.

SOURCE 16
An engraving of threshing by steam engine in the late nineteenth century. Corn was fed into the top of the machine and grain poured out of the bottom into sacks

SOURCE 17
A steel works at Barrow-in-Furness in the late nineteenth century

Transport

- Railways served all parts of Britain. They helped to make Britain more united.
- Many canal companies and turnpike trusts had been driven out of business. The railways were a faster method of transport than canals or roads for both passengers and goods.
- The journey from London to Edinburgh took 30 hours by boat, at least 46 hours by road and nine hours by train.
- Bicycles were a common sight and cars had been invented – although they were not allowed to go faster than fourteen miles per hour.

Culture

■ School was compulsory for all five- to twelve-year-olds, both boys and girls.
■ Many more people could read and write.
■ There were ten universities in England, five in Scotland, one in Ireland and one in Wales.
■ Newspaper and book publishing was expanding.

SOURCE 19 A photograph of a council school in 1908

Politics

■ Most men could now vote, but women could not.
■ Parliament included many MPs from the growing industrial towns and fewer from country areas.
■ The government in London and local authorities now played a large part in everyone's life. They had improved living and working conditions.

1. Using the figures on pages 2–7, draw a graph showing how a) Britain's population, and b) the death rate in Britain, changed between 1750 and 1900.

Now, working in pairs, look back over pages 2–7.

2. In which category was there most change between 1750 and 1825? In which category was there least change?
3. Now look at the period between 1825 and 1900. Which category saw most change? Which category saw least change?
4. Now look at the period 1750–1900 as a whole. Which category saw most change?
5. Why do you think there was more change there?
6. Of all the changes mentioned on pages 2–7 which do you think was the most important? Give reasons for your choice. See if other people in the class agree with you.
7. When would you rather have lived: 1750, 1825 or 1900?

SOURCE 20
An architect's cross-section through the Victoria Embankment in London around 1900, showing water and gas mains (1), telegraph cables, a sewer (2) and the new Metropolitan underground railway (3)

SOURCE 21 An express train in 1897

Why did businesses grow?

BUSINESSES come in many different sizes. Look at Sources 1–3, which all show businesses that were doing well in the nineteenth century.

1. Which business do you think employs most people?
2. Roughly how many people do you think work in each business?
3. What machinery do you think is used in each business?

SOURCE 1 A photograph of an ice-cream man in the 1890s

SOURCE 2
A fish and poultry shop in 1900. The people posing for the photograph are the shop owner and the shop assistant

SOURCE 3 A nineteenth-century drawing of an iron foundry

Factor 1: the market grows
More people want to buy what the business sells, because:
■ the population is increasing
■ people have more money spend
■ the business takes its products to new places where they have not been sold before, so that people over a larger area can buy them
■ the business advertises its products
■ the business cuts its prices, so that more people can afford its products.

Factor 2: production grows
The business produces more, because:
■ suppliers of RAW MATERIALS improve their extraction methods so that raw materials are cheaper or better and available in larger quantities
■ transport improves, so raw materials are cheaper and the supply is more reliable
■ the business takes on more workers, and builds bigger buildings for them to work in
■ the business trains its workers so that they can produce things more efficiently
■ the business uses new technology to produce goods faster.

Factor 3: investment grows
The business has more money to INVEST because:
■ banks or other businesses lend it to them
■ individuals who have money to spare invest it in the business in the hope of making big profits and improving their lifestyle or status
■ the business makes profits.

SOURCE 4 The story of Josiah Wedgwood's pottery business at Etruria in Staffordshire

Josiah Wedgwood started work as a potter aged nine.

He saved £20 and set up his own business aged 28. He hired the best workers and worked them hard.

He produced good pottery at low prices. People flocked to buy it.

Yet all the finest pottery, the kind that the rich wanted, was still imported. Wedgwood thought that he could compete there too.

It's the best there is.

POTTERY FROM CHINA

He was a great inventor. He invented new machines and new glazes which he kept secret from his rivals.

He produced high quality fine china.

He built a new factory next to a canal, to cut transport costs and to carry his fine china safely around Britain and Europe.

He reinvested his profits in better factories and a fine village for his workers.

He opened a new shop in London. The King and Queen bought his china.

1. Find something in your home, your school or nearby which was made in the nineteenth century.
2. Try to work out where it was made and what materials were used in making it.
3. Make a class display of nineteenth-century products.

The Darbys of Coalbrookdale

Why Coalbrookdale?

IN THE 1700s Coalbrookdale in Shropshire became the centre of a flourishing new iron industry. It had a history of iron making, but only on a small scale.

---

1. Using Sources 1 and 2 explain why Coalbrookdale was a good place to make iron.

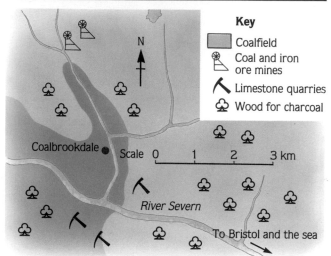

Key
- ▢ Coalfield
- ⚙ Coal and iron ore mines
- ⛏ Limestone quarries
- ♣ Wood for charcoal

SOURCE 1 The area around Coalbrookdale in 1700

SOURCE 2 Iron making in 1700

Abraham Darby I

Around 1700 Abraham Darby was working in Bristol, making brass cooking pots. However, these pots were rather expensive for poor people to buy. Darby had worked out a way of making cheaper pots out of cast iron and he thought that there would be a big market for them. All Darby needed was a regular supply of cast iron.

However, at that time the iron industry had problems. There was not enough charcoal for the furnaces. Coal had been tried instead, but the sulphur in it ruined the iron. Darby thought he had the answer. He knew a lot about the malt industry and how it had replaced coal with coke (coal with the sulphur taken out). Maybe coke could be used for iron making as well.

In 1708 he bought a derelict iron works in Coalbrookdale and tried out his ideas. The cast iron he made was not of a high quality. It couldn't be hammered into different shapes to make tools and machines. But for the cast iron pots it was perfect. The demand in Britain and in America was enormous. Darby's business went from strength to strength.

---

1. Give each of the following factors a mark out of ten for its importance in Darby's success:
   - knowledge of the market
   - new technology and ideas
   - luck
   - finding a good location.
   Write a sentence to explain each mark.

Abraham Darby II

Thirty years later Abraham Darby's son took over the business. He made a big breakthrough by improving the quality of the cast iron. Now it could be hammered into shape for tools and machinery. For the first time, coke-produced iron was as good as iron smelted by charcoal. What's more, it was much cheaper, and it could be produced in much larger quantities. Darby could sell all the iron he could produce.

Darby also borrowed huge amounts of money to pay for improvements at Coalbrookdale.
- He built six new blast furnaces.
- He bought up the local iron ore and coal mines.
- He built a horse-powered tramway from the mines to the furnaces and the river. Each waggon carried as much as twenty horses had done before.
- He used steam pumps to pump water to the water wheels which fired his furnaces. His furnaces could run all year – even when the river was low. Darby was the first iron maker to use steam pumps.

SOURCE 3 A painting of Coalbrookdale by François Vivares, 1758

1. Describe in detail what you can see happening in Source 3.
2. Do you think Source 3 gives a realistic impression of Coalbrookdale?

Abraham Darby III

Abraham Darby III took over the business in the 1770s. As the business grew he needed to attract more workers. So he took various measures. At a time of food shortages he bought up local farms to grow food for his workers. He paid higher wages than workers could earn in nearby potteries, farms or mines. He built good houses for his workers.

However, Darby III's real success was in making Coalbrookdale itself famous. He built an iron bridge over the river Severn – the first of its kind in the world. He used it to advertise the uses of iron. Artists, engineers and sightseers came to Coalbrookdale to see this 'wonder of the modern world'.

SOURCE 4 A Coalport jug showing the iron bridge, 1856

Activity

The Darbys borrowed a lot of money to finance their business.

Work in threes. Choose one Darby each. Write a letter from 'your' Darby to a partner who might lend you money. Explain what ideas you have for making the business successful, and why he or she should invest in it.

In your letter make sure you cover the three factors mentioned on page 8:
■ increasing the market for your product
■ increasing your production
■ increasing the amount of money you INVEST in your business.

Compare the three letters. What are the similarities and differences from generation to generation? Was the secret of the Darbys' success the same in each case?

11

What made Richard Arkwright successful?

Richard Arkwright's story

RICHARD Arkwright was born in 1732. His father was a tailor in Lancashire.

Coming from a tailor's family, Arkwright knew a lot about the cloth industry. He knew that weaving had been speeded up by a new invention called the 'flying shuttle' in 1733. He also knew that spinning was still a slow process. There was plenty of cotton being imported, but spinners could not turn it into yarn quickly enough to supply the speeded up weavers. Arkwright could see the importance of speeding up spinning as well. In the 1760s he began to work on an invention that might do it.

Other inventors were doing the same. James Hargreaves invented the 'spinning jenny' in 1764. It was powered by hand. Using a 'jenny', a single spinner could produce eight threads at once. However, it was a complicated machine to work, and the thin thread which it produced was not very strong.

By 1768 Arkwright had perfected his own spinning machine (see Source 3). Unlike the 'jenny', it couldn't be operated by hand – it was so heavy that it took horse power to drive it. Nor could it produce the high-quality thread that the 'jenny' produced. However, it was much simpler to operate and the thick thread it produced was much stronger.

Arkwright wanted to set up a factory to use his spinning machine. He also wanted to protect his invention by a 'patent' (this would mean that anyone else who wanted to use it would have to get his permission and pay him). But to get a patent and to set up a factory he needed money. So he went into partnership with two merchants and two stocking manufacturers in Nottingham. In 1769 they helped him buy a patent for fourteen years, and to set up his 'spinning frame' in a factory in Nottingham. It was powered by horses walking round and round in a circle.

The spinning frame could also be driven by a water wheel. In 1771, Arkwright and his partners built a cotton spinning mill at Cromford in Derbyshire. The water wheel was turned by a fast flowing stream which had been built to drain the local lead mines. The spinning frame now became known as the 'water frame'.

In 1750 spinning was usually done in the home. Weaving was often done in a small workshop where there was room for several looms. This was known as the Domestic System

A spinning wheel turns cotton, flax or wool into yarn or thread. Spinning was usually done by women

A weaving loom turns the yarn into cloth. Weaving was usually done by men

SOURCE 1 Spinning and weaving in 1750

Activity

You have been asked to write an advertisement for thread produced by the 'spinning frame'. Write a short advertisement describing its advantages over thread produced by the 'spinning jenny'.

The water frame was very successful. Several more machines were installed in the factory and then more mills were built, at Cromford and around Britain.

Arkwright's factories made lots of money. His ideas were copied by many MANUFACTURERS in Britain and in other countries. Arkwright tried to make these people pay him to use his invention and he became very unpopular. His patents were also challenged. Some people claimed that he had 'borrowed' his ideas from other inventors. But Arkwright also became very rich. He bought a country estate and built himself a large mansion. When Arkwright died in 1792 his fortune was worth about half a million pounds.

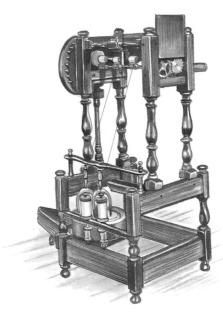

SOURCE 3 Arkwright's spinning frame

SOURCE 4 Written by Viscount Torrington in his diary, 1790

I saw the workers issue forth at seven o'clock [in the evening], a wonderful crowd of young people . . . a new set then goes in for the night, for the mills never leave off working . . .

These cotton mills, seven storeys high, and filled with inhabitants, remind me of a first rate man of war [a fighting ship]; and when they are lighted up, on a dark night, look most beautiful.

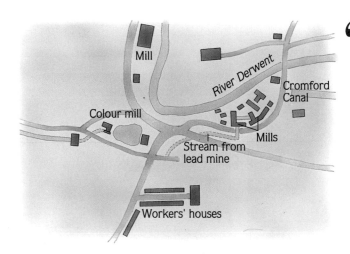

SOURCE 2 Plan of Cromford

1. Draw a timeline for the period 1730–1800. Study Arkwright's story on this page and mark on your timeline the important stages in the development of Arkwright's business.
2. Compare Sources 2 and 5. Can you work out whereabouts on the map the artist of Source 5 was standing when he drew the picture?

What were Arkwright's mills like?

In the DOMESTIC SYSTEM most workers worked at home. At Cromford they worked in specially built factories. People reacted in different ways to these new mills.

SOURCE 5 Illustration of the first Cromford mill from the *Mirror* magazine, 1836

SOURCE 6 From a tourist guide to Derbyshire, published in 1939

. . . The fortress-like appearance of the old mills suggests that the inventors feared attack.

WHAT MADE RICHARD ARKWRIGHT SUCCESSFUL?

SOURCE 7 Cromford mills, painted in 1789 by Joseph Wright of Derby. He was an artist who painted many pictures of industry

SOURCE 8 A photograph of Cromford mills today

1. Choose one of Sources 5, 7 and 8, and write a paragraph describing the scene it shows. Describe the building in as much detail as you can.
2. Show your description to another person in the class and see if they can work out which picture you are describing.
3. Explain in your own words the different impressions that Sources 4 and 6 give of Cromford mills.
4. Which of these impressions is supported most by Sources 5, 7 and 8?
5. Suggest reasons why these sources give different impressions of the mills.

Why was Arkwright successful?

SOURCE 9 Adapted from the diary of Sylas Neville, an eighteenth-century traveller, written in 1781

Arkwright appears to be a man of great understanding. He knows how to make people do their best. He not only rewards them, but gives special clothes to the most successful men and women, which makes people want to copy them.

He also gives two balls at the Greyhound [a hotel in Cromford, built by Arkwright] to the workmen and their wives and families with a week's holiday at the time of each ball. This makes them hardworking and sober all the rest of the year.

SOURCE 10 Written by Matthew Boulton, a successful businessman, in a letter to his partner, James Watt, in 1781

Arkwright swears he will take the cotton spinning abroad, and that he will ruin those Manchester Rascals [who had used his invention without his permission]. It is agreed by all who know him that he is a Tyrant.

SOURCE 11 Written by another successful businessman, Josiah Wedgwood, in a letter to James Watt in 1785

Mr Arkwright . . . invites me to come and see him as often as I can, although he tells me he at present shuns [avoids] all company because it robs him of his time and breaks in upon his plans. And besides, he is no company for people who visit him, for whilst they are talking to him upon one subject he is thinking upon another, and does not know what they say to him.

SOURCE 12 Written by Viscount Torrington in his diary, 1790

66 *The landlord of the Greyhound Hotel has a grand assortment of prizes, from Sir R. Arkwright, to be given at the year's end to such bakers, butchers, etc, as shall have best supplied the market . . .*

They show Sir Richard's prudence and cunning; for without ready supplies, Cromford could not prosper . . . 99

SOURCE 13 Written by a painter, Joseph Farington, in his diary in 1801 about child workers at Richard Arkwright's mills at Cromford

66 *In the evening I walked to Cromford, and saw the children coming from their work . . . I was glad to see them look in general very healthy, many with fine, rosy complexions.*

These children had been at work from six or seven o'clock this morning and it was now near seven in the evening. The time for resting allowed them is at twelve o'clock 40 minutes, during which time they dine.

One boy of ten or eleven years of age told me his wages were 3s 6d a week – and a little girl told me her wages were 2s 3d a week . . .

These children are employed in Mr Arkwright's works in the week days, and on Sundays attend a school where they receive education. They came to chapel in regular order and looked healthy and well and were decently clothed and clean . . . 99

SOURCE 14 Written by the historian Edward Baines in his *History of Cotton Manufacture in Great Britain*, published in 1835

66 *That he might not waste a moment Arkwright generally travelled with four horses, and at a very rapid speed.*

His businesses in Derbyshire, Lancashire and Scotland were so extensive and numerous as to show at once his astonishing power of doing business and his all-grasping spirit.

In many of these businesses he had partners, but he generally managed in such a way that whoever lost, he himself was a gainer.

So unbounded was his confidence in the success of his machinery, and in the national wealth to be produced by it, that he would say that he would pay off the government's debt. 99

SOURCE 15 Written by a historian, T.S. Ashton, in his book *The Industrial Revolution*, published in 1948

66 *Although he did not have any great inventive ability, Arkwright had the character and robust sense that are traditionally associated with his native county – with little, it may be added, of the kindliness and humour that are, in fact, the dominant traits of Lancashire people.* 99

SOURCE 16 Written by a historian, E.J. Hobsbawm, in *Industry and Empire*, published in 1968

66 *The water frame was not the original idea of the man who patented it, Richard Arkwright, an unscrupulous operator who – unlike most real inventors of the period – became very rich.* 99

1. Using sources 9–16, draw up a list of five words to describe Arkwright's character.
2. Which aspects of his character were most important to his success as a businessman?
3. Look closely at the dates of the sources. Arkwright died in 1792. When were Arkwright and his achievements a) most admired, and b) most criticised? Was it:
   ■ in his lifetime
   ■ in the nineteenth century
   ■ in the twentieth century?
4. Why do you think people in these three periods had different views on Arkwright?

1. Under each of the following headings: money, treatment of workers, awareness of markets, and developments in technology, write a paragraph summarising how that factor helped Arkwright to be successful. Refer to the information and evidence on pages 12–15 to support your views.

Activity

It is 1792. You have to write an obituary for Sir Richard Arkwright, who has just died. Use the information and sources on pages 12–15 to describe his life. Include quotations from people who knew him. Try to decide what the most important reason was for Arkwright's success.

Children in the mills

Where did the workers come from?

IF BUSINESSMEN like Richard Arkwright were going to develop their businesses they needed people to work for them. This was a difficult problem. The textile mills were often in remote places by the fast flowing streams which provided the water power. Where did the workers come from?

> 1. Using the information and sources on this page, list the different kinds of people factory owners tried to recruit for their workforce.

Many of the early mill owners employed large numbers of children. This was not shocking. In the DOMESTIC SYSTEM children had worked at home. Some of the children in the mills were 'apprentices'. These children were often orphans, who were sent to the mills by the authorities who looked after them in the large towns. The factory owner agreed to feed and clothe them. They lived in an 'apprentice house' near the mill. Overseers were given the job of making the children work as hard as possible. The more work the children did the more the overseers were paid

Other child workers were the sons and daughters of adult workers. One employer, David Dale (see Source 2) sent advertisements out to the Highland areas of Scotland where there was a lot of poverty and unemployment. He invited whole families to come and work for him. Despite the problems they faced (some spoke only Gaelic), many came. Dale provided housing for families if they had more than three children who could work in the mills. By 1793, 1157 people were working at New Lanark. Of these, 795 were children (68 per cent of the workforce): 275 – mainly apprentices from Edinburgh and Glasgow – lived in the mills themselves; 103 came from the old village of Lanark about one mile away; 400 lived with their parents in the houses built by Dale at New Lanark.

Children had many advantages as mill workers. They were paid less than adults, and apprentices were not paid at all. Children were also more agile, so it was easier for them to crawl under the machines to repair broken threads.

Cotton Mill, Cromford, 10th Dec. 1771.

WANTED immediately, two Journeymen Clock-Makers, or others that understands Tooth and Pinion well: Also a Smith that can forge and file.—Likewise two Wood Turners that have been accustomed to Wheel-making, Spole-turning, &c. Weavers residing in this Neighbourhood, by applying at the Mill, may have good Work. There is Employment at the above Place, for Women, Children, &c. and good Wages.

N. B. A Quantity of Box Wood is wanted: Any Persons whom the above may suit, will be treated with by Messrs. Arkwright and Co. at the Mill, or Mr. Strutt, in Derby.

SOURCE 1 An advertisement placed by Richard Arkwright in the *Derby Mercury*, December 1771

SOURCE 2 A letter written in 1791 by a mill owner, David Dale, to his agent about how he was finding workers for his mills at New Lanark, twenty miles from Glasgow

66 *I have already done all that you suggest with regard to the Highland emigrants. As soon as I learned that they wished to stay in this country I sent two friends to them and invited old and young to come to this place. I have sent in waggons a number of families to Lanark and the rest are now in my house . . .*

I have information that there are persons crossing the islands to entice the poor people to go to America. I have therefore wrote to several persons to send information to all places where people are proposing to leave their native country to advertise to them that they may have work [here] in the Lowlands, and I have pledged myself to build houses at Lanark for 200 families and to give them work. 99

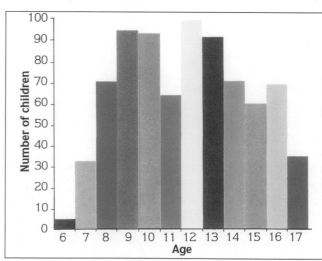

SOURCE 3 Graph showing the ages of the children working in the mills at New Lanark in 1793

How were the child workers treated?

SOURCE 4 Inside a cotton spinning factory in the 1840s

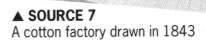

▼ **SOURCE 5** Punishing child workers – an engraving made in 1840

▲ **SOURCE 7**
A cotton factory drawn in 1843

SOURCE 8 Leonard Horner, a factory inspector, describes what happened to a young girl in a textile factory

❝*She was caught by her apron, which wrapped around the shaft. She was whirled round and repeatedly forced between the shaft and the carding engine. (Her right leg was found some distance away.)*❞

SOURCE 6 Pauper apprentices in an early nineteenth-century spinning factory – an illustration from a novel written in 1840

1. Look at Sources 4–8. What dangers can you see for the workers?

SOURCE 9 An early nineteenth-century cartoon by Robert Cruikshank

SOURCE 10 An extract from the *Memoir of Robert Blincoe*. Robert Blincoe was an orphan who worked in the mills as an apprentice from the age of seven. He became so deformed because of the work that he left and worked for himself at home. He published his memoir – under the name of John Brown – in 1828. This extract describes his first day at work

They reached the mill about half-past five [in the morning]. The moment he entered the doors, the noise appalled him, and the stench seemed intolerable.

The task first given him was to pick up the loose cotton that fell upon the floor. Apparently nothing could be easier and he set to eagerly, although much terrified by the whirling motion and noise of the machinery, and not a little affected by the dust and flue with which he was half suffocated.

Unused to the stench he soon felt sick and by constantly stooping, his back ached. He therefore sat down, but this he soon found was strictly forbidden. His taskmaster gave him to understand he must keep on his legs. He did so, till twelve o'clock. Blincoe suffered greatly with thirst and hunger.

SOURCE 11 In 1833 Robert Blincoe was invited to give evidence to Parliament about conditions in the mills

I have seen the time when two handles of a pound weight each have been screwed to my ears. Then three or four of us have been hung on a cross-beam above the machinery, hanging by our hands. Mind, we were apprentices without a father or mother to take care of us. Then we used to stand up, in a skip, without our shirts, and be beat with straps. Then they used to tie up a 28-pound weight to hang down our backs.

1. Read Sources 10 and 11. Robert Blincoe had to stop working in the factory because he became deformed. He gave these accounts later when he was an adult. Do you think they are reliable?

SOURCE 12 Mark Best, an overseer, describes the straps

They are about a foot and half long, and there is a stick at the end; and that end they beat with is cut into five or six thongs.

SOURCE 13 Elizabeth Bentley, aged 23, was questioned by a Parliamentary Committee in 1831. She began work in a mill in Leeds when she was six years old

Q: Explain what you had to do.
A: When the frames are full, they have to stop the frame, and take the flyers off, and take the full bobbins off, and carry them to the roller, and then put the empty ones on.
Q: Does that keep you constantly on your feet?
A: Yes there are so many frames, and they run so quick.
Q: Suppose you flagged a little, what would they do?
A: Strap us. The girls had black marks on their skin many a time, and their parents dare not come to him about it, they were afraid of losing their work.
Q: In what part of the mill did you work?
A: In the card-room. It was very dusty. The dust got upon my lungs, I got so bad in health. When I pulled the baskets all heaped up the basket pulled my shoulder out of its place and my ribs have grown over it. I am now deformed.

SOURCE 14 Mr John Moss, who was in charge of apprentice children at Backbarrow Mill was questioned by a Parliamentary Committee at the House of Commons in 1816

Q: Were any children employed at the mill?
A: There were 111. All parish apprentices, mostly from London, between the ages of seven and eleven.
Q: What were the hours of work?
A: From five o'clock in the morning till eight at night.
Q: What time was allowed for meals?
A: Half an hour for breakfast and half an hour for dinner.
Q: Would the children sit or stand at work?
A: Stand.
Q: Were they usually tired at night?
A: Yes, some of them were very tired. I have frequently found some asleep on the mill floor.
Q: Were any children injured by machines?
A: Very frequently. Very often their fingers were crushed and one had his arm broken.

2. Many parents let their children work in these conditions. Does this mean they were cruel and didn't care about their children?

SOURCE 15 John Hall, overseer at a mill in Bradford, was questioned by the same Parliamentary Committee

At the top of the spindle there is a fly goes across and the child takes hold of the fly by the left hand and he throws the left shoulder up and the right knee inward; he has the thread to get with the right hand and he has to stoop his head down to see what he is doing. All the children I have seen that are made cripples by this work are bent in the right knee.

SOURCE 16 Joseph Hebergam, aged seventeen, was questioned about his work in a mill in Huddersfield

After I had worked for half a year I could scarcely walk. In the morning my brother and sister used to take me under each arm and run with me, a good mile, to the mill. If we were five minutes late, the overlooker would take a strap and beat us till we were black and blue. I have seen my mother weep at me sometimes, but she would not tell me why she was weeping.

SOURCE 17 Fines that could be imposed on spinners in Tyldesley in 1823. From a pamphlet circulated by strikers

Offence	Fine
Any spinner found with his window open	1s
Any spinner found dirty at his work	1s
Any spinner found washing himself	1s
Any spinner heard whistling	1s
Any spinner being five minutes after last bell rings	1s
Any spinner having a little waste on his spindles	1s
Any spinner being sick and cannot find another spinner [to replace him]	6s

Activity

Work in pairs. First make a list of all the bad points about children working in the mills. Then design a handbill to be sent to all employers calling on them to improve conditions for children. Choose the most important points from your list to go on the handbill and one illustration from pages 17-18. Be ready to explain why you have chosen these ones. Then write a letter from an employer replying to your handbill.

Robert Owen: a better way to run a factory?

ROBERT OWEN was born in 1771 in Wales. He was the son of a tradesman. He received some schooling and then worked in a draper's shop selling cloth. In 1787 he moved to Manchester. He did well, becoming the manager of a large spinning mill when he was still only twenty. In 1799 he bought the cotton mills in New Lanark, Scotland, from his father-in-law, David Dale. Owen took over the day-to-day management of the mills. He ran them very successfully. They made large profits.

In his time David Dale had been generally looked upon as a good employer. His apprentices were well fed and even spent two hours a day at school – though this was after thirteen hours at work. But Owen became convinced that he needed to improve conditions. He wrote about the children, 'Many of them became dwarfs in body and mind, and some of them were deformed.'

Owen made many improvements at New Lanark. He wrote descriptions of the situation he found when he arrived at New Lanark and the changes he introduced there himself.

SOURCE 1 From *A New View of Society*, written by Robert Owen in 1813

66 *When I arrived the workers possessed almost all the vices and very few of the virtues of a social community. Theft and the receipt of stolen goods was their trade, idleness and drunkenness their habit . . . I formed my plans accordingly . . .*

The system of receiving apprentices from public charities was abolished; permanent settlers with large families were encouraged, and comfortable houses were built for their accommodation.

The practice of employing children in the mills of six, seven and eight years of age was stopped, and their parents advised to allow them to acquire health and education until they were ten years old.

The children were taught reading, writing and arithmetic, during five years, that is, from five to ten, in the village school, without expense to their parents . . .

Those employed became hardworking, temperate, healthy, faithful to their employers, and kind to each other . . . 99

SOURCE 2 From Owen's autobiography *The Life of Robert Owen*, published in 1857

66 *Before I arrived at New Lanark the retail shops, in all of which spirits were sold, were great nuisances. All the articles sold were bought on credit at high prices . . . The qualities were most inferior, and they were sold to the workpeople at very high prices.*

I arranged superior stores and shops, from which to supply every item of food, clothing, etc. which they required. I bought everything . . . on a large scale, and . . . supplied to the people at the cost price. The result of this change was to save them in their expenses full 25 per cent . . .

The effects soon became visible in their improved health and superior dress, and in the general comfort of their houses. 99

SOURCE 3 A painting of the New Lanark Institute in 1825

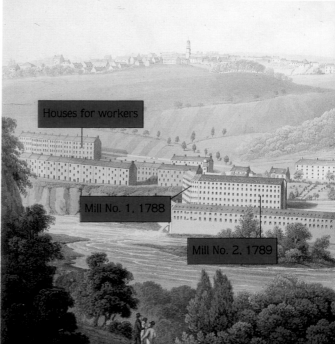

Houses for workers

Mill No. 1, 1788

Mill No. 2, 1789

SOURCE 4 A contemporary description of one of the rooms in the 'Institute for the formation of character' at New Lanark, opened in 1816

" *The walls are hung round with the representations of the most striking zoological and mineralogical specimens, including quadrupeds, birds, fishes, reptiles, insects, shells, minerals, etc. At one end there is a gallery adapted for the purpose of an orchestra and at the other are hung very large representations of the two hemispheres. This room is used as a lecture and ballroom and it is here that dancing and singing lessons are daily given.*

The lower storey of the building is divided into three apartments. It is in these that the younger classes are taught reading. "

SOURCE 5 A painting of New Lanark in the early 1820s. The red labels mark features introduced by David Dale and the blue labels mark features introduced or improved by Robert Owen

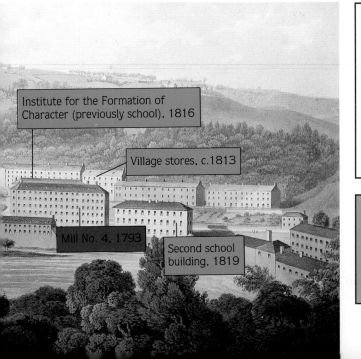

Institute for the Formation of Character (previously school), 1816

Village stores, c.1813

Mill No. 4, 1793

Second school building, 1819

Could Robert Owen's ideas work?

Robert Owen believed that if factory owners treated their workers better they would work better, and the factory owners would make bigger profits. He also thought that by improving the environment and providing education he would improve the character of his workers. In 1819 he persuaded Parliament to pass a Factory Act to improve conditions in the mills. But because of the opposition of other factory owners it did not go as far as he wanted.

Gradually Owen decided that the basic problem was that factory owners were too selfish. They competed with one another to make big profits. They did not care about society in general. Owen believed that if co-operation replaced competition a better world could be created for everyone. He suggested that the unemployed should work together in co-operative villages.

In 1824 he went to the USA to set up a new co-operative community called New Harmony. He spent £40,000 of his own money, but it was not a success. However, when he returned to Britain in 1829 he found that his ideas had gained much support among working-class people. He helped set up one of the first national trade unions – the Grand National Consolidated Union – which anyone could join. Its aim was to fight for better pay for workers. Soon 800,000 people had joined. But in 1834 the union collapsed because of opposition. For the rest of his life, until his death in 1858, Owen concentrated on writing and lecturing about these ideas. He did not die a rich man, but for many people he was a hero – 'the first SOCIALIST'.

Boulton and Watt: who was more important?

SOURCES 1–3 are about one factory during the late eighteenth and early nineteenth centuries. See how much you can work out about the factory from these sources alone. For example:

■ What form of power was used in this factory?
■ Why was it sited where it was?
■ What did it produce?
■ In what ways was it different from a modern factory?

SOURCE 1 The Soho Works, an engraving made in 1800. The caption lists products produced by the Soho Works in 1800

SOURCE 2 From Swinney's Birmingham Directory, 1774

> The building consists of four squares, with shops, warehouses, etc. for a thousand workmen, who in a great variety of branches, excel in their various departments; not only in the making of buttons, buckles, boxes, trinkets, etc. . . . but in many other arts . . .
>
> The number of ingenious mechanical contrivances they avail themselves of, by the means of water mills, much facilitates [makes easier] their work, and saves a great portion of time and labour . . . Their excellent ornamental pieces have been admired by the nobility and gentry, not only of this kingdom but all Europe: and are said to surpass anything of the kind made abroad.

SOURCE 3 A map of Birmingham made in 1828 by J. Pigot Smith, showing the location of the Soho Works

The factory was the Soho Works at Handsworth near Birmingham. It was built in 1764 by Matthew Boulton. A partner also helped provide some of the money. The factory was really a collection of smaller workshops in which craftsmen turned out a broad range of products.

The Soho Works is most famous today as the place where steam engines, which pumped water from mines and later provided power for machinery in factories, were built. This happened as a result of the link between two individuals, Matthew Boulton and James Watt. The story of their partnership is told in Source 4.

Activity

Divide your page into two halves, headed 'Boulton' and 'Watt'. Using Source 4 list the ways in which they each contributed to their successful partnership.

Who do you think was more important to their success, Boulton or Watt?

SOURCE 4

THE STORY OF BOULTON & WATT

1. An engineer, Thomas Newcomen, had produced an improved steam engine in the early eighteenth century. Many of his engines were bought by the owners of coal and tin mines.

2. James Watt was working as an instrument maker at Glasgow University. In 1769 he patented an invention which made Newcomen's steam pump work more quickly while using less fuel.

3. Watt and a partner set up a company to produce these engines, but his partner went bankrupt.

4. Watt was desperate for money to develop his invention. In 1774 he went into partnership with Matthew Boulton.

5. They had precision parts made for Watt's engines by the Shropshire iron manufacturer, John Wilkinson. Boulton and Watt began to assemble engines at the Soho Works.

6. Boulton had to borrow money to pay for the manufacture of Watt's engines. It was a long time before he was out of debt.

BOULTON AND WATT: WHO WAS MORE IMPORTANT?

7
They sold the engines to the owners of coal mines in Staffordshire and Shropshire and tin mines in Cornwall.

8 Watt's pump—like all steam pumps—produced up-and-down movement. To turn machinery, rotary movement was needed. Boulton realised that there would be a very large market for a rotary steam engine.

9 Watt worked on the problem but it was William Murdoch, the foreman at the Soho Works, who thought of a solution.

10 The rotary steam engine was patented in 1782. Soon it was being used in many industries, including brewing and textiles. At Soho, Boulton used rotary engines to power coin presses in a new part of his factory called the Soho mint.

11 Boulton opened a new factory, called the Soho Foundry, in 1790. All the parts for the steam engines could now be made on one site, and this part of the firm's business expanded rapidly.

12 When Boulton died in 1809, he had a fortune of £150,000.

13 Watt was not interested in developing the steam engine for use on the roads or in boats. But other inventors such as William Murdoch gradually improved Watt's engine until it could be used for pulling trains.

How did Matthew Boulton work?

SOURCE 5 Written in 1989 by a modern historian, Eric Hopkins, in *Birmingham: The First Industrial Town in the World*

66 It is true that as a capitalist Boulton always seemed able to raise large sums of money. Both his first and second wives were heiresses and each brought to the marriage (and to the firm) a fortune of £14,000. In 1767 he mortgaged his wife's property for £4000, and in the mid 1770s he sold landed property to Lord Donegal for £15,000. Many other loans to help the firm were raised from time to time, both locally and in London, and even in Amsterdam. All in all, at least £60,000 was borrowed.

However, the need for these frequent borrowings was brought about by the simple fact that in spite of the glittering facade provided by Boulton's activities, the firm of Boulton and Fothergill was often near to bankruptcy . . . Things were so bad in 1778 that only a loan of £23,000 secured on the engine business saved the firm from financial ruin. 99

SOURCE 6 Adapted from a letter Boulton wrote to his business agent

66 I wish to know the taste, the fashions, the toys, both useful and ornamental, the implements, vessels, etc, etc, etc, in all the different parts of Europe, as I should be glad to work for all Europe . . .

If in the course of your future travelling you can pick up for me any metallic ores or fossil substances or any other curious natural productions, I should be much obliged to you. I am fond of all those things that have a tendency to improve my knowledge in the mechanical arts. 99

SOURCE 7 Written by the writer James Boswell after a visit to the Soho Works

66 I shall never forget Mr Boulton's expression to me: 'I sell here, Sir, what all the world desires to have – POWER.' 99

SOURCE 8 Adapted from a letter from Boulton to Watt, written in 1781

66 The people in London, Manchester and Birmingham are steam mill mad . . . The most likely line for the use of our engine is in mills, which is certainly a sizeable field. 99

SOURCE 9 Written in 1980 by a modern historian, Victor Skipp, in *A History of Greater Birmingham*

66 At a time when pauper children were regularly apprenticed at seven, Boulton refused to employ any child under twelve. He had the inside of his workshops whitewashed regularly to ensure light and cleanliness, and took particular care over ventilation. Even more unusual was his introduction in 1792 of a social insurance scheme, with wage-related payments and benefits. 99

1. What impressions of Boulton's character do you get from Sources 5–9?
2. How many of the factors listed on page 8 can you see working in the success of his business?

Activity

You have been asked by Madame Tussaud's, the famous waxworks museum, to help them design an exhibition called 'Great entrepreneurs of the eighteenth and nineteenth centuries'.

Look back over pages 9–25. Choose one businessman who you think should be included in the display. Then design the exhibit. Think about what kind of exhibit would best show his character and the secrets of his success.

Will you show him in his office, out in his factory with his workers, in a workshop with an inventor, or at home enjoying himself?

Then write a caption of about ten lines to go with the exhibit, explaining what this businessman has done to be included in the exhibition of 'Great entrepreneurs'.

How did farmers produce more food?

Farming in 1750

INDUSTRY needed workers and workers needed food. Between 1750 and 1825 the population of Britain almost doubled, and the number of people living in towns – who couldn't grow their own food – was increasing rapidly. So Britain's farmers needed to grow more food. Britain didn't import much food, so it *had* to rely on British farmers producing more. Was British farming up to it?

How farmers produced food varied a lot from region to region. In highland areas, where the soil was too poor to grow crops, farmers mainly kept animals. In lowland areas crops were more important than animals, although animals from highland areas were brought down to the rich pasture of the lowland areas to be fattened up.

In many villages farming techniques had changed little since the Middle Ages, as you can see from Source 1, which shows a lowland village, Ashill in Norfolk. Most of the land was divided into open or common fields where the people of Ashill worked. A few people owned or rented their own farms, but most farmers did not think much about how to make money from their land. They grew just enough food for their families and the village.

1. Pick three features in Source 1 that might prevent the farmers in Ashill increasing food production. Give reasons for your choice.

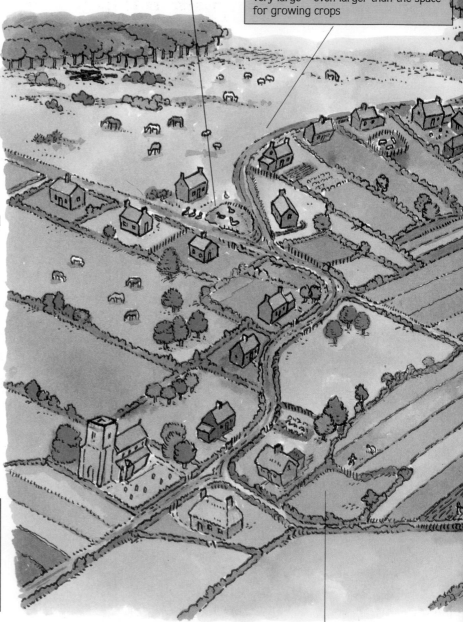

On remote parts of the common there were bushes and trees. The poorer people collected firewood here

Many poor people kept geese on the part of the common next to their cottage and on the village pond

The commons. Cows were grazed on the commons by villagers who had 'common rights'. Other villagers probably grazed their animals on the commons as well, although they had no legal right to do so. The big landowners grazed their sheep here, too.

In some other villages where the soil was poor these commons might be very large – even larger than the space for growing crops

Most people lived in cottages near the centre of the village, close to the medieval church and the rectory

Some privately owned ENCLOSED land. Used for growing crops and grazing animals

SOURCE 1 A reconstruction drawing of Ashill, Norfolk in 1750

The two manor houses and the other large farmhouses were rented out to tenant farmers. It was these tenant farmers who employed the labourers from the village

Enclosure in Ashill

To grow more food in Ashill the farmers needed to reorganise the land. Or so the big landowners said. In 1785 they asked Parliament to pass an Act to allow them to ENCLOSE the commons and the common fields. An Enclosure Act would divide up all the land and individual farmers would then look after and improve their own patch. The landowners told Parliament that enclosure would benefit everybody. All over the country landowners were saying the same thing: between 1750 and 1825 five million acres of land in Britain was enclosed. The idea was that it would make it possible to grow more food. Let's see if this really happened.

Pigs and chickens were probably kept in the farm yards and cottage gardens

Most people in the village were agricultural labourers. Farming tasks were mainly done by hand. Some tasks such as threshing grain (beating it to remove the husks) kept the farm workers busy throughout the winter

Most machines were made of wood. Wooden ploughs were pulled by horses. There was little new machinery. The farmers could not afford to INVEST in it, and on their thin strips of field machines would be difficult to use anyway

The same crops were grown as in the Middle Ages – wheat and barley, oats and peas.

On the ENCLOSED land some farmers had done away with the fallow year by growing turnips and clover. (Turnips absorb goodness from deep down in the soil and allow the top soil to rest. Clover adds nitrogen to the soil). Some farmers had tried this in the common fields, but it led to disputes with other farmers who wanted to graze their animals there during the fallow year

The open or common fields. Crops were grown here. To keep the soil fertile part of the land was left fallow (empty) each year and used for grazing animals. Animals were also grazed here during the winter

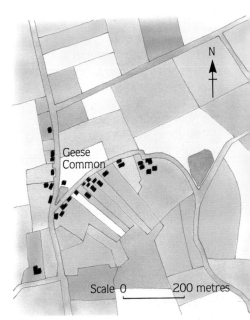

SOURCE 2 Part of Ashill after enclosure

SOURCE 3 In 1804 Arthur Young made these observations about the effects of enclosure on Ashill

66
■ *The number of cows had decreased.*
■ *There were 39 acres of common land for the poor, but owing to abuse of the land they did not get much benefit from it.*
■ *The production of corn had increased to an extraordinary degree.*
■ *Improvement had in general been great.*
■ *Land, which before enclosing was worth very little, had now been sold for up to £40 an acre.*
99

1. Compare Sources 1 and 2. How did enclosure change this part of Ashill?
2. Look at Source 3. According to Arthur Young, did enclosure help the farmers of Ashill to grow more food?

HOW DID FARMERS PRODUCE MORE FOOD?

Changes

Enclosure was only one of the many changes in farming in the eighteenth century. Landowners all over the country were experimenting with new ideas. Many of the ideas, such as introducing new crops, were only possible after the land had been enclosed. In some parts of the country the changes took place very slowly, but farming in Britain in 1850 was very different from farming 100 years earlier.

SOURCE 6 A horse-powered threshing machine

New crops were grown. Turnips, swedes or clover made ideal feed for animals. But just as importantly, they were crops that put nourishment back into the soil, so a fallow year was no longer needed. In the first half of the eighteenth century farmers were encouraged to use the 'Norfolk Four Course Rotation' (wheat–turnips–barley–clover) by major landowners such as Lord Townshend.

Clay and lime were increasingly used as a fertiliser.

Tools and equipment were improved. New, stronger ploughs were made of iron. Tools also became cheaper and more widely available as the iron industry grew.

Some hand tasks were speeded up by new machinery. A horse-drawn hoe and seed drill were designed by Jethro Tull. A horse-powered threshing machine was developed at the end of the eighteenth century.

Enclosure meant that land could be used more efficiently. Farmers also had more freedom to make improvements, because only one farmer was responsible for decisions about how a field was used, rather than many farmers who might not agree.

SOURCE 4 Improvements in farming in the eighteenth century

As the population of Britain grew, so did the demand for food. The price of food went up.

Animals got bigger. By careful breeding and better feeding farmers such as Robert Bakewell developed stronger, healthier and heavier farm animals. In 1710 the average weight of cattle sold at Smithfield meat market was 320 pounds. In 1795 it had more than doubled to 800 pounds.

Farmers realised that they could make money by making their land more efficient and productive.

Farm owners realised that if they INVESTED in improving their farms, they could raise rents. Farming was becoming a profitable business. Landlords let their farms only to tenants who would use the new methods successfully.

Information about the new methods was spread by agricultural writers such as Arthur Young, and Agricultural Societies were founded.

SOURCE 5 A Surrey pig in 1798. It was four feet high, eight feet nine inches long, had five inches of fat all over and weighed nearly half a ton

1. How were the problems you identified in question 1 on page 26 solved by eighteenth-century farmers?
2. Which of the changes in Source 4 do you think would be most important for increasing food production?

Case study: Thomas Coke

Thomas Coke (pronounced Cook) owned land at Ashill. He enclosed most of his land and rented it out to tenants. He also kept one farm to work himself, where he tried out many of the new farming methods. Of course, most of the actual work was done by the men and women labourers who were employed on the farm. Sources 7–10 describe how Coke improved his estate and his farm.

SOURCE 9 Thomas Coke inspecting his Southdown sheep, 1808

SOURCE 7 Adapted from a letter written by Sir James Caird in 1852

❝The present superiority of Norfolk in improved farming is due to Coke. He offered his farms to men of money and intelligence. He introduced clover. An improved stock of cattle and sheep was kept. The Norfolk Rotation was started.❞

SOURCE 8 From a school textbook, *Britain since 1700* by R.J. Cootes, published in 1968

❝Coke . . . followed in Townshend's footsteps, using clay, marl [clay with lime] and manure to increase the fertility of the soil . . . Then he set out to educate his tenants . . . They were made to use certain crop rotations and were forbidden from growing two successive corn crops on the same soil.

Every year Coke held a sheep shearing festival and awarded prizes to farmers who showed new ideas. His 'sheep shearings' attracted visitors from many parts of Europe and set the pattern for future agricultural shows.❞

SOURCE 10 Written by Arthur Young, following visits to Coke's estates

❝**1801**   Mr Coke's South Down [sheep] flock at Holkham is generally known to be excellent. They are remarkably good, of the largest size, straight, fine woolled, clean.
1804   Mr Coke has the most powerful roller for grass lands I have ever seen. He also has a very large machine, which cost £600. Besides threshing, it grinds corn, works two chaff cutters, and breaks oil cake . . . Some of the crops were immense, particularly barley.❞

1. Look at the agricultural improvements described in Source 4. How many of these were adopted by Coke, according to Sources 7–10?

Who improved Holkham?

In his day, Thomas Coke was regarded as the man who brought all the new ideas and improvements to Holkham. Modern historians wonder whether his role has been exaggerated, and they have looked at what farming in the area was like before Coke took over.

SOURCE 11 Written in 1975 by a modern historian, R.A.C. Parker, in *Coke of Norfolk*

❝. . . It is wrong to think of the agriculture of Norfolk as backward before 1776. The Norfolk Rotation was present before 1776. Sown grasses and clover were common . . . Marl had been familiar for a very long time . . . and there were excellent farmers, investing a lot of money . . .

Where did these errors and exaggerations begin . . .? The person chiefly responsible seems to have been none other than Coke of Norfolk himself . . . Coke was a very old man . . . Old men forget facts and remember fancies, especially about the scenes and events of their youth . . .

Coke was the largest landowner in Norfolk. His power aroused envy and opposition . . . Coke's political opponents accused him of causing unemployment and high prices. The picture of his fertilising a desert waste, causing wheat to grow where only rabbits and rye were found before, was developed in reply to his critics.❞

1. According to Source 11, has Thomas Coke's role been exaggerated?
2. Suggest reasons why historians like the ones in Sources 8 and 11 disagree about Coke's importance.

29

Did Britain have the raw materials it needed?

BRITAIN'S growing industries needed a constant supply of RAW MATERIALS. Fortunately, the country was rich in many raw materials. So when improved iron production methods or new steam engines were developed, the necessary raw materials, such as coal, were there waiting to be exploited. Other raw materials, such as the cotton for the booming textile industry, needed to be imported. Source 1 shows you where the most important supplies came from.

1. Look at Source 1. Which raw materials were mainly imported? Which were mainly home produced?
2. Look at Source 2. What raw materials would be needed to make each object?
3. ■ 'Britain's wealth of raw materials did not in itself lead to the Industrial Revolution.' Do you agree?

SOURCE 1 The main sources of Britain's raw materials in the eighteenth and nineteenth centuries

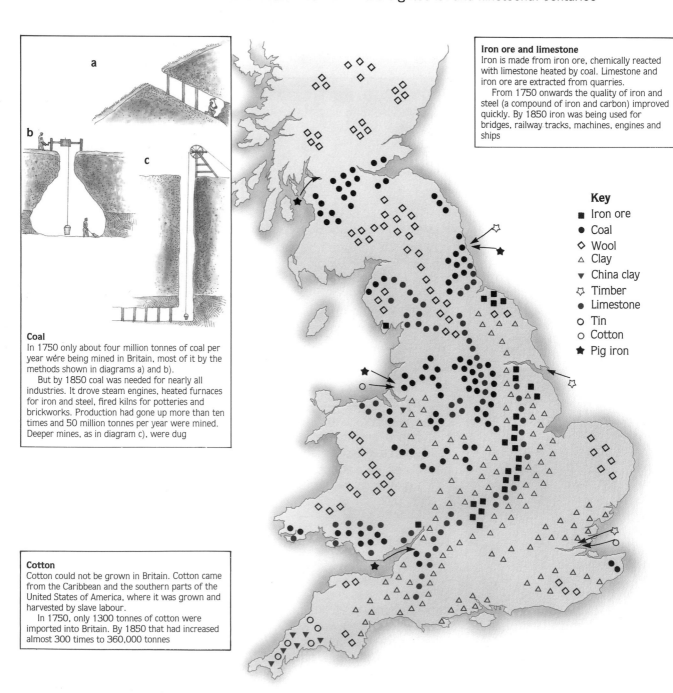

Iron ore and limestone
Iron is made from iron ore, chemically reacted with limestone heated by coal. Limestone and iron ore are extracted from quarries.
  From 1750 onwards the quality of iron and steel (a compound of iron and carbon) improved quickly. By 1850 iron was being used for bridges, railway tracks, machines, engines and ships

Key
- ■ Iron ore
- ● Coal
- ◇ Wool
- △ Clay
- ▼ China clay
- ☆ Timber
- ● Limestone
- ○ Tin
- ○ Cotton
- ★ Pig iron

Coal
In 1750 only about four million tonnes of coal per year were being mined in Britain, most of it by the methods shown in diagrams a) and b).
  But by 1850 coal was needed for nearly all industries. It drove steam engines, heated furnaces for iron and steel, fired kilns for potteries and brickworks. Production had gone up more than ten times and 50 million tonnes per year were mined. Deeper mines, as in diagram c), were dug

Cotton
Cotton could not be grown in Britain. Cotton came from the Caribbean and the southern parts of the United States of America, where it was grown and harvested by slave labour.
  In 1750, only 1300 tonnes of cotton were imported into Britain. By 1850 that had increased almost 300 times to 360,000 tonnes

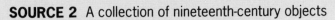

SOURCE 2 A collection of nineteenth-century objects

A fountain

A pottery plate

Men's and women's clothes in the 1830s

A steam locomotive

A post box made in the 1870s

Did transport need improving?

To GROW, Britain's industries needed good, reliable, extensive, cheap transport systems. Heavy RAW MATERIALS such as coal, cotton and iron had to be brought to the factories. The finished goods had to be delivered all over Britain and abroad. Businessmen and women had to be able to travel to sell their goods.

Was the transport system in the eighteenth century good enough? Judge for yourself.

Water transport in 1750

One way of moving goods was to use water transport – rivers and the sea. This was cheaper than road transport and much better for carrying bulky goods. Large amounts of coal were taken from Tyneside to London by sea using sailing ships. Rivers were also used for heavy goods, such as stone and corn.

Source 1 shows the navigable rivers in 1750. Attempts had been made to improve these rivers. For example, those with too many bends or with obstructions such as weirs had been made navigable by digging new channels. Others had been extended by means of man-made cuts.

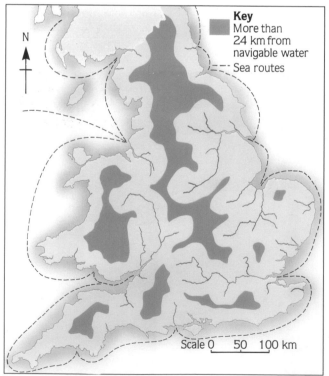

Key
More than 24 km from navigable water
--- Sea routes

Scale 0   50   100 km

SOURCE 1 Navigable rivers and sea routes in 1750. The shaded areas are parts of the country which are more than 24 km from a navigable river

1. Water transport was cheap and efficient for heavy goods. What do you think were its disadvantages?

Road transport in 1750

SOURCE 2 A packhorse train in the eighteenth century

SOURCE 3 A wide wheeled goods waggon

SOURCE 4 A nineteenth-century engraving of a mail coach in a snowdrift

1. Look at Source 3. In 1753 the government passed laws against waggons with wheels less than nine inches wide. Why did they want the wheels of waggons to be so wide?

Road traffic was growing rapidly and local parish officials were unable to cope with the increasing need for road repairs. In 1750 the roads were in a worse state than they had been in the Middle Ages. Travellers sometimes reported water up to their saddlebags. Coaches often sent footmen ahead with an axe to clear the way of bushes and trees.

There were a growing number of regular stage coach services for passengers and stage waggons for goods, but many only ran in the summer. Journeys took about twice as long in the winter as they did in the summer. Even in the best conditions the fastest coach took six and a half days to travel from London to Newcastle. There was also the danger of highwaymen.

The roads were also used for carrying some heavy goods, often by long strings of packhorses. Heavy waggons used the better roads. But they travelled at only two or three miles an hour – a slow walking pace.

How were roads improved?

In some places business people and local residents joined together to form turnpike trusts. Parliament gave them control over a section of road. They set up gates and toll houses and charged people to use the roads. The money they raised was used to improve the road, or even to build new roads.

The number of turnpike trusts grew quickly: from 520 in 1770 to almost 1000 in 1830. But even by 1830 they only controlled 22,000 miles out of a total of 105,000 miles of important roads.

Some trusts employed surveyors, who developed ways of building stronger roads that stood up better to heavy traffic. One of these surveyors was John McAdam, who worked for many turnpike trusts in the late eighteenth and early nineteenth centuries. He realised that roads needed strong foundations and good drainage. See if you can work out from Source 7 how he provided these.

On these improved roads stage coaches could travel faster, changing horses every ten to fifteen miles, and could keep to a regular timetable. Mail coaches (which also carried passengers) now delivered mail around the country more quickly. By 1810 journeys took only a third of the time that they had taken in 1750.

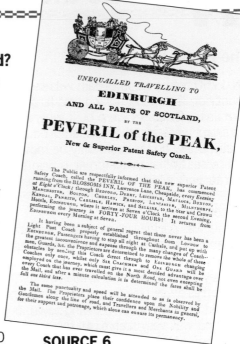

SOURCE 6
An advertisement from 1831 for an express stage coach

SOURCE 5 Written by Arthur Young in 1771

❝Let me warn all travellers who decide to travel through this terrible northern country to avoid this road like the devil. They will meet here with ruts which actually measured four deep and floating with mud in the summer. What can it be like after a winter? The only mending is the tumbling in of some loose stones which serve to jolt the carriage around. I passed three carts broken down in eighteen miles.❞

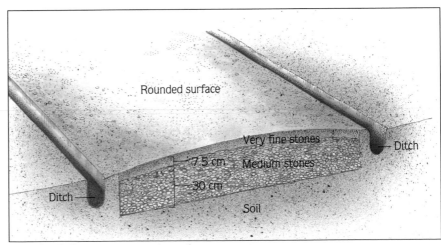

Rounded surface

Very fine stones

7.5 cm   Medium stones

30 cm

Ditch

Ditch

Soil

SOURCE 7 A cross-section of a McAdam road

2. How good was road transport in 1750? Organise your answer under the following headings: speed, carrying goods, comfort. Support your answer with evidence from Sources 2–5.

1. Who did the road improvements described above benefit more: passengers, or INDUSTRIALISTS wanting to move heavy goods?

Why was the Bridgewater Canal built?

The problem

IN 1750 transport in Britain was so bad that each county or region in England was largely self contained. Factories were built where the RAW MATERIALS were and the finished products were sold locally. Bulky goods could only be moved along rivers and by sea. What MANUFACTURERS wanted was a means of transport which would improve their supply of raw materials and open up trade with different parts of the country.

This was particularly true of the North West of England, around Liverpool and Manchester:

■ The Duke of Bridgewater owned coal mines at Worsley. He sold his coal to Manchester, eleven kilometres away (see Source 1). It was needed for use as fuel in homes in the growing town, because firewood was very scarce. All the coal had to be carried on horseback or by road waggon. This meant it was only delivered in small quantities and was expensive.

■ The port of Liverpool served the industries in Manchester and the surrounding towns (see Source 2). Into Liverpool came the essential raw materials, and out of Liverpool went the manufactured goods which Britain sold to the world. It was in the interests of both Liverpool and Manchester to improve transport between the two towns.

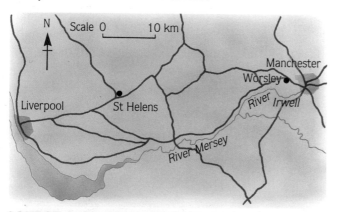

SOURCE 1 The area around Liverpool and Manchester in 1750

SOURCE 2 Liverpool's main trade

Coming into Liverpool	Leaving Liverpool
cotton from America	iron goods
yarn from Ireland	cotton goods from
tobacco from Virginia	Manchester
timber	salt from Cheshire
coffee	pottery from
rice	Staffordshire
rum	
indigo	

The solution: the Bridgewater Canal

How could the transport in this area be improved? The Duke of Bridgewater thought he had the answer. He decided to build a canal from his collieries in Worsley to Manchester, and he brought in the canal builder James Brindley to do it for him.

The Worsley to Manchester section of the Bridgewater Canal was completed in 1765. By this time the Duke was already planning an extension in the opposite direction, so that his boats could also sail to Liverpool. This was opened in 1776.

The Duke of Bridgewater had seen canals on the continent. He also knew about a nearby canal which had been built to connect St Helens to the River Mersey.

In 1759 the Duke persuaded Parliament to pass an Act which allowed him to build the canal.

The Duke employed James Brindley to advise him on how to build the canal. Brindley was a millwright, had a good understanding of machines and was good at solving practical mechanical problems.

Most of the canal was level but ten 'pound locks' were needed in the last mile to take it down to join the River Mersey. Pound locks had been used on the continent since the fourteenth century and in England since the sixteenth century.

The Duke had to find a way for the canal to cross the River Irwell. Brindley built an aqueduct to carry the canal over it, the first of its kind in Britain.

At Worsley one of the Duke's staff had the idea of extending the canal underground so that the coal could be loaded straight into boats inside the mine.

The Duke had to borrow huge sums of money to pay for the canal.

SOURCE 3 How the Bridgewater Canal was built

SOURCE 4 A contemporary writes about the plans for the canal

It will be the most extraordinary thing in the kingdom, if not in Europe. The boats in some places go underground, and in another place over a river without communicating with its waters.

SOURCE 5 An engraving from 1794 showing the aqueduct which carried the Bridgewater Canal over the River Irwell

WORSLEY BASIN

SOURCE 6 The entrance to the Duke's underground colliery canals

The results

The Bridgewater Canal brought down the price of coal in Manchester from twelve shillings a ton to six shillings. This was a great help to the people living in Manchester, who used coal to cook with and to keep their houses warm. It also allowed factories to introduce steam engines to replace water power.

As soon as the extension to Liverpool was built, finished goods could be moved between Manchester and Liverpool at one sixth of the cost of road transport. The Duke of Bridgewater charged other businesses for the use of the canal and soon cotton was travelling by canal to Manchester and manufactured goods were sent to Liverpool.

Liverpool grew rapidly as a port. In 1748 only 456 ships used Liverpool. In 1800 it was 4746 and by 1825 it was 19,837. In 1792 Liverpool imported only 503 bags of American cotton. In 1822, just 30 years later, 289,989 bags came in. Before American supplies had been developed cotton had come from Turkey to London and then by road to the north!

For James Brindley, the success of the canal meant he was soon involved in a much bigger enterprise, to connect up all the great rivers of Britain with canals in a Grand Trunk Network. You can see on page 40 how this was done.

SOURCE 7 Written by Thomas Telford, another great canal builder, in 1804

❝*Canals are chiefly used for the following purposes:*
First: For conveying the produce of mines to the sea-shore.
Second: Conveying fuel and raw materials to some manufacturing towns and districts, and exporting manufactured goods.
Third: Conveying groceries and merchant-goods for the consumption of the district through which the canal passes.
Fourth: Conveying fuel for domestic purposes; manure for the purposes of Agriculture; transporting the produce of the districts through which the canal passes, to the different markets; and promoting agricultural purposes in general.❞

---

1. Using all the information on these two pages:
   a) make a list of factors which show that the canal was needed
   b) make a list of factors which show the importance of James Brindley.
2. If the Duke had not employed Brindley, how likely is it that he could still have built the canal?

Activity
Design a poster showing the advantages an area will gain if a canal is built through it.

How was the Liverpool and Manchester Railway built?

The problem

BY 1820 INDUSTRIALISTS could transport their goods between Liverpool and Manchester in several ways.

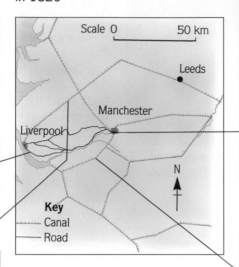

SOURCE 1 Methods of transport between Liverpool and Manchester in 1820

By road

By 1800 the 36-mile road from Liverpool to Manchester was packed with waggons and packhorses – 70 packhorses left one Liverpool inn in a day! Passengers had 22 regular coaches a day. The journey took three hours. The road was looked after by a number of TURNPIKE TRUSTS, but it was often in a very poor condition.

Rates for transporting goods between Liverpool and Manchester:
- all goods 40s a ton

By the Leeds and Liverpool Canal

As you can see, this canal went the long way round to Manchester – 58 miles had to be travelled. It was particularly used for carrying bulky goods such as coal, brick, lime and timber.

Rates for transporting goods between Liverpool and Manchester:
- all goods 9s 2d a ton

By the Mersey and Irwell Navigation

This had made the two rivers navigable. It was 43 miles long. It carried imported goods such as cotton and sugar and home produced goods such as grain, stone, timber and coal. On the lower part of the Mersey, as it approached the sea, boats could be delayed by tides, wind and storms. Higher up at the Manchester end they could be held up by lack of water in the river. The journey often took 36 hours!

Rates for transporting goods between Liverpool and Manchester:
- cotton 20s a ton
- sugar 16s 8d a ton
- grain 13s a ton

By the Bridgewater Canal

This was 46 miles long. Boats using this canal could be delayed by tides and storms in the Mersey. In winter the canal could be blocked by ice. One of the other drawbacks of the Bridgewater Canal was that the Duke of Bridgewater owned nearly all the land along the bank and he did not allow other companies to build warehouses there.

Rates for transporting goods between Liverpool and Manchester:
- cotton 18s 4d a ton
- sugar 13s 4d a ton
- grain 12s 6d a ton

By 1820 all kinds of raw materials which were due to be sent to towns like Manchester were piling up in the Liverpool docks, where they might be left for weeks. The traders complained that there were not enough barges, there were hold-ups at the locks, and the canal companies were charging very high rates. Because there was more than enough traffic to keep all the routes busy all the time, the canal companies did not have to compete by setting low rates.

Activity

You are an industrialist who has to move goods between Liverpool and Manchester. Which route would you use? Are you happy with it?

The solution: the Liverpool and Manchester Railway

In 1822 a Provisional Committee of Liverpool and Manchester industrialists was set up to plan the building of a railway.

Horse-drawn waggons running on rails had been used at coal mines for over 200 years. The first passenger railway in Britain was opened in 1807 at Oystermouth in South Wales. In 1825 the engineer George Stephenson opened the first passenger steam railway in England, between Stockton and Darlington.

The Committee had heard about Stephenson's work at Stockton. It invited him to be the engineer for the Liverpool and Manchester Railway.

Stage 1: raising money

In 1824 the Liverpool and Manchester merchants formed the Liverpool and Manchester Railway Company. This was a JOINT-STOCK COMPANY. The estimated cost of building the railway was £300,000, so the company issued 3000 SHARES which people could buy at £100 each. If the railway was successful the shareholders would get some of the profits.

Stage 2: raising support

The next job was to win the support of the local people and to persuade Parliament to give permission to build the railway.

The local industrialists and merchants prepared their arguments for the railway. Leaflets, posters, letters to the press and public meetings were used to present their point of view. They wrote to local MPs and even elected the Mayor of Liverpool as Chairman of the Company to get the support of the Council.

Those people opposed to the railway also got themselves organised with leaflets and letters to the press. The opposition was led by powerful local landowners: the Earls of Derby and Sefton, and the Duke of Bridgewater. They all owned land along the planned route. When Stephenson and his men tried to survey the route they were turned off the land and even attacked. They ended up carrying out the survey at night by torchlight!

Arguments for the railway
■ The owners of mines in St Helens would be given a direct link with Liverpool and could export their coal all over the world.
■ Farmers would be able to send their produce to market more quickly and cheaply.
■ Manufactured goods and raw materials would be carried for half the cost of canal travel in one sixth of the time.
■ The railway would be more reliable than the canal because canals could be closed by frost, drought, wind and tide, goods got damaged by the water, and there were not enough barges.
■ The cost of coal in Liverpool would go down.
■ Passengers could travel more quickly and cheaply.
■ Irish linen, corn and butter could be better transported to markets in Yorkshire.

Arguments against the railway
■ Hunting would be ruined.
■ Cows wouldn't graze within sight of the locomotives.
■ Women would miscarry at the sight of the locomotives.
■ Farm land, crops and buildings would be burned and destroyed by the sparks.
■ Smoke would badly affect vegetation and gardens.
■ The smoke and soot would get into to people's houses in Liverpool and Manchester.
■ It would cause havoc in Liverpool and Manchester where it would cross lots of streets.

Stage 3: getting Parliament's permission

By 1825 the survey was done, the route was chosen and the costs worked out.

But you could not just go out and build a railway. You needed permission from Parliament.

In 1825 Parliament began to debate the plan for the railway. As you can see in the boxes below, various groups sent petitions to Parliament for and against the railway.

Some of the groups which sent petitions to Parliament in support of the railway
■ corn merchants in Dublin, Ireland
■ merchants of the City of Cork in Ireland
■ Liverpool merchants in the West Indian and East Indian trade
■ Liverpool Ship Owners' Association
■ merchants, manufacturers and traders of Leeds, Bradford and Dewsbury.

Some of the groups which sent petitions to Parliament against the railway
■ the Earls of Derby and Sefton
■ the Leeds and Liverpool Canal Company
■ smaller landowners along the railway route
■ Barton Road Turnpike Trustees
■ the owners of the Bridgewater Canal
■ the Mersey and Irwell Navigation Company.

1. Pick one group from each of these boxes and say why you think it supported or opposed the railway.

Activity

Divide into groups. Plan a campaign, with posters and letters, for or against the railway.

HOW WAS THE LIVERPOOL AND MANCHESTER RAILWAY BUILT?

The outcome

Parliament rejected the plan.

One important reason for this was that the company insisted that steam locomotives, rather than horses, should be used to pull the trains. Many people saw these as monsters. Few people could imagine this monster travelling at the enormous speed of ten miles per hour without the boiler exploding, the engine and carriages leaving the track, or all the passengers and goods being shaken to pieces.

The MPs were also doubtful whether a way could be found to build the railway over Chat Moss, a large area of marsh on the proposed route (see Source 6).

Activity

Although Parliament has rejected the plan, you can ask it to consider it again. What changes will you make to the plan to give you a better chance of getting it through next time?

See if you have made the same changes as the company itself did.

A second attempt

In 1826 the Company decided to present a new plan to Parliament. It made changes to the plan so that there would not be so much opposition.

The route was changed:
■ to avoid much of the land of the Earls
■ to leave Liverpool by tunnel so no streets had to be crossed
■ to stop at Salford rather than going right into Manchester.

Other changes were made as well:
■ The question about steam engines was left open.
■ Canal owners were given the chance to buy shares in the railway (and so to share any profits).

This time Parliament said yes. The rates and fares were also fixed by Parliament (see Source 2).

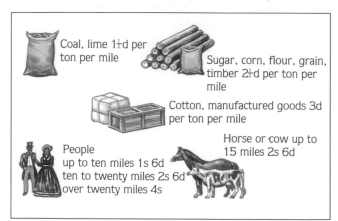

Coal, lime 1½d per ton per mile

Sugar, corn, flour, grain, timber 2½d per ton per mile

Cotton, manufactured goods 3d per ton per mile

Horse or cow up to 15 miles 2s 6d

People
up to ten miles 1s 6d
ten to twenty miles 2s 6d
over twenty miles 4s

SOURCE 2 Rates and fares fixed by Parliament

Building the railway

Stephenson had to plan and then build embankments, cuttings, bridges, engines and machinery. Sources 3–7 on these two pages show how he solved the various problems which he faced.

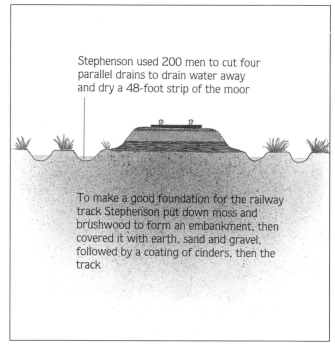

Stephenson used 200 men to cut four parallel drains to drain water away and dry a 48-foot strip of the moor

To make a good foundation for the railway track Stephenson put down moss and brushwood to form an embankment, then covered it with earth, sand and gravel, followed by a coating of cinders, then the track

SOURCE 3 Cross-section of the railway on Chat Moss

SOURCE 4 The Sankey Viaduct, which was built to carry the railway over the Sankey Brook

1. Explain how each of the following helped towards the successful building of the railway:
   ■ the needs of Liverpool merchants and Manchester factory owners
   ■ the decision by the company to change its plans in 1826
   ■ the skills of George Stephenson.
2. Which one was the most important?

Near Liverpool a tunnel had to be bored through almost a mile and a quarter of solid rock.

SOURCE 5
The entrance to the 2250-yard tunnel into Liverpool at Edgehill

▲ **SOURCE 6**
The route taken by the railway

SOURCE 7
Navvies at work on the 100-foot deep Olive Mount cutting

The company decided to use a steam locomotive rather than horse power. It ran some trials at Rainhill to decide which locomotive to use. In October 1829 about 15,000 people turned up to watch Stephenson's 'Rocket' winning the trials. It went as fast as fifteen miles per hour when pulling stones and passengers and 28 miles per hour without.

The railway opened in September 1830.

Was the railway a success?

First class trains left each city at 7.00 a.m., 10.00 a.m., 1.00 p.m. and 4.30 p.m. Second class trains left at 8.00 a.m. and 2.00 p.m. The trains carried about 120 passengers, and the journey took an hour and 40 minutes.

SOURCE 8 From the annual register in 1832, two years after the railway opened

> All the coaches have stopped running. The canals have reduced their prices by 30 per cent. Goods are delivered in Manchester the same day as they arrive in Liverpool. By canal it took three days. The saving to manufacturers in Manchester, in the transporting of cotton alone, has been £20,000 a year. Coal pits have been sunk and factories established along the railway, giving greater employment to the poor. The railway pays one fifth of the poor rates in the parishes through which it passes. The transportation of milk and garden produce is easier. Residents along the line can use the railways to attend their business in Manchester and Liverpool with ease and little expense. No inconvenience is felt by residents from smoke or noise. The value of land on the line has gone up because of the railway. It is much sought after for building.

SOURCE 9 Travel on the new railway

	Passengers	Goods (tons)	Coal (tons)
1830	71,951	1,433	2,630
1835	473,847	230,629	116,246

Activity

Design a poster advertising the railway to potential customers.

1. Explain whether each of the following people could benefit from the Liverpool and Manchester Railway:
   - a merchant in Liverpool selling cotton
   - a canal owner
   - a Manchester cotton mill owner
   - an unemployed person in Liverpool
   - a farmer on the railway route.
2. Look back at the arguments on page 37 for and against building the railway. According to Source 8, who was right: the supporters or the opponents of the railway?

Changing transport

New roads

In 1750 there were 3000 miles of turnpike roads. By 1800 there were almost 20,000 miles (see Source 1). Turnpike roads shortened journey times for passengers. For example:

London to	1750	1825
Edinburgh	10–12 days	46 hours
Newcastle	5 days	36 hours
Carlisle	4½ days	32 hours
York	4 days	20 hours
Manchester	3½ days	18 hours
Liverpool	3½ days	22 hours
Exeter	3 days	18 hours
Birmingham	2–3 days	15 hours
Bristol	2½ days	11 hours
Norwich	1½ days	12 hours
Oxford	1½ days	6 hours
Brighton	1 day	4 hours

These new roads were more suitable for coaches carrying passengers than for heavy waggons carrying industrial goods.

Key

— Turnpike roads in 1750
— Turnpike roads in 1770

SOURCE 1 Turnpike roads in 1750 and 1770

New waterways

In 1750 almost the only inland waterways were the navigable rivers. If these great rivers could be connected up it would make it possible for boats to cross Britain from one end to the other.

Source 2 shows you how this was done to create the Grand Trunk System. Many industries, such as the iron industry in Coalbrookdale on the River Severn and the pottery industry in Stoke-on-Trent, benefited. For example, the pottery industry needed china clay from Cornwall. This could now be brought to Stoke-on-Trent via Liverpool, instead of overland by waggon. The Wedgwoods at Etruria used to send their china to London, Liverpool and Hull by packhorse. But this method jolted the china around too much. Canal transport was a much smoother and safer way to transport fragile goods.

The success of the early canals set off a period of 'canal mania'. Many new canals were built, even in rural areas where they were not really profitable. By 1840 there were nearly 3000 miles of canals in England and Wales and 200 miles in Scotland. But waterways had many limitations. In the eighteenth century the boats were pulled by horses or by people. Even when steam-driven canal boats came in, they still only averaged a few miles per hour because they had to slow down at locks. They were no good for passengers and the network still did not cover the whole country. Very few new canals were built after 1840.

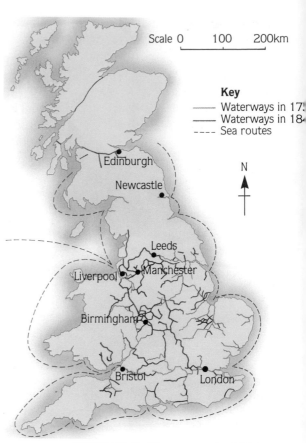

Key

— Waterways in 17[...]
— Waterways in 18[...]
---- Sea routes

SOURCE 2 Waterways in 1750 and 1840

Coastal shipping

Well into the nineteenth century coastal shipping remained an important method of moving goods and people. Ports like London, Liverpool, Bristol and Glasgow were also growing industrial centres and needed goods, fuel and raw materials. Coal was the most valuable coastal trade, but grain, stone and slate were also important.

In the early nineteenth century steamships were developed, which could travel much faster than sailing ships. This led to an increase in passenger traffic. In 1849 twice as many passengers travelled from Edinburgh to London by steamship as travelled by train.

New railways

After the success of the Liverpool and Manchester Railway a period of 'railway mania' followed, from 1844 until 1848. Hundreds of companies were set up, and thousands of miles of track were laid.

Everyone thought there was easy money to be made from INVESTING in a railway company. Merchants and MANUFACTURERS urgently wanted railways to provide faster and cheaper transport for their goods.

Many of the railway companies were small-scale and local, and the various companies often used different gauges (widths) of track. Through travel between areas was therefore difficult. A standard gauge for the whole country was introduced in the 1860s. The main-line network was largely complete by 1875 and by 1900 most of the main lines had been connected up by branch lines to create the network shown in Source 3.

The success of the railways gradually destroyed horse-drawn transport and canals. The railways helped to change the face of

Britain. Commuter trains into the big cities and towns allowed workers to live further out of town, and suburbs were created. Fast cheap trains to the coast meant that ordinary people could take cheap holidays or day trips to the seaside. Seaside resorts grew up. In 1811 the journey from London to Brighton took six hours by stage coach and cost £1; in 1841 it took two hours by train and cost four shillings. The railways also improved the supply of fresh food into towns.

SOURCE 4
The Railway Station, a painting by William Frith, 1862

SOURCE 5 From the *Railway News*, 1864

❝In the early morning we see the supplies for the London markets rapidly unloaded by these night trains; fish and food, Aylesbury butter and pork, apples, cabbage and cucumber. No sooner do these disappear than at ten-minute intervals arrive other trains with Manchester pails and bowls, Liverpool cotton, American provisions. Later in the morning stones, bricks, iron girders and steel pipes arrive.❞

Activity

Work in groups of four. Each of you choose one of the following journeys:
■ taking cloth from Manchester to London
■ taking coal from Newcastle to London
■ taking stone from Leeds to London
■ taking your family of five from London to Cardiff.
Decide on a route and method of transport for 1750, 1840 and 1900. Give reasons for your choice.

Compare your answers with others in the group. How do the routes and methods of transport used change between 1750 and 1900?

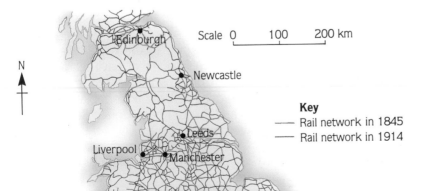

Scale 0   100   200 km

Key
— Rail network in 1845
— Rail network in 1914

SOURCE 3 The rail network in 1845 and 1914

Empire and trade

DURING the seventeenth and eighteenth centuries Britain's overseas trade grew quickly. As you can see from Source 1, by the end of the eighteenth century Britain had trading links throughout the world. Some of the most important trade was with its COLONIES, which included vast, rich countries such as India. This trade made the merchants an enormous amount of money, which they could spend or INVEST back in Britain. In the next four pages we will be investigating how Britain's trade helped the INDUSTRIAL REVOLUTION to get going.

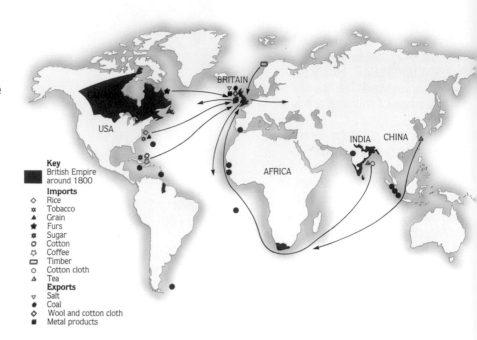

Key

British Empire around 1800

Imports
◇ Rice
✿ Tobacco
▲ Grain
★ Furs
✹ Sugar
○ Cotton
♧ Coffee
▭ Timber
o Cotton cloth
△ Tea

Exports
▽ Salt
● Coal
◇ Wool and cotton cloth
■ Metal products

SOURCE 1 Britain's trade and Empire around 1800

The Industrial Revolution and the slave trade

The most important part of Britain's trade in the late eighteenth century was the slave trade. This trade had a great impact on Britain:

■ It brought into Britain new imports like sugar and coffee, which changed many people's eating and drinking habits.

■ It brought in RAW MATERIALS such as cotton, which were vital for Britain's growing industries.

■ It provided many jobs in Britain by creating a market abroad for British goods.

■ It produced enormous profits, some of which were invested in new inventions and industries in Britain.

See if you can see examples of each of these on pages 42–44.

Around the middle of the eighteenth century three new imports began to have a great impact on people's eating habits: coffee, tea and sugar. In London there were coffee shops everywhere. These were places to meet friends for a chat and to read the newspapers. Meanwhile, tea was fast becoming the national drink. Both these drinks have a naturally bitter taste, and large amounts of sugar were used in them. Sugar was also added to many other things: bread, porridge and puddings, for example. In 1700 the British ate four pounds of sugar per person. By 1800 this had risen to eighteen pounds. The British were developing a 'sweet tooth', and rapidly losing their teeth as a result.

Most tea came from China (and later India), but coffee and sugar, along with many other goods, came from the West Indies and were produced by the work of slaves.

Sugar cane had been brought to the West Indies in 1493 by Christopher Columbus. By 1516 the first sugar grown in the West Indies was being shipped back to Europe. When the British conquered many of the West Indian islands they set up huge sugar plantations. Many British families made their fortunes from sugar plantations.

Workers were needed for these huge plantations. The plantation owners found their workers in Africa. They were brought over to the West Indies as slaves.

It was also slave labour that gave the people of Britain cheap cotton. The vast cotton imports into Liverpool (see page 35) came from plantations in the West Indies and the southern United States farmed by African slave labour.

SOURCE 2 Written in 1729 by a British merchant, Joshua Cree

❝ Our trade with Africa is very profitable to the nation in general. The supplying our plantations with Negroes is of extraordinary advantage to us, that the planting of sugar and tobacco, and carrying on trade there could not be supported without them. All the great increase of the riches of the kingdom proceed chiefly from the labour of Negroes in the plantations. ❞

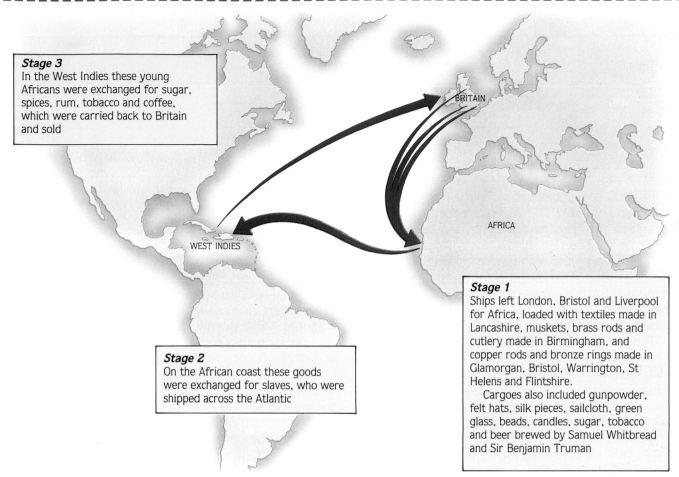

Stage 3
In the West Indies these young Africans were exchanged for sugar, spices, rum, tobacco and coffee, which were carried back to Britain and sold

BRITAIN

AFRICA

WEST INDIES

Stage 1
Ships left London, Bristol and Liverpool for Africa, loaded with textiles made in Lancashire, muskets, brass rods and cutlery made in Birmingham, and copper rods and bronze rings made in Glamorgan, Bristol, Warrington, St Helens and Flintshire.

Cargoes also included gunpowder, felt hats, silk pieces, sailcloth, green glass, beads, candles, sugar, tobacco and beer brewed by Samuel Whitbread and Sir Benjamin Truman

Stage 2
On the African coast these goods were exchanged for slaves, who were shipped across the Atlantic

SOURCE 3 The Trade Triangle

Industrial expansion and the slave trade

The Trade Triangle (see Source 3) was a very clever system. The ships never sailed empty and everyone made lots of money:

■ the ship owners who sold the slaves. The numbers of slaves transported were incredible, e.g. 610,000 to Jamaica in 1700–86 and 800,000 to St Domingue in 1680–1776. The profits for the ship owners were huge – often more than £5000 profit per boatload
■ the plantation owners in the West Indies. In 1780 the West Indies supplied two thirds of the cotton imported into Britain
■ the factory owners in Britain, who had found a market for their goods. In 1770 one third of Manchester's textiles were exported to Africa and half to the West Indies, where the cloth was used for blankets and clothes for the slaves.

Some powerful people such as John Gladstone (the father of William Gladstone, a nineteenth-century Prime Minister) made their wealth from slave ships and slave plantations. But every person in Britain who smoked or used sugar or worked in one of the factories also benefited. By 1788 £200,000's worth of goods were being sent to Africa each year. Of this £180,000's worth was for buying slaves. About

18,000 men, women and children earned their livelihood by making these goods in the factories. In 1753 there were 120 sugar refineries in England, all providing new jobs.

The two most important cities involved in this trade triangle were Bristol and Liverpool. In the 1730s the average voyage from Bristol, picking up 170 slaves in Africa, made a profit of £8000 – an enormous sum of money in those days (see Source 5 over the page).

SOURCE 4 Written by Malachy Postlethwayt in 1746

❞ *The extensive employment of our shipping to and from America, and the daily bread of most of our British manufacturers, are owing mainly to the labour of Negroes.*

The Negro trade is the main source of wealth and naval power for Britain. ❞❞

EMPIRE AND TRADE

SOURCE 5 Written by a historian, J.F. Nicholls, in 1881

" There is not a brick in Bristol that was not cemented with the blood of a slave. Sumptuous mansions and luxurious living was made from the sufferings and groans of the slaves bought and sold by Bristol merchants. "

In 1700 Liverpool had been a small sea port with a population of 5000. In 1709 Liverpool slave traders set out on their first voyage to buy and sell slaves. By 1771 there were 106 ships a year sailing from Liverpool, which between them carried 282,000 slaves. In the 1790s Liverpool's slave trade alone accounted for fifteen per cent of Britain's entire overseas trade. By 1800 Liverpool was a successful booming city of 78,000 people.

The slave trade provided many jobs in Liverpool. By 1774 there were eight sugar refineries and fifteen rope factories. There were many factories making chains, anchors, and iron, copper and brass goods for the slave ships. Half of Liverpool's sailors were involved in the slave trade.

Money poured into Liverpool from the slave trade. Banks did well by lending money to traders, but slave merchants also used their profits to set up Liverpool's most important banks. In the 1780s Liverpool made a profit from the slave trade of over £1 million a year. The trade was so profitable that it was not just the rich who wanted a share in it. Many people bought a share in a slave ship.

SOURCE 6 Written in 1795 by J. Wallace in *A General and Descriptive History of the town of Liverpool*

" It is well known that many of the small vessels that carry about 100 slaves are paid for by attornies, drapers, ropers, grocers, barbers and tailors. "

SOURCE 7 Written in 1907 by a historian, R. Muir, in *A History of Liverpool*

" The slave trade helped every industry, provided the money for docks, enriched and employed the mills of Lancashire. Beyond a doubt it was the slave trade which raised Liverpool from a struggling port to be one of the richest and most prosperous trading centres in the world. "

SOURCE 8 From a history of Liverpool written by the city's public librarian and paid for by the city to celebrate the 750th anniversary of the city's charter in the 1950s

" In the long run, the triangular trade operation based on Liverpool was to bring benefits to all, not least to the transplanted slaves, whose descendants have subsequently achieved in the New World standards of education and civilisation far ahead of their countrymen whom they left behind. "

Some of the merchants, slave traders and plantation owners who made fortunes through the slave trade INVESTED some of their profits in industrial developments in Britain. For example:

■ James Watt's work with steam engines was partly financed by money from the West Indian trade.

■ Anthony Bacon, a slave trader, invested money in iron foundries and coal mines in South Wales.

■ Thomas Harris, a Bristol slave trader, invested in the iron works in Dowlais in South Wales.

■ West Indies merchants financed iron works in South Yorkshire producing iron rails for colliery waggon ways.

■ The company which built the Liverpool and Manchester Railway included John Moss (who owned a sugar plantation) and John Gladstone (who owned slave ships and sugar and coffee plantations).

1. Sources 5 and 8 give different views about the slave trade. Suggest possible reasons why they differ.
2. Which of the writers of Sources 5 and 8 do you agree with?
3. Under the following headings make a list of all the ways British industry and British people benefited from the slave trade:
   ■ raw materials for British factories
   ■ changed living habits and diet
   ■ new jobs in Britain
   ■ profits invested in British industry.
4. Which of these statements do you agree with most?
   ■ 'Without the slave trade the Industrial Revolution would not have happened.'
   ■ 'Without the slave trade the Industrial Revolution would have got off to a slower start.'
   ■ 'Without the slave trade the Industrial Revolution would have happened in exactly the same way.'

Why did London need new docks?

During the eighteenth century Britain's trade of all kinds went from strength to strength. In 1800 Britain was the world's wealthiest trading nation. London was the greatest port in the world, and London's docks were the busiest in the world. Tea, coffee, pepper, spices, silks, porcelain, timber and many other goods flooded into London from overseas. Goods manufactured by Britain's new industries also flooded into London, for export. The London docks were crammed with ocean-going ships.

Added to this were the thousands of ships which were involved in the coastal trade between London and other parts of Britain. Bulky goods such as grain, building materials or coal were usually brought to London by ship, even from nearby Kent. The amount of coal brought to London from Newcastle and Sunderland tripled during the eighteenth century. In 1800 the London docks were crowded with coal barges, timber barges, and thousands of smaller boats.

All these boats headed for the Pool of London, the area between the Tower of London and London Bridge (see Source 10). It soon became clear that London's docks could not cope. There were not enough quays for boats to dock against, so they had to be moored four or five abreast in midstream. Over 3000 small boats called lighters continuously ferried their cargoes to and from the quays. This led to long delays, which lost the merchants money. Also, because the quays were piled high with cargoes, the docks made easy pickings for thieves.

SOURCE 10 The Pool of London early in the eighteenth century

By the end of the eighteenth century London merchants were demanding that new docks be built. They wanted deep water docks which ocean-going ships could enter, with plenty of warehouse space. In 1799 over 100 West Indies merchants set up a company to build new docks for the West Indies trade. They would use the docks themselves, but would also charge other merchants to use them. The new docks were opened in 1802 on the Isle of Dogs. All West Indies trade went there. More new docks were soon built (see Source 9).

---

1. Using your own research find out where the goods in Source 9 came from. Source 1 on page 42 and Source 1 on page 30 will help you.
2. Choose three imports which were needed by Britain's industries. Explain your choice.
3. Choose three imports which would affect the way people ate or dressed. Explain your choice.

SOURCE 9 New docks built in London, 1800–1900

Name	Date built	Goods handled
West India Docks	1802–6	sugar, rum, tea, hardwood, timber, fruit, coffee
London Docks	1805	wine, wool, rice, sugar, brandy, tobacco
Surrey Docks	1805	softwood timber, wheat, foodstuffs
East India Dock	1806	tea, silks, spices, porcelain
St Katherine's Docks	1828	tea, ivory, wool, sugar, rubber
Poplar Docks	1852	coastal coal
Royal Victoria Dock	1855	meat, grain, tobacco, vegetables, passengers
Millwall Dock	1868	grain
Royal Albert Dock	1880	meat, grain, tobacco, vegetables, passengers
Tilbury Docks	1886	coal, grain, passengers

Why there and why then?

WHY DID the INDUSTRIAL REVOLUTION happen where and when it did? Historians disagree about the answer to this question. On this page there are many possible reasons suggested by historians, but as you will see not everyone agrees how important each one is. You have already looked at some of these factors in detail. Now you can make up your own mind about them.

Read the historians' statements carefully. Then, working in groups:

1. Choose statements ('for' or 'against') that could be applied to the case studies of businessmen such as Richard Arkwright or Matthew Boulton on pages 9–25.
2. Draw a flow diagram showing the ways in which any of the six factors are connected.
3. Design a wall display headed 'What caused the Industrial Revolution?' Choose suitable pictures to put on it.
4. Write an essay entitled 'What caused the Industrial Revolution?' Try to include your own view as to which causes were more important than others.

Because . . . Britain's population was growing

For:
■ The more people there were, the more goods businesses could sell to them
■ The growing population provided the extra labour to work in the new industries

Against:
■ Many people in Britain were too poor to be able to buy the products made by British industry
■ The new industries often started in places where there were not many people to work in them

Because . . . Britain had plenty of raw materials

For:
■ There was plenty of the raw materials needed to make iron and steel, which were used to make machines and railways
■ There was plenty of coal to drive steam engines to power machinery in the factories

Against:
■ The raw materials were very difficult to extract. They were not always where they were most needed and they were slow and expensive to transport
■ These raw materials had been around for thousands of years, but there had been no Industrial Revolution

Because . . . Britain's farmers grew more food

For:
■ They grew more food to feed the growing population, particularly the town population, which did not grow its own food
■ The profits made by some farmers and landowners were invested in industry or in transport improvements such as canals
■ Farmers and farm workers earned more and so had more money to spend on goods produced by industry

Against:
■ Some landowners actually tried to stop industry developing in their area
■ Many of the improvements in agriculture happened long after the changes in industry had started

Because . . . Britain's Empire and overseas trade were growing

For:
- People involved in overseas trade made money, which was invested in developing British industry and transport
- New supplies of raw materials were opened up, e.g. cotton from America
- A big new market was created for British goods overseas. This meant new factories were needed and new jobs were created.

Against:
- Profits from trade were sometimes spent on land and property instead of being invested in industry

Because . . . Britain's transport was improved

For:
- Better transport made raw materials cheaper, and made the supply more reliable
- Better transport also enlarged the markets and made the finished goods cheaper
- Better transport allowed new ideas and inventions to spread more quickly

Against:
- Industrial developments began well before the great improvements in transport
- Many landowners opposed improvements in transport if the routes ran across their land

Because . . . there were new ideas and new inventions in industry

For:
- There were great individuals, industrialists and inventors, who saw how to make businesses out of new inventions

Against:
- A lot of money was needed to develop new inventions. It was as easy to go bust financing a new invention as it was to make profits

Was there an Industrial Revolution?

So FAR in this book we have focused on how industry changed between 1750 and 1850. But did all industries change in the same way? We are going to approach this question by looking at what happened to the DOMESTIC SYSTEM.

In 1750 most industrial work was carried out in people's homes. Historians therefore call it the Domestic System.

The impression many people have is that:
- the Domestic System was an ideal one, where workers controlled their own lives
- the Industrial Revolution totally replaced the Domestic System with an inhuman Factory System.

SOURCE 1 Written in 1833 by P. Gaskell

Down to 1800 the majority of workers laboured in their own homes. The spinning wheel was to be found in almost every house . . . These were undoubtedly the golden times of manufacturing. By the work carried out under a man's roof he retained his respectability and earned wages which were enough not only to live comfortably upon, but which enabled him to rent a few acres of land.

SOURCE 2 From an article in the magazine *History Today*: April 1983

At the centre of most people's picture of the Industrial Revolution stands the dark satanic mill, where an exploited and dispirited army of men, women and children is engaged for starvation wages in an endless round of drudgery: the pace of their labour is determined by the persistent pulse of the steam engine; the sole beneficiary of their efforts is the grasping factory master.

SOURCE 4 Weaving in a factory, 1834

---

1. What do Sources 1–4 suggest were the differences between the Domestic System and the Factory System?

What was the Domestic System really like?

Under the DOMESTIC SYSTEM a MANUFACTURER bought raw materials and hired labourers to make the finished products in their own houses. For example, in the 1830s the Dixons of Carlisle employed 3500 handloom weavers, scattered all over the north of England and Scotland. These domestic workers were wage earners. They were not their own bosses. Even though they were all working in their own homes rather than in a single factory, it was still a system of mass production. In bad times the employers would cut pay rates, but because the workers were so scattered they could not organise themselves to demand better pay and conditions.

Not many of the workers were skilled craftsmen. Much of the work was just repetition of a few simple movements, such as sewing buttons onto shirts.

All the family was involved. The women, and children from the age of six or seven, worked long

SOURCE 3 A contemporary illustration of a weaver working at home

SOURCE 5 A forge for making nails. It is attached to the family's home. The whole family is involved in the work

hours. In fact, in the textile industry 75 per cent of the workers were women and children.

Fathers were often in charge of the family's work. Like factory overseers they made their family work hard for long hours. Some historians believe that the Factory System improved family relationships, because it stopped the father behaving like an overseer.

Under the Domestic System there were also many small workshops. Children were often sent to work in these as APPRENTICES. It was not uncommon for children to become apprentices at seven years of age and go on until they were 21.

Did the Factory System take over?

It is too simple to say that the Factory System replaced the Domestic System overnight. The two overlapped for a long time. For example, the first spinning factories produced yarn which weavers working at home turned into cloth.

In the nineteenth century, however, all stages of the textile industry were mechanised, and in textiles the Domestic System did disappear. But in other industries such as rope-making, nail-making, hat-making or hosiery the Domestic System was used until well after 1850. Some of the newer industries, such as cardboard box making, also used the Domestic System.

1. Look at Sources 7–9, which come from the nineteenth century. Explain what is happening in each picture.
2. Where is the work taking place: in a factory, in a home, or somewhere else?

Activity

Work in pairs.

One person should prepare evidence to support the statement 'Change was more important than continuity in the Industrial Revolution'.

The other should prepare evidence to support the statement 'Continuity was more important than change in the Industrial Revolution.'

SOURCE 6 From a Government report on domestic weaving workshops in 1833

66 *Draw-boys and girls work as long hours as the weavers, that is, as long as they can see; standing on the same spot, barefooted, on an earthen cold damp floor in a close damp cellar, for thirteen or fourteen hours a day.*

1. Which of Sources 1–6 give the most and least favourable impressions of the Domestic System?
2. Make a list of the similarities between the Domestic System and the Factory System.
3. Which would you rather have worked in?

SOURCE 7

SOURCE 8

SOURCE 9

The story of two families

OVER the next few pages we are going to look at a range of case studies of people and places, investigating how things changed between 1750 and 1900 and asking 'Was life getting better?'

This will be a difficult question to answer, because we all have different ideas about what makes life better. And people in the nineteenth century probably had different ideas from people today.

Activity

Work in groups. Under the following headings, make a list of questions which you could ask someone in order to measure their quality of life: jobs, prices, health, home life.

One way to explore how people's lives were affected by all the changes between 1750 and 1900 is to look at the history of one family.

On 17 November 1887, Charles Herbert Glover married Emily Eyles at Worcester. You can see them at the bottom of page 51. These are extracts from their family history. You might be able to find out similar information about your own family.

Work in pairs.
1. Work out:
   - how old each couple were when they got married
   - how long each person lived
   - how many children each family had (remember babies who died).
2. Do any of these figures show a pattern of change over the period?
3. Do these family histories provide evidence that people were becoming more mobile? For example, think about how far apart the homes of people getting married were, and how far people moved during their lives.
4. List all the jobs people did.
5. Do these two family histories show movement from farming jobs in the country to industrial and commercial jobs in towns?
6. Compare the lives of the people at the beginning of the story with those at the end. Who had the better life?

Charles Herbert Glover's family

Matthew Glover (1780–1858) was the fifth child in a family of six. He lived and worked in Alverthorpe, two miles from Wakefield in Yorkshire. Like his father he was a butcher. He rented fields, where he probably kept his animals ready for slaughter. He did well in his business and bought some land in Alverthorpe.

In 1806 he married **Ann Wood** (1783–1846), who also came from Alverthorpe. They had four children, three sons and a daughter.

Their second son was **Matthew Henry Glover** (1817–1884). He did not inherit his father's business. Instead, he was APPRENTICED to a draper (a cloth-dealer) in Wakefield.

In 1848 he married **Elizabeth Barker** (1822–c.1865) of Pontefract (nine miles from Wakefield). Her father was a farmer and sold malt to the brewing industry. They had six children.

By 1851 Matthew Henry Glover had his own shop in Wakefield selling linen and silk. He employed fourteen people.

By 1861 he was a woollen manufacturer, employing 47 people at a mill near the centre of Leeds. He lived in a suburb of Leeds.

By 1871 Matthew Henry had moved to a farmhouse with 40 acres of land on the edge of Leeds. Elizabeth had died.

By 1881 Matthew Henry had set up an engineering and machine making firm in Leeds.

His second son was **Charles Herbert Glover** (1850–1906). He did not inherit his father's business.

With his brother he moved to New Cross in London. With money given to them by their father they set up a very successful timber import and sawmill business.

An accident at work made him blind. Despite this, he made frequent trips by ship to Sweden to buy timber. It was on one of these trips that he met **Emily Eyles** (1854–1915), who was returning to England after a short holiday.

Charles Herbert Glover and Emily Eyles ▶

Emily Eyles' family

Hope Eyles (1797–1865) was the youngest of five children. He married **Jane Gibson** (1798–c.1865) in Old Sodbury in Gloucestershire in 1819. Jane came from the nearby market town of Chipping Sodbury. They had six children.

They moved to Chipping Sodbury. The 1841 CENSUS lists Hope as a freestone mason; he probably worked at the quarry nearby. A Directory of 1842 lists Jane as a straw bonnet maker.

In 1851 Hope was working as a master baker and in 1861 as a carrier. He was also one of the Overseers of the Poor for Chipping Sodbury.

Samuel Eyles (1820–1890) was Hope and Jane's eldest child. He moved to Bristol (twelve miles away), where he worked as a wheelwright.

In 1844 he married **Matilda Ann Marsh** (1820–1883). Matilda's family had been market gardeners in Chipping Sodbury.

By the time of the 1851 census Samuel and Matilda lived in the village of Brokenborough about fifteen miles from Chipping Sodbury. They had twelve children. Three died as babies. Their household included a 'monthly nurse' to look after a one-day-old baby and a maidservant. Samuel had a coachmaking business which employed three men.

By 1871, they had moved to Worcester (about 50 miles away). Samuel had developed a new paint spraying process, and in 1869 he sent his two sons to the United States to advertise and sell it. One stayed there permanently.

In about 1882 the business closed and Samuel became a travelling salesman based in Worcester.

Matthew Henry Glover

Samuel Eyles

Emily Eyles (1854–1915) was born at Brokenborough. She was Samuel and Matilda's sixth child.

Her mother died in 1883. She and her sisters probably helped look after their father. She also spent some time in Wales as a paid 'companion' for a married woman. Afterwards, she took a holiday in Sweden with a friend, and on the return journey met **Charles Herbert Glover**. They married on 17 November 1887 and had three children.

Did life in the countryside get better?

Life in the village before 1850

YOU will remember the village of Ashill in Norfolk from pages 26–29 of this book. Source 2 shows the centre of the village in detail.

Most people in Ashill were farm labourers. From dawn until dark they did hard, physical work on the land. Horses were kept to pull ploughs and harrows, but nearly all other work, including sowing, harvesting and threshing, was done by hand.

Harvest time was the climax of the farming year. Many workers, including children, were needed then. It was an opportunity for families to earn a little extra money.

People in Ashill who were not farm labourers still depended on the farmers for their work. The blacksmith and the carpenter made and repaired farm tools and equipment. The miller ground the village's corn.

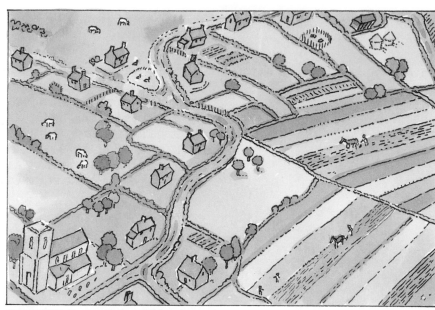

SOURCE 2 Ashill in 1780

SOURCE 3 Inside a farm labourer's cottage in the eighteenth century

SOURCE 1 Written by a historian, Rowland Parker, in his book *The Common Stream*, 1975

“*In the eighteenth century farming was still the be-all and end-all of village life, and village life was still the life of the vast majority of English people. The majority of the men in the village were labourers with a weekly wage. Sanitation and hygiene cost nothing except the trouble of getting a bucket of water. Travel cost them nothing because they walked.*”

SOURCE 4 An early nineteenth-century picture of the rape seed harvest (rape seed provided oil for lamps) in Yorkshire

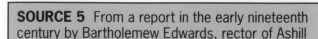

SOURCE 5 From a report in the early nineteenth century by Bartholemew Edwards, rector of Ashill

“*Ashill: population 547 . . . One school, taught by a man, and two by women, in which about 60 children are educated . . . The poorer classes want [lack] education.*”

1. Look at Source 4. Can you see:
   - the crop being brought for threshing
   - threshing with flails
   - removing the straw with wooden forks
   - cleaning the seed by shaking it?

2. In no more than ten lines describe the main features of life in a village in the early nineteenth century.

Enclosure

The first big change Ashill experienced was the ENCLOSURE of its land in 1786. As you saw on page 27 the big landowners supported this enclosure, but they claimed that everybody would benefit.

> **SOURCE 6** An anonymous letter, left in the gateway of the rectory of Ashill in 1816
>
> 66 *To the gentlemen of Ashill:*
> *This is to inform you that you have brought us under the heaviest burden and under the hardest yoke we ever knowed: You do as you like, you rob the poor of their commons rights, plough the grass up that God sent to grow, that a poor man may feed a cow, pig, horse or ass; lay muck and stones on the road to prevent the grass growing.*
> *There is five or six of you have gotten the whole of the land in this parish in your own hands and you would wish to be rich and starve the poor of the parish. Gentlemen, we mean to circulate your blood.* 99

> **SOURCE 7** From *The Agricultural Revolution 1750–1880* by J.D. Chambers and G.E. Mingay, 1966. The authors are commenting on the effects of enclosure across the country as a whole
>
> 66 *Enclosure meant more food for the growing population, more land under cultivation, and on balance, more employment in the countryside; and enclosed farms provided the framework for the new advances of the nineteenth century.* 99

1. Does the fact that Sources 6 and 7 disagree about the effects of enclosure mean that one of them is wrong?
2. Why do you think Source 6 was sent anonymously?
3. Compare Sources 6 and 7 with Source 3 on page 27. Which of these three sources is the most reliable for finding out about the effects of enclosure in Ashill?
4. Which of the following are likely to have benefited from enclosure in Ashill:
   - a rich landowner who rented out land to tenant farmers
   - a tenant farmer who paid rent to a landowner
   - a small landowner who had common rights
   - a farm labourer who grazed animals on the common?

Hard times

During the wars with France (1793–1815) there was a great demand for food and farmers prospered. When the wars ended, life for the farm labourers became harder. Some farmers had to sack some of their workers, and workers who kept their jobs had their wages reduced.

In 1831 agricultural labourers across much of southern and eastern England rioted. They attacked the new threshing machines which were taking away their winter work. They set fire to farm buildings and hay stacks. In 1834 the reform of the Poor Law made things worse. Instead of the poor being given bread or extra money, they were sent to workhouses, where families were split up and conditions were harsh.

SOURCE 8 A cartoon entitled *The home of the rick burner*, published in 1844

> **SOURCE 9** A letter sent to a farmer, signed by 'Swing'. Many different groups of desperate labourers signed their threats to the farmers 'Captain Swing', hoping to frighten them
>
> 66 *Sir,*
> *This is to acquaint you that if your threshing machines are not destroyed by you directly we shall commence our labours. Signed on behalf of the whole.*
> *Swing* 99

1. Does Source 8 fully explain why farm workers sent letters like the one in Source 9?

DID LIFE IN THE COUNTRYSIDE GET BETTER?

Did life get better after 1850?

By the middle of the nineteenth century prosperity had returned to farming. On many farms improvements had been made to increase production. But from the 1870s onwards British farmers faced increased competition from farmers in America, Australia and New Zealand. The prices farmers could get for their produce fell. Wages fell too. Many people stopped working on the land and moved. The population of Ashill decreased.

> **SOURCE 10** From an account of a meeting in Ashill in 1892, attended by 70 labourers and six farmers
>
> " Labourers have decreased in numbers the last few years. Some have gone to the colonies, some to the mines, some to the towns.
>
> The hours of work for labourers in the summer are from 6.00 a.m. to 6.00 p.m. In the winter they work from light to dark. As a rule they go on working till they cannot see to do any more.
>
> Most men here are employed regularly summer and winter. Wages have been the same for two years.
>
> The cottages are very fair and have gardens. Most men live near their work. The furthest a man has to go is one and a half miles. The water supply is good, but some have to go a little way to fetch it.
>
> The relations between employer and employed are good. "

> **SOURCE 11** From *White's Directory*, 1883, which lists the occupations of property owners in Ashill
>
> " Allcock, Miss Emily, infant schoolmistress
> Allcock, Thomas, wheelwright
> Amos, Charles, blacksmith
> Coker, William, carpenter
> Dennis, William, miller
> Darsley, John, farmer and beerhouse owner
> Franklin, John, brick and tile maker
> Grimmer, Henry, grocer and Post Office
> Horsley, Robert, farmer and threshing machine proprietor
> Lockwood, William, baker
> Sear, Edward, farmer and road surveyor
> Smith, George, joiner and builder. "

> 1. Which of these jobs would have been done in Ashill in 1750?

By 1900 all the children in Ashill went to school. The National School had been built in 1848 for 100 children, and an Infants School was built in 1876 for 60 children. Source 12 gives some extracts from the reports of the inspectors who visited the National School.

> **SOURCE 12** Extracts from the inspectors' reports
>
> " **1878** The order is very far from being satisfactory, the children being much given to both talking and copying during the examination. Foolscap paper should be obtained, and the children should often be examined on paper. The style of putting down the sums is bad. Writing too needs improvement.
>
> **1883** I regret to report that I can see very few signs of improvement. Reading is very poor. Arithmetic is bad throughout. The school is very far below the average of country schools . . . one tenth to be deducted from the grant to the school for faults of instruction.
>
> **1885** The school continues in an unsatisfactory condition. I am glad to hear that Mr Allcock is about to retire, as the work now required in Elementary Schools is evidently beyond him.
>
> **1886** The school has made great progress during the past year. Writing is good throughout. Reading much more intelligent. Arithmetic is very much improved. Needlework should be taught according to the instructions.
>
> **1888** The lower part of the school is excellent. In the higher there is some falling off. Grammar and Repetition very good. The condition of the school does Mr Sykes much credit. "

> 2. In what ways did the education provided in Ashill improve between 1800 and 1900?
> 3. What were the causes of these improvements?
> 4. Look at Source 13. Did the appearance of Ashill change much between 1750 and 1900?
> 5. In what ways did rural life improve? Consider work and living conditions.
> 6. Did everyone benefit from these improvements?
> 7. Are there any ways in which life had not changed much by 1900?

SOURCE 13 An artist's reconstruction of the centre of Ashill in 1900

SOURCE 14 A steam-driven threshing machine in Norfolk in the late nineteenth century

SOURCE 15 A steam plough being tested in 1871

How did Merthyr Tydfil change?

MERTHYR Tydfil is in a hilly area of South Wales. Before 1750 it was a small village, but during the 1750s it became one of the centres of the British iron industry.

From 1800 onwards the iron industry grew rapidly. It supplied cannon for the wars with France and rails for the growing railway network. Many eye-witnesses recorded their impressions of Merthyr, as you can see in Sources 1–4.

> 1. List as many changes as you can that took place in Merthyr between 1750 and 1900.
> 2. Were these changes for the worse, for the better, or a combination of the two? Support your answer with evidence from Sources 1–4.

People at work in the Merthyr iron works

SOURCE 5 From a description of Richard Crawshay's iron works written by Benjamin Malkin in 1803

66*His house is surrounded with fire, flame, smoke and ashes. The noise of the hammers, rolling mills, forges and bellows incessantly din and crash upon the ear. The machinery of this establishment is gigantic; and part of it is worked by water.* 99

SOURCE 1 Written by John George Wood in 1811

66*Merthyr Tydfil is but a village, but it enjoys the title of town . . . Its appearance . . . is very inferior, being chiefly composed of the huts and cottages of the workmen, belonging to the various iron works, erected upon the spur of the occasion, without plan or design, producing a confusion.* 99

SOURCE 6 From a description by W. and S. Sandys, 1819

66*We could see men moving among the blazing fires, and hear the noise of huge hammers, clanking of chains, whiz of wheels, blast of bellows, with the deep roaring of the fires . . . the effect was almost terrific when contrasted with the pitchy darkness of the night.* 99

SOURCE 2 From *The Cambrian Tourist or Post Chaise Companion through Wales*, a guidebook written in 1828

66*It is without form or order . . . yet here there is a larger population that any town in Wales can boast; its markets are large . . . its shopkeepers are thriving; and all that seems to be required to make the town one of the most respectable in Wales is a little attention to order and cleanliness.* 99

SOURCE 3 Written by a visitor in 1848

66*The footways are seldom paved, the streets are ill-paved and with bad materials, and are not lighted. The drainage is very imperfect; there are few underground sewers, no house drains, and the open gutters are not regularly cleaned out. Dustbins and similar receptacles for filth are unknown; the refuse is thrown into the streets.* 99

SOURCE 7 *Inside the rolling mills of Cyfarthfa Iron Works*, a painting by Penry Williams, 1825: The owner's home can be seen in the background, on the far right

SOURCE 4 From *Black's Picturesque Guide to Wales*, 1881

66*The town was, until lately, a shapeless, unsightly cluster of wretched dingy dwellings; but has in recent years undergone much improvement . . . It now contains some regular, well-built streets, a court-house, a market-house, several elegant private residences, a large number of respectable shops, four churches, and not fewer than 36 dissenting chapels.* 99

SOURCE 8 A painting of an iron works near Merthyr Tydfil at night, by Thomas Hornor, 1819

SOURCE 10 Puddlers, painted in about 1900

1. Look at Sources 5–8. What features described in Sources 5 and 6 can be seen in Sources 7 and 8?
2. What do you think was the attitude to the iron industry of the people who produced Sources 5–8?

The iron industry provided many jobs. Some jobs were highly skilled and quite well paid. Others were unskilled and poorly paid. As well as jobs in the iron works, many jobs were created by the iron industry for workers in the coal and ironstone mines.

The skilled jobs were done by men; the unskilled jobs were done by men, women and children.

Most workers worked twelve-hour shifts, but some of the skilled workers worked eight-hour shifts. Skilled workers earned four times as much as unskilled workers. Workers had to spend part of their wages at a shop run by the ironmaster (the owner of the iron works). In 1800 the workers at the Penydarren iron works attacked their employer's shop, claiming that the prices charged were too high.

Skilled workers were provided with houses, on a fixed rent, while unskilled workers had to find their own places to live as best they could.

SOURCE 9 A description of the work of the 'coke girls', from the Morning Chronicle, 1850

Seven or eight young women in coarse, sleeved pinafores, handkerchiefs tightly bound over their heads, battered hats, bristling with frayed feathers, blue stockings, and, in some instances, masculine overalls – some helping to unload the trucks [of coal] that came up the shaft, and others pottering with shovels about the 'tip'.

SOURCE 11 A description of rolling iron from an article on Merthyr in the Morning Chronicle, 1850

The rough bar is next snatched by huge pincers and swung with a vigorous arm upon iron rollers, of great strength and thickness, and in rapid motion, through which it passes – being grasped on the other side by a man holding huge tongs, suspended by a chain to the roof, who returns it over the rollers to the workman on the other side, who next puts it through a second and smaller groove in the rollers – and so on till the bar is lengthened to the proper extent, and reduced to the required width . . . The bar is generally twelve feet long and three inches wide, and whilst red hot and flexible as a thong of leather, it is dragged out by boys and sometimes by girls. The whole of this process takes less time than it has occupied the reader to peruse this account of it.

3. Study Sources 9–11 and the list of other jobs which your teacher will give you.
a) Which would be skilled jobs and which would be unskilled?
b) Which of the jobs described on this page would you rather have had? Give as many reasons for your choice as you can.
4. You have just moved from working on a farm in the country to a job in the iron industry in Merthyr. Explain whether or not your life has improved, and why.

Housing and health

Most of the houses in Merthyr were built by private builders. They built the houses as cheaply as possible and then rented them out at the highest rents they could get. Some of the houses were shared by several families, who had only two rooms each. But even these were better than the cellar rooms or the overcrowded common lodging houses where the poorest families lived.

---

1. Look at Sources 12 and 13. Make a list of housing problems in nineteenth-century Merthyr.

SOURCE 14 Rhyd-y-car Terrace. One third of the houses in Merthyr were built by the ironmasters (owners of the iron works) to attract skilled workers to work for them. Rhyd-y-car Terrace was built by the ironmaster Richard Crawshay between 1800 and 1820

SOURCE 12 From an article on Merthyr in the *Morning Chronicle*, 1850

"The best houses are of two stories, have four small sash windows (which are never opened).
On the ground floor there is a roomy kitchen with a stone floor; adjoining is a small room, just large enough to contain a four-post bed, a chest of drawers, a small corner cupboard, two chairs, a window table. The ceiling is not plastered, and the rafters are used for hanging up the crockery and the household utensils. Above stairs are two bedrooms, one large and the other small.
There is no strip of garden, no back door, no toilet, no drain, nor any pump for the supply of water. The street in front receives every kind of filth and rubbish."

SOURCE 15 In 1980 the oldest houses in the terrace were moved to the Welsh Folk Museum, near Cardiff. They were restored and furnished to show what the houses would have looked like at various times during the nineteenth century

SOURCE 13 From the report of a Government Inspector, 1849

"■ Some of the worst dwellings are those called 'the cellars'. These are small two-roomed houses, in a hollow between a road and a vast cinder heap. In these miserable tenements, with nothing in front or between them but stagnant pools and house refuse, it is said that nearly 1500 living beings are congregated.
■ On visiting Michael Harrington's lodging house I found 45 inmates, but many more come in to sleep at nights. There are no beds, but all the lodgers lie on the ground or floor. The children were sleeping in old orange boxes, or they would be liable to be crushed in the night by persons rolling over them. Each party had with them all their possessions – heaps of rags, bones, salt fish, rotten potatoes, and other things. The stench was sickening."

SOURCE 16
A coal miner's home, drawn in 1875

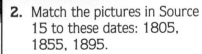

SOURCE 17 From an article on Merthyr in the *Morning Chronicle*, 1850

a) About the best paid skilled workers' houses

66 *These are, for the most part, the very type of cleanliness and order. They are stuffed with furniture: a fine mahogany clock, a showy mahogany chest of drawers, a set of mahogany chairs with solid seats, a glass-fronted cupboard for the display of china, glass and silver spoons . . . for the principal room.*

The women . . . are always scrubbing the rooms, polishing the furniture.

b) About an average coal miner's home

Among the furnishings I noticed: one chest of drawers, on which stood a tea tray, and a few books, including a Bible, the Young Woman's Companion, *the* Popular Story Teller, *etc. On the books were a clothes and hair brush; and hanging on the wall above was a small looking glass. [Also] two tables, three chairs, a cradle, a Dutch clock without a case, and over the fireplace brass candlesticks, a coffee pot and the like. In a small back window there hung a canary in his cage . . .* 99

2. Match the pictures in Source 15 to these dates: 1805, 1855, 1895.
3. How did the inside of a Rhyd-y-car Terrace cottage change between 1805 and 1855?
4. What changed between 1855 and 1895?
5. In which period did the more important changes take place?
6. Do any of the changes suggest that life at Rhyd-y-car Terrace was getting better? Explain your answer.
7. Can some of the changes be explained by changes in fashions? Which ones?

8. Does the 1855 reconstruction in Source 15 match up with the details in Sources 16 and 17?
9. Can you suggest reasons why there are differences?

Activity

You are an old woman living in Merthyr Tydfil in 1855. You are describing to your young grandchild what has changed since you came here in 1790.

What will you say? Draw up a list of changes and say how you feel they have affected your life.

Beside the seaside!

Changes: 1750–1900

UNTIL 1750, Brighton was a small seaside town. The main industry was fishing. Then in 1750 Dr Richard Russell, a Brighton doctor, published a book called *The Use of Sea Water in Diseases of the Glands*. He argued that bathing in seawater and drinking it were good for health. Wealthy people came to Brighton to follow his advice, and 'bathing machines' were provided for their use. Other doctors came to the town and built warm and cold baths.

SOURCE 1 The Royal Pavilion in Brighton, designed to look like an Indian palace and completed in 1821

In 1783 the Prince of Wales came to Brighton for the first time. He liked the town and bought property there, and he later employed the architect John Nash to build the spectacular Royal Pavilion.

The royal interest established Brighton as one of the most fashionable places to visit. From 1800 until 1830 it was mainly a resort for the wealthy upper classes.

---

1. Look at the maps in Source 2. Which shows Brighton in 1779 and which shows it in 1824? Explain your answer.
2. List five important changes between 1779 and 1824.

Sake Deen Mahomed

The Royal Pavilion (see Source 1) was designed to look like an Indian palace. India was the most important and most successful colony in the British Empire at the beginning of the nineteenth century. Indian ways were beginning to have an effect on many aspects of British life, as you can see from this case study of a famous Brighton businessman, Sake Deen Mahomed.

He was born in India in 1749, and came to Britain with a British army officer whom he had worked for in India. He moved to Brighton to set up his business – 'warm, cold and vapour baths'. He also introduced the practice of 'shampooing'.

In order to overcome white people's prejudice against him, he offered to treat influential clients without charge. This proved very successful, and he soon had many customers. The King gave him the title 'Shampooing Surgeon to His Majesty George IV' and made him superintendent of the baths at the Royal Pavilion.

In 1822 Mahomed wrote a respected medical book. It described the many patients he had treated successfully. It included cures for asthma, rheumatism, sciatica, lumbago and loss of voice.

After his retirement in 1843 his son Arthur Akhbar Mahomed continued to run the baths in Brighton until the 1870s.

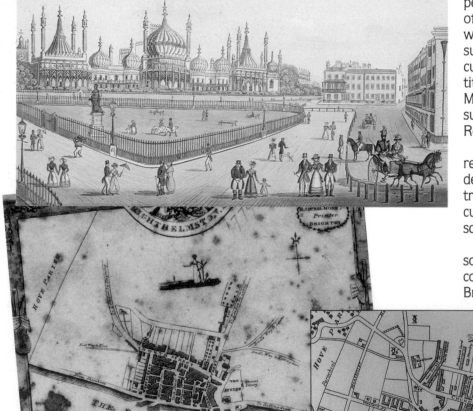

SOURCE 2 Brighton in 1779 and 1824

▲ **SOURCE 3**
A nineteenth-century picture of Mahomed's Baths

Brighton as an upper-class resort

Most of the new developments from 1750 until 1830 were designed for rich visitors. 'Assembly rooms' were created where upper-class ladies and gentlemen could meet, eat and dance together. A 'Master of Ceremonies' was appointed to direct the entertainments at these assemblies.

SOURCE 6 The Assembly Room at the Castle Inn in Brighton in 1776

SOURCE 4
Sake Deen Mahomed

SOURCE 5 A description of the baths written by a modern historian, Rosina Visram, in 1986

66 *... The patients first lay in a steaming aromatic herbal bath; having sweated freely, they were then placed in a kind of flannel tent with sleeves. They were then massaged vigorously by someone outside the tent, whose arms alone penetrated the flannel walls.* 99

1. Suggest reasons for Sake Deen Mahomed's success in Brighton.
2. What difficulties might he have had to face?

SOURCE 7 Facilities introduced at Brighton, 1750–1830

66 **1754** Regular 'assemblies' at the Castle Inn
1760 Two circulating libraries in operation
1761 Second assembly room opened
1764 First theatre established
1766 Ballroom built at the Castle Inn
1767 Master of Ceremonies appointed
1769 First indoor baths opened
1786 'Mahomed's Warm, Cold and Vapour Baths' opened
1790 New theatre opened
1793 Pleasure gardens (modelled on those in London) opened
1806 Larger theatre opened
1821 Brighton Pavilion completed
1823 Lamprell's swimming baths opened
1823 The first pier – the 'Chain Pier' – opened. 99

Activity
Design an advertisement for Mahomed's baths. You could include the treatment people might receive and the benefits it might bring them, and mention famous customers and other attractions.

Swimming in the sea was popular. Men and women had to swim from separate parts of the beach. 'Bathing machines' (wooden huts on wheels) were used for changing in, and were wheeled into the sea before the bather came out. The men swam naked.

BESIDE THE SEASIDE!

◄ SOURCE 8
A cartoon by George Cruikshank called *Mermaids at Brighton*, 1820

SOURCE 9
West Cliff, Brighton, drawn by C.W. Wing around 1810

SOURCE 10
A cartoon by George Cruikshank called *Beauties of Brighton*, 1826. It shows rich and famous people of the time, including the Duke of York and Duke of Gloucester, walking in front of Brighton Pavilion

> **1.** Use Sources 6–11 to write a description of Brighton as a holiday resort in the late eighteenth and early nineteenth centuries.

Brighton as a popular resort

All over the country the coming of the railways brought seaside resorts within the reach of ordinary people. London was the biggest city in the world: when the London–Brighton railway opened in 1841, millions of people were suddenly only two hours' train ride away from the seaside. For the first time, the 'day tripper' appeared in Brighton. In 1837 stage coaches brought 50,000 travellers to Brighton in a whole year. In 1850 the railway carried 73,000 in one week.

To start with it was mainly middle-class visitors who came to Brighton. To cater for them large hotels were built. As the town grew, industries developed alongside the holiday trade, and slums developed too. Brighton's population grew from 7339 in 1801 to 24,429 in 1821. In 1881 its population was 107,546.

In the late nineteenth century many working-class holiday-makers began to come to Brighton as well. The middle classes and working classes preferred holidays in the summer, so the upper classes tended to come in the autumn and winter when the town was less crowded.

◄ SOURCE 11 The Chain Pier in 1833. It was originally built for passengers to get on and off the steamboats that ran along the coast. But the public could pay 2d to walk on it. More money was raised from the promenades than from the steamer passengers. Later, shops and silhouettists sold their wares on the pier

SOURCE 12 Facilities introduced in Brighton, 1830–1900

1864 Grand Hotel completed
1866 Second pier (West Pier) opened
1872 Marine aquarium opened
1883 Opening of an electric railway along the sea front
1900 Palace Pier completed, replacing the Chain Pier

SOURCE 13 From a poem published in the nineteenth century

I took the train to Brighton – I walked beside the sea,
And thirty thousand Londoners were there along with me.

SOURCE 16 Brighton beach in the 1890s

SOURCE 17 A lion in a cage and a goat cart at Brighton around 1900

SOURCE 14 A painting called *To Brighton and back for 3s 6d*. The stage coach fare had been £1 and it took all day. The train left at 7.00 a.m. and arrived in Brighton at 9.00 a.m.

1. What point are Sources 13, 14 and 15 all making about Brighton in the second half of the nineteenth century?
2. Does the evidence of Source 16 support this point or not?
3. Do you think that Brighton was a better place in 1900 than it was in 1800?

Activity

Choose one of these tasks.
A. 'We had a lovely time . . .' Write a letter beginning with this sentence, which a child might have written describing a holiday in Brighton in the 1890s.
B. 'I am disgusted to report . . .' Write a letter beginning with this sentence, which an elderly adult might have written to a Brighton newspaper describing a day trip to Brighton in the 1890s.

SOURCE 15 A cartoon from *Mr Punch at the Seaside* – 'A Quiet Drive by the Sea'

What are Victorian values?

WHEN looking back at the nineteenth century – and particularly at the Victorian era – people see different things.

Some people look back longingly. They see the grand hospitals and schools which the Victorians built. They respect the Victorians' pride in being British. They agree with the Victorians' idea that people should improve their own situation, rather than depend on the government. They admire the Victorians.

Other people deeply despise the values of Victorian Britain. They argue that Victorian bosses treated their workers like slaves. They dislike Victorian snobbishness. They criticise the way Victorians were prejudiced against peoples from other countries or races. When they use the word 'Victorian' they mean 'old-fashioned' or 'intolerant', or 'uncaring'.

SOURCE 1 On a television programme during the General Election campaign in 1983, Margaret Thatcher, who was then Prime Minister, had the following conversation with a member of the audience

Member of audience You have expressed an approval for 'Victorian values'.

'Victorian times' creates for me images of child labour, women as second-class citizens, rigid class barriers, almost impossible poverty traps and a set of values which rejected fun and generally kept people in their place.

Now I would like to know why you are so attracted to the values of these times.

Mrs Thatcher I think you have mixed up, if I might respectfully say so, some of the 'conditions' with some of the 'values'.

In fact, during Victorian times, as you know, conditions improved. That was the great improvement in industry, the great expansion in industry, which gave us a chance to have a rising standard of living.

Almost every school that we were replacing when I was Minister for Education used to be a school that had been given by voluntary effort in Victorian times. So too the hospitals. So too even the prisons.

It was a time when you had great self-reliance – you lived within your income – great honesty, great duty, a great increase in Empire, and a great increase in self-confidence as a nation.

Yes, there were very difficult and dark things. But the fact was that we were creating the extra wealth with which to improve those conditions. That time was the greatest time of improvement.

1. Look at Source 1. List as many differences as you can between Mrs Thatcher's view of Victorian times and the view of the member of the audience.
2. Try to explain why people today still have such different points of view about life in Victorian times.
3. You now know a lot about the Victorians. Do you admire them?

Victorian values

Your values are the things you think are important. Sources 2–12 here and over the page show what some Victorians thought was important.

SOURCE 2 A painting by William Powell Frith called *Many Happy Returns of the Day*. It shows a middle-class home in 1880

SOURCE 3 *Work*, a painting by Ford Madox Brown, 1863

SOURCE 4 Written by a Frenchman, Hippolyte Taine, who visited Britain in the 1860s, about the middle-class men he met

"It was obvious to me that their happiness consists of the following: home at six in the evening; an agreeable and faithful wife; tea; four or five children clambering over their knees; and respectful servants."

1. Look carefully at Source 3. Describe what is happening in the painting in as much detail as you can. Make sure you describe the different types of people: e.g. the navvies, the intellectuals, the mother, the girl looking after her urchin brothers and sisters, the beggar, the rich man and woman.
2. Choose two characters which the artist seems to approve of and two which the artist seems to disapprove of. Explain your choice.
3. What message is the artist trying to give?

WHAT ARE VICTORIAN VALUES?

SOURCE 5 From an article written by G.H. Law in 1831

"*The Almighty has given to his creatures different abilities and strengths, both of mind and body. There must be the Thinker, the Politician, the Craftsman, and . . . at the same time, the hewers of wood and the drawers of water. On the combined operation of all . . . depends the proper working, and the harmony, of the great machine of the world.*"

SOURCE 6 A poem from a Victorian book called *Divine and Moral Songs for Children*

"*Have you not heard what dreadful plagues,
Are threatened by the Lord,
To him who breaks his father's laws,
Or mocks his mother's word?

What heavy guilt upon him lies!
How cursed is his name!
The ravens shall pick out his eyes
And eagles eat the same.*"

1. Discuss in pairs what you think the message of the artist is in a) Source 7, and b) Source 8.

SOURCE 8 An engraving called *Myself? Or the children?* It shows a working man, and was published in 1872 to illustrate a Christmas story

SOURCE 7 *Kit's Writing Lesson*, painted in 1852 by R.B. Martineau. Boys who wanted office jobs had to practise their handwriting until it was perfect

SOURCE 9 Written by Dr Hodgson, whose views on education were widely respected in the nineteenth century

" There is a strong male instinct that a learned or even over-accomplished woman is one of the most intolerable monsters in creation. "

SOURCE 11 Written by a school inspector in the 1870s

" The habit of obedience to authority . . . may tend to teach the working classes a lesson which many so sadly need in the North of England . . .

Submission to authority, deference to others . . . those are the real marks of manly self-respect and independence. "

SOURCE 12 A report of the activities of Carr's Lane Chapel in Birmingham in 1859

" We now raise nearly £500 per year. For the Colonial Missionary Society we raise £70. For our Sunday and day schools (with nearly 2000 children), we raise £200. We support two town missionaries at a cost of £200.

Our ladies also help in orphan mission schools. They work for the poor of the town. We also have night schools for young men and women, and Bible classes. "

CROMER URBAN DISTRICT.

BYE-LAWS
AS TO
PUBLIC BATHING

The following are the appointed Stands for Bathing Machines.

No. of Stand.	Description or limits of Stand.	Sex to which appropriated.
1	Between the Doctor's Steps Groyne and the Cart Gangway - - - - -	FEMALE
2	Between the Doctor's Steps Groyne and a point 100 yards to the East thereof— Before the hour of 8 a.m. daily - - After the hour of 8 a.m. daily - -	MALE MALE & FEMALE
3	To the East of a point 200 yards to the East of the Doctor's Steps Groyne, being 100 yards East of the Easternmost limit of Stand No. 2 - - - -	MALE
4	To the West of Melbourne House Groyne— Before the hour of 8 a.m. daily - After the hour of 8 a.m. daily - -	MALE MALE & FEMALE

GENTLEMEN bathing in the Mixed Bathing Ground must wear a suitable costume, from neck to knee.

Copies of the Bye-laws may be obtained at the Offices of the Council. Persons offending against the Bye-laws are liable to a Penalty of £5.

SOURCE 10 Laws about bathing at the seaside resort of Cromer in 1898

2. Using Sources 2–12 find at least one quality that a 'typical' middle-class Victorian man looked for in each of the following:
   - his wife
   - his children
   - his home life
   - society in general.
3. Do you think all Victorian men had these values?
4. What do sources 2–12 tell us about the role of Victorian women?
5. Make a list of as many Victorian values as you can. Discuss in class whether they are all good values.

Activity

Working in groups, create a piece of drama that shows Victorian children how they should behave and perform it to the rest of the class. Use Sources 2–12 for ideas. Your teacher will help you to get started.

WHAT ARE VICTORIAN VALUES?

Expansion, trade and industry: a cause for celebration?

Britain's Empire, trade and industry all grew steadily during Queen Victoria's reign (1837–1901). By the mid-nineteenth century, so many goods were exported from Britain that it was known as 'the workshop of the world'. By the end of the century its Empire was the biggest in the world. Many Victorians were deeply proud of this Empire, and saw bringing British goods and British values to 'less civilised' countries as one of the greatest British achievements.

> **SOURCE 13** Adapted from an article by Joseph Chamberlain, Britain's Colonial Secretary, in *Scribner's Magazine*, 1898
>
> 66 *In countries where the great majority of the population are natives, the only sure way to develop the resources of the country is to provide the native population with white superintendents, and with rulers and administrators who will bring the knowledge they have derived from their experience in a higher civilisation to their task of running that country . . . who will always be led by the standards and ideals which they have been brought up to respect. This is the root idea of British dominion in the tropics.* 99

> **SOURCE 14** From a guide to the London and Birmingham and Grand Junction Railway, 1839
>
> 66 *It is a proud feeling to an Englishman to know that the products of the thousand busy hands and whirling wheels around him are destined to increase the comfort, refinement or splendour of nations spread far and wide over the globe.* 99

> **1.** According to Sources 13 and 14, what values lay behind the development of the British Empire?

The Great Exhibition in 1851 expressed many people's feelings of pride in all Britain's achievements. The exhibition was the idea of Victoria's husband, Prince Albert. All the countries of the world would display their products and inventions in a huge, futuristic building of glass and iron called the Crystal Palace (see Source 15). It was built in Hyde Park in London.

Everything about the Great Exhibition was big. The Crystal Palace was so enormous that it enclosed some large trees which grew in the park. It took 4500 tons of iron and nearly 300,000 panes of glass to build it. Fourteen thousand exhibitors showed off over 100,000 products from all over the world. The biggest displays, however, were of British products.

Over six million people visited the Great Exhibition, many coming on excursion trains on the new railways. It was the grandest exhibition that the country (or the world, for that matter) had ever seen.

> **SOURCE 16** From an exhibition guide, 1851
>
> 66 *. . . Thousands of little engines were hard at work, and ingeniously occupied in the manufacture of all sorts of useful articles from knife handles to envelopes . . .*
>
> *In this great park of machinery, a thoughtful observer could easily discover the distinctive character of the English nation.* 99

SOURCE 15 The Crystal Palace at the opening of the Great Exhibition, a print made in 1851

SOURCE 17 Contemporary paintings of the stands inside the Great Exhibition, showing some of the exhibits on display

Activity

Work in pairs.

Millions of British people came on excursions to London to visit the Great Exhibition. Many also came from overseas. Use Sources 15–17 to design two leaflets with text and pictures to advertise the exhibition.

One of you should design a leaflet for people in Britain. The other should design a leaflet for people coming from other countries.

Compare your ideas, and explain any differences.

Were the British racist?

The case of the slave ship *Zong*

On 6 September 1781 the slave ship *Zong* sailed from the coast of Africa bound for Jamaica. On board were seventeen white crewmen and about 440 African slaves.

By the end of November the *Zong* was nearing Jamaica. By this time seven of the crew and more than 60 slaves had died. Many of the other slaves were badly ill. But instead of heading for Jamaica with all possible speed Collingwood, the captain, started to sail in the opposite direction! He knew that when he reached Jamaica no one would want to buy the sick slaves. This would mean that the owners of the ship would lose money. Collingwood also knew that the slaves, like any ship's cargo, were insured, but that the insurance company would not pay up if the 'cargo' died from natural causes. So if the slaves kept dying and more became ill the owners would lose all their money.

Collingwood hit on what he thought was a brilliant idea. He called the ship's officers together to tell them about it. He said that if they threw the sick slaves overboard the owners would be able to claim money back from the insurance company. They could pretend that they were running out of drinking water and that they had to save the water for the fit slaves, who would then have a better chance of surviving. He also said that the sick slaves would be quickly put out of their misery.

After some argument the officers agreed and over the next few days 133 sick slaves were thrown overboard. Some of them put up a fight and were chained before being thrown overboard. Some, seeing what was going to happen, jumped overboard themselves rather than be thrown. One of the officers later stated that on 1 December, after 42 slaves had been thrown overboard, it rained heavily all day. When the *Zong* arrived in Jamaica on 22 December it had 420 gallons of water left.

The owners claimed the insurance money for the lost cargo on the grounds that the ship had run out of water so some of the slaves had to be killed in order to save the crew and the other slaves. The insurance company refused to pay and the case went to court.

Sources 1 and 2 are extracts from the trial. Sources 3–5 are from the eighteenth century and show the conditions on slave ships such as the *Zong*.

SOURCE 1 From a speech by Lord Mansfield, the Chief Justice

> *The case of slaves was the same as if horses had been thrown overboard.*

SOURCE 2 From a speech by the owners' lawyer during the court case

> *What is all this talk of human people being thrown overboard? This is a case of goods. It is a case about throwing over of goods. They are goods and property.*

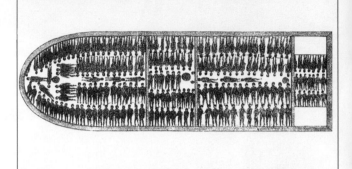

SOURCE 3 A plan of the interior of a Liverpool slave ship. It was drawn by Thomas Clarkson, who campaigned to abolish the slave trade. The picture is quite accurate. As you can see every space is filled

SOURCE 4 A nineteenth-century illustration of young male slaves being shipped to America

SOURCE 5 An eighteenth-century illustration of slaves being packed below decks for the Atlantic crossing

Activity

Work in pairs.

One of you should write a speech for the ship owners' lawyer to give in court.

The other should write a speech for the insurance company's lawyer to give in court. Think about the reasons that the insurance company would have for refusing to pay. Was it because what had happened was cruel and terrible? Or was it because the ship owners were trying to cheat the insurance company? Or were there other reasons?

Use Sources 1–5 to help you.

Conditions on the slave ships

When you study evidence such as Sources 3–5 about the conditions on slave ships like the *Zong* you will not be surprised that so many slaves fell ill.

We should then add to this picture the thought of the ship out on the sea rolling around on the waves. The slaves would be terrified, many would be seasick or have dysentery. The lavatory was often a large bucket 60 centimetres across and 75 centimetres deep. Many of the slaves could not reach it, so the floor was soon a quagmire.

SOURCE 6 Written by Alexander Falconbridge, a doctor, after a visit to a slave ship

The floor was covered with blood and mucus and resembled a slaughterhouse. After fifteen minutes I was so overcome by the heat, stench and foul air, that I nearly fainted. With assistance I got back on deck.

SOURCE 7 Written by an ex-slave trader, John Newton, in his *Journal of a Slave Trader*, 1788

The poor creatures, thus cramped for want of room, are likewise in irons, for the most part both hands and feet, and two together, which makes it difficult for them to turn or move, to rise or lie down, without hurting themselves.

The ship owners wanted the slaves to be in good condition when they reached the West Indies, so the slaves were probably fed as well as was possible under the awful conditions. Twice a day a small bucket of food was handed to each group of ten slaves. The slaves usually had to scoop the food out with their filthy hands. When the weather was good they might be fed on deck.

SOURCE 8 Falconbridge describes the slaves' meals

These consist chiefly of horse beans, boiled to a pulp; of boiled yams and rice, and sometimes a small quanity of beef or pork. They sometimes have a sauce of palm oil, mixed with flour, water and pepper.

Some of the slaves simply gave up the struggle to stay alive and refused to eat. Others committed suicide. Slave revolts on ship were common, especially soon after leaving the coast of Africa. By the end of the eighteenth century the death rate amongst slaves during the voyage was about 55 per cent.

Most ships had fewer women slaves. They were kept, unchained, in the smaller spaces between the decks, with the child slaves.

SOURCE 9 An eighteenth-century illustration of a slave rebellion at sea

SOURCE 10 Alexander Falconbridge's comments on the treatment of women slaves

On board some ships, the common sailors are allowed to have intercourse with such of the black women whose consent they can get. The officers are allowed to indulge their passions among them as they like, and sometimes are guilty of such brutal excesses, as disgrace human nature.

1. Slaves only fetched a good price in the West Indies if they were healthy. Why did the ships' captains treat the slaves in the ways described?

WERE THE BRITISH RACIST?

Slavery on the sugar plantations

Although many people in Britain benefited from slavery (as we saw on page 43), they had little idea of how the slaves were treated on the ships. They also knew virtually nothing of the life the slaves led on the sugar plantations in the West Indies. Sources 11–22 give us an impression of this life.

When the slave ships reached the West Indies the slaves were cleaned up ready to be sold. One ship's captain, who had a batch of slaves suffering from dysentery, told the doctor to block the anus of each slave with rope.

After the sale, most of the slaves were immediately taken to work on sugar plantations.

SOURCE 14
A poster advertising a sale of slaves alongside household goods

> **SOURCE 11** A description by Olaudah Equiano, who was sold as a slave
>
> *On a given signal the buyers rushed at once into the yard where the slaves are confined, and make choice of that parcel that they liked best. The noise and clamour increased the worry of the terrified African. In this manner are relations and friends separated, most of them never to see each other again.*

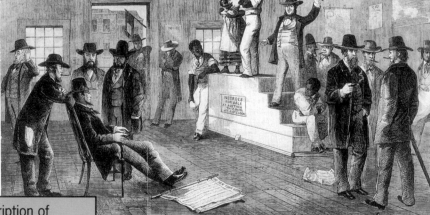

SOURCE 12 A nineteenth-century print of a slave family being auctioned

> **SOURCE 13** A contemporary description of plantation work in 1807
>
> *The slaves are divided into three classes called gangs; the first of which consists of the most healthy and strong, both of the males and females, whose chief business is, before crop time, to clear, hole, and plant the ground; and during crop time to cut the canes, feed the mills, and attend to the manufacture of the sugar.*
>
> *The second gang is composed of young boys and girls and pregnant females who weed the canes and do other light work.*
>
> *The third gang consists of young children, attended by an old woman, who collect green food for the pigs and sheep and weed the garden.*

> **SOURCE 15** The slaves' day
>
> *5.30 a.m. Go to fields taking their breakfast with them, register called, then work till 8.00 a.m.*
> *8.00 a.m. Breakfast: boiled yam, eddoes, okra, all seasoned with salt and pepper. Any latecomers arriving are whipped*
> *8.30–12.00 a.m. Work*
> *12.00–2.00 p.m. Rest and dinner: salted meat or pickled fish*
> *2.00–6.00 p.m. Work*
> *6.00 p.m. Allowed to return to their huts*
> *Night-time During the harvest season work in the mill and boiling houses throughout the night*

SOURCE 16 A report by a visitor to a plantation in Jamaica in the eighteenth century

The punishments are:

For rebellions, burning them by nailing them down on the ground with crooked sticks on every limb, and then apply the fire by degrees from the feet and hands, burning them gradually up to the head, whereby their pains are great.

For crimes of a lesser nature, gelding [castrating] or chopping off half of the foot with an axe.

For running away, they put iron rings of great weight on their ankles, or pothooks about their necks, which are iron rings with two long hooks riveted to them, or a spur in the mouth.

For negligence, they are usually whipped by the overseers with laice-wood switches, being first tied up.

SOURCE 17 An advertisement for a runaway slave in the Jamaica Royal Gazette, 1782

MARIA, a washer, bought from James Elford, the initials of whose name she bears on one of her shoulders – she eloped in October and has been seen in Port Royal.

The slaves' hard work, and their poor diet and living conditions, all led to a low life expectancy (the average age at death). The slaves' average life expectancy was only 26. The death rate among babies was particularly high: 25 per cent of all babies died of tetanus before they were ten days old. Then there were smallpox, measles and whooping cough, which could all be fatal. Nobody bothered to register a baby's birth until it had survived for several weeks.

SOURCE 18 A modern photograph of a man wearing a neck ring, which was worn by slaves as a punishment for 24 hours a day

SOURCE 19 Treadmills like this were introduced to the West Indies as an 'improved' form of punishment

SOURCE 20 A painting from 1823 showing a white overseer supervising field slaves cutting sugar cane

WERE THE BRITISH RACIST?

SOURCE 21 The mill, where rollers squeezed the juice out of bundles of sugar cane

SOURCE 22 In the boiling house: the slaves are clearing the scum off the juice, which flows into cooling trays under the windows

Activity

You are a plantation owner who has decided to sell your plantation and slaves. Design a brochure to attract buyers.

1. Do you think that slave ship captains and plantation owners were deliberately cruel to the slaves? Were they wicked people?
2. If people back in Britain had known about the conditions on the ships and plantations what might their reactions have been?
3. Some people in Britain called factory work 'white slavery'. Compare the lives of these black slaves with the lives of workers in British factories described on pages 16–19. Start by making a list of the conditions that each group suffered.

Were the Victorians racist?

In the early nineteenth century slavery was abolished (a story which we study in depth on pages 82–85). People in Britain saw the abolition of slavery as proof that Victorian values were more ENLIGHTENED than those of earlier times. But did the Victorians believe that black and white people were equal?

In the Victorian period there were over 10,000 black people living in Britain. Although some of them were successful and some played important roles in working-class organisations such as the CHARTISTS (see page 92), most were very poor and life was a grim struggle. Many were beggars, while others, like the teacher in Source 25, found it very difficult to do the job they were trained for.

SOURCE 23 Written by Dr Robert Knox in 1850 in his book *The Races of Men*, which was based on his popular public lectures

Look at the negro, so well known to you. Is he shaped like any white person? Is the anatomy of his frame, of his muscles, or organs like ours? Does he walk like us, think like us, act like us? Not in the least. What a hatred the white people have for him.

Can the blacks become civilised? I should say not.

SOURCE 24 From an article written by an American visitor to London in the early nineteenth century

A few days since, I met in Oxford Street a well dressed white girl walking arm in arm with a negro man who was as well dressed as she. As there are no slaves in England perhaps the English have not learned to regard negroes as a degraded class of men, as we do in the United States, where we have never seen them in any other condition.

SOURCE 25 A reference for a black applicant for a teaching job in Gloucestershire in the early nineteenth century

Unfortunately he is a native of the West Indies, which circumstance, added to a family of nine children, has kept him down in the world. Where a dark complexion is not objected, he would make a very valuable schoolmaster.

SOURCE 26 Written by the writer and historian Thomas Carlyle in 1867

❝One always rather likes the nigger, a poor blockhead with good dispositions and affections. He is the only savage of all the coloured races that doesn't die out on sight of the white man, but can actually live beside him. The Almighty maker has appointed him to be a servant.❞

▶ **SOURCE 27** A cartoon called *Lowest life in London*, by George Cruikshank, 1820

SOURCE 29 From a letter written to *The Times* by a British army officer serving in India

❝I must say that I have been struck with the arrogant and repellent manner in which we often treat natives of rank, and with the unnecessary harshness of our treatment of inferiors. The most scrubby mean little representative of the white race . . . regards himself as infinitely superior to Indians with a genealogy [family history] of 1000 years.❞

SOURCE 30 Written by the novelist Charles Dickens in 1848

❝Between the civilised European and the barbarous African there is a great gulf. To change the customs of civilised men is most difficult and slow; but to do this with ignorant and savage races is a work which requires a stretch of years that dazzles in the looking at.❞

SOURCE 28 The cover of *The Wonderful Adventures of Mary Seacole*, 1857. Mary Seacole was born in Jamaica and trained as a nurse. In 1853 Britain desperately needed nurses in the Crimea, in Russia, where the British army was fighting. Mary Seacole applied to go, but the army turned her down. She went out all the same, set up her own hospital and saved many injured soldiers. When she returned to Britain she was famous but poor. A four-day festival was held in London to raise money for her

1. Make a list of all the racist attitudes you can find in Sources 23–30.
2. Is there any evidence in these sources that some white people did treat black people decently?

1. Write a letter, either as a nineteenth-century white person justifying how black people are treated, or as a twentieth-century historian explaining whether the British in the eighteenth and nineteenth centuries were racist.

Did the Victorians care?

DURING the nineteenth century upper-class and middle-class people became more aware of the conditions in which the poor worked and lived. Most people thought these conditions should be improved, but they could not agree how to do it.

> **SOURCE 1** From *Christian Charity*, a book written by J.B. Sumner in 1847
>
> " *Tell the rich in this world, that they must do good, that they should be ready to give, willing to help. In a world like ours there will always be poverty . . . There will always be many naked to be clothed, many hungry to be fed, many sick to be relieved.* "

> **SOURCE 2** From *The Illustrated London News*, 10 March 1866
>
> " *The gift of a quarter of a million pounds bestowed on the poor of London has been used for building healthy and comfortable homes for working-class families, let at a cheaper rate than normal . . . Peabody Square, Islington, has 240 flats of one, two or three rooms, with baths and laundries, good supplies of water and gaslight, shafts for the removal of rubbish, and perfect drainage and ventilation.* "

> **SOURCE 3** Adapted from a best-selling book called *Self-help*, written by Samuel Smiles in 1859
>
> " *Self-help is the root of all genuine growth in the individual. Whatever is done for men and classes takes away the stimulus and need of doing it for themselves . . . The most that institutions can do is to leave man free to improve his individual condition.*
>
> *No laws can make the idle work, the spendthrift save, or the drunk sober.* "

1. Which of Sources 1–3 are in favour of people taking action to improve conditions for the poor?
2. Make a list of all the ways to help the poor suggested by Sources 1–3.

The workhouse

The changing use of the workhouse in the nineteenth century tells us a lot about Victorian values. Before the Victorian period, each parish had to look after its own poor. Those who could not work (the old, mothers, the handicapped) were given small sums of money. Children were often trained in a local trade. Poor people who were fit to work were given either 'indoor relief' or 'outdoor relief'.

■ Indoor relief: the poor were given work in workhouses. They were provided with looms and tools and raw materials with which they made goods to sell.

■ Outdoor relief: in some parts of the country the poor were given 'tickets'. If they could find a job locally they handed over the ticket to the employer who paid the same amount as they would have received from the parish. There was also the problem of people who were working but did not earn enough to feed their families. In some places their wages were topped up by the parish according to the size of their family and the price of bread.

1. Do you think the poor were well looked after?
2. Do you think the poor were being encouraged to work hard?
3. Is there any way in which employers could misuse outdoor relief?

These different systems were very expensive. By 1830 about £7 million a year was being spent on the poor. This had to be paid for by the property owners in each town, through their local tax called 'rates'. Many rate-payers claimed that they were paying people to be lazy and to avoid work. In 1834 the Poor Law Amendment Act was passed by Parliament. Outdoor relief was abolished, and instead the poor would now all be put into workhouses. The conditions in the workhouses were intended to be so grim that only those genuinely in need of help would apply to enter.

> **SOURCE 4** Written by Edwin Chadwick, who headed the government commission investigating the reform of the Poor Law
>
> " *The existing laws are destructive of the industry of labourers and the wealth of the employers and of the owners of property.*
>
> *If no relief were given to the able-bodied except in well regulated workhouses, the worst of the existing evils of the system would disappear.* "

SOURCE 5 Written in the nineteenth century by John Beecher

The inferior classes must be forced to see how demoralising and degrading poor relief is and how sweet and wholesome is that independence which is earned by perseverance and honest hard work.

SOURCE 6 Government regulations for workhouses, 1835

Admission of paupers
The pauper [poor person] shall be thoroughly cleansed and shall be clothed in a workhouse dress.

Every pauper shall be searched and all articles taken from him.

Classification of paupers
The paupers shall be classed as follows. To each class shall be assigned a separate ward or building. There each class shall remain without communication with those of another class.
- *infirm men*
- *able-bodied men and youths above fifteen years*
- *boys above the age of seven and under fifteen*
- *infirm women*
- *able-bodied women and girls above the age of fifteen*
- *girls above the age of seven and under fifteen*
- *children under seven years of age*

The master shall allow the father or mother of any child in the same workhouse to have an interview with that child.

SOURCE 8
The women's ward in a workhouse, 1843

SOURCE 9 A description of the Lambeth workhouse by Charles Chaplin, who went to live there when he was six

I didn't know what was happening until we entered the workhouse gate. Then it struck me; for there we were made separate, Mother going in one direction and we in another. How well I remember the first visiting day; the shock of seeing Mother in workhouse clothes. How forlorn and embarrassed she looked. In one week she had aged and grown thin.

Breakfast
7oz. of bread
1½ pints of gruel

Dinner
1½ pints of beef and vegetable soup

Supper
6oz. of bread
2oz. of cheese

SOURCE 10 The typical workhouse diet

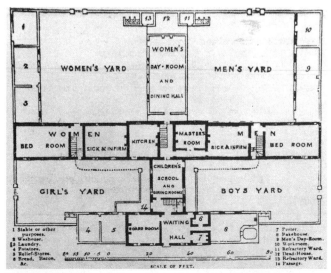

SOURCE 7 From the plans drawn by the Poor Law Commissioners to show what the new workhouses should be like

SOURCE 11 The daily routine for children in the workhouse

	8.30–12.00	12.00–1.00	1.30–6.00
Girls	learning to read and write	dinner	knitting and sewing
Boys	work in the card room	dinner	reading and writing in the schoolroom

DID THE VICTORIANS CARE?

SOURCE 12 The dining hall at St Pancras workhouse in London in 1900

SOURCE 13 Workhouse regulations, 1835

66 *The following offences are to be punished:*
- *making a noise when silence was ordered*
- *using obscene language*
- *refusing to work*
- *pretending to be sick*
- *climbing over the boundary wall of the workhouse.*

The limits to punishments are as follows:
- *No child under twelve years of age shall be punished by confinement in a dark room.*
- *No corporal punishment shall be inflicted on any male child except by the schoolmaster.*
- *No corporal punishment shall be inflicted on any female child.*
- *No corporal punishment shall be inflicted on any male child, except with a rod approved of by the Guardians of the workhouse.* 99

1. From the information and sources on the last three pages, list as many reasons as you can why the Victorians wished to change the system of looking after the poor.
2. Many Victorians claimed they wanted to change the system in order to help the poor better. Do you think this was their main reason?
3. Study Sources 6–13 here and on the previous page. How do they show the aims of the Victorians being carried out?

Activity

Work in pairs. You are visitors to a workhouse in the middle of the nineteenth century. One is a critic of the system and the other a supporter. Each of you should describe and comment on what you see during your visit. Your teacher will give you some ideas

The story of Harriet Kettle

Harriet Kettle spent most of her early life in Victorian institutions. Because she caused a lot of trouble we know a lot about her early life! Here is a brief outline of some of the events of her life. Your first task will be to construct a more detailed timeline of her life from the information in Sources 14–20.

1839 Harriet was born in a Norfolk village, the daughter of a farm labourer.
1845 Her mother died insane. Her father neglected her.
1851 Harriet was living in the workhouse at Gressenhall.
1864 She was discharged from the Norfolk Lunatic Asylum.
1865 She married an agricultural labourer and over the next few years had four children.
1891 By now Harriet was a grandmother.

SOURCE 14 From workhouse records, 28 April 1851

66 *. . . Harriet Kettle was again brought before the Board [of Guardians of the Poor Law Union] charged with repeated disobedience of the schoolmistress and was ordered to be kept in a separate apartment for six hours a day for four days.* 99

1. Draw a timeline to show Harriet Kettle's life.
2. How was Harriet Kettle punished in the workhouse?
3. Suggest why she was sent to the lunatic asylum. Do you think she was insane?
4. Did the people in charge of the institutions where she lived try to understand her?

Activity

■ 'Harriet Kettle's problems were all her own fault.'

■ 'Harriet Kettle was not to blame for her problems.'

Get into pairs, one supporting the first statement and the other supporting the second statement. Who can put up the strongest argument?

Which statement would most Victorians have supported?

SOURCE 15 From workhouse records, 7 January 1856

66 Harriet Kettle violently refused to perform the work ordered by the Master because she was refused clothes to leave the workhouse. 99

SOURCE 16 From Little Walsingham prison records, 11 July 1856

66 The prisoners have been orderly and respectful, with the exception of Harriet Kettle, whose conduct has been most violent and disobedient and who has lately become a suicidal lunatic. 99

SOURCE 17 From records of the County Lunatic Asylum, 16 July 1856

66 Kettle, Harriet. Admitted 16 July 1856. Her case is put down to a naturally bad temper and from her irregular life, she having been a girl on the town [a prostitute] in Norwich for some years before her committal to prison for having assaulted the master of a workhouse . . . 99

SOURCE 18 From workhouse records, 28 March 1859

66 The Clerk called the attention of the Guardians to the prosecution of Harriet Kettle . . . on a charge of attempting to set fire to the workhouse. 99

SOURCE 19 From the *Norfolk Chronicle*, 31 March 1860

66 The prisoner Harriet Kettle exhibited the utmost excitement, and acted as though she was insane. She declared she would take her own life and that no man should conquer her.

The prisoner was charged with attempting to set fire to the Mitford and Launditch Union House at Gressenhall on 20 November 1858.

The master of the workhouse stated that on the day named his attention was called to the prisoner's beating the assistant matron in the dining hall. He assisted in removing the prisoner, and put her into a separate apartment. She then declared that she would burn down the 'b—y building', and soon after he went into the room, and found some straw on the floor which had been ripped out of a bed in the room. The straw had just been set fire to. He put the fire out. She was subsequently taken before a magistrate.

The Master of Thorpe Lunatic Asylum said he did not think she was insane, but that she was subject to violent fits of passion, especially when thwarted.

The learned judge summed up saying it was quite possible for the prisoner to behave in this violent manner for the purpose of escaping punishment.

The jury found her guilty. The prisoner was sentenced to eighteen months' hard labour. 99

SOURCE 20 From the records of the County Lunatic Asylum, 10 July 1863

66 Harriet Kettle was admitted 10 July 1863. She was brought up in Gressenhall Workhouse, which she left while still quite a girl. From this point her evil courses date. Inheriting a bad disposition and violent passions, deprived of a mother's care, and being brought up surrounded by the moral effluvia [filth] of a workhouse, a place unfavourable to any advance in rectitude, it is not surprising that when set free in the world she got into trouble.

She is very short, and small, neat and tidy in her person, quick and intelligent. Her features are somewhat coarse, the lips thick, and her face has a repulsive look, showing cunning, low breeding.

She blames the world for some of her follies, and says she could not earn a living honestly, not being strong enough for service. She has had a cough a long time, is thin and frequently spits blood. 99

The Victorians and women workers

YOU have already studied working conditions in the textile factories (see pages 16–19). Conditions in other workplaces, such as coal mines, were also very bad. One of the leading campaigners for reform was the politician Lord Shaftesbury. He had a difficult job because many people thought the government had no right to interfere with the factories.

However, child workers were regarded as a special group who needed protection and in 1833 their working hours were restricted, as you can see in Source 1.

Many employers and MPs still argued that the government should not interfere with the working hours of adults, who should be able to work for as long as they chose. But gradually campaigns by Shaftesbury and his supporters persuaded Parliament that women also needed protection and should be regarded as a special case. From 1842 various reforms were passed limiting the hours worked by women. These are summarised in Source 1.

Sources 2–9 suggest that there were a number of reasons why people wanted to reform women's working hours.

SOURCE 2 From a speech by Lord Shaftesbury in 1827

I am bound to try to do what God has put into me for the benefit of England. To help the advancement of religion and the increase of human happiness.

SOURCE 3 A woman and a child working in a Lancashire mine

SOURCE 1 The main reforms in the nineteenth century

WORK: 9 hours   SCHOOL: 2 hours

1833 Factory Act. In textile factories:
- no children under nine allowed to work
- children aged between nine and thirteen limited to nine hours per day, and had to attend two hours' school per day
- fourteen- to eighteen-year-olds limited to twelve hours' work per day

WORK: 6½ hours   SCHOOL: 3 hours

1842 Mines Act banned employment of all women and girls and all boys under ten in coal mines

1844 Factory Act. In textile factories:
- children aged between eight and thirteen limited to six and a half hours' work per day, and had to attend three hours' school per day
- women limited to twelve hours' work per day

1847 Factory Act. In textile factories:
- women limited to ten hours' work per day

1867 Factory Act. This extended the previous Factory Acts to all places of industry with more than 50 employees

SOURCE 4 An extract from a letter by Richard Oastler to a Leeds newspaper in October 1830

Thousands of our fellow creatures, both male and female, are at this very moment existing in a state of slavery more horrid than are the victims of the hellish system of colonial slavery. They are forced not by the cart whip of the negro slave-driver, but by the equally appalling strap of the overlooker.

SOURCE 5 Two extracts from the report of the 1842 government commission, led by Lord Shaftesbury, which investigated conditions in the coal mines. The contents of this report horrified people all around the country

a) An account by Betty Harris, aged 37

I have a belt around my waist and a chain passing between my legs and I go on my hands and feet. The road is very steep, and we have to hold by a rope. The pit is very wet and I have seen the water come up to my thighs. I have drawn till I have had the skin off me. The belt and chain is worse when we are in the family way [pregnant].

b) A report by one of the commissioners

The men work in a state of perfect nakedness, and are in this state assisted in their labours by females of all ages, from girls of six years old to women of 21, these females being themselves quite naked down to the waist. In one pit, the chain, passing high up between the legs of two of these girls had worn large holes in their trousers and any sight more indecent can hardly be imagined – no brothel can beat it.

SOURCE 6 From a speech by Lord Shaftesbury

Everything runs to waste; the house and children are deserted; the wife can do nothing for her husband and family; she can neither cook, wash, repair clothes, or take charge of infants.

Dirt and ignorance are the portion of such households. Females are forming various clubs gradually gaining all those privileges of the male sex. They meet together to drink, sing and smoke. They use disgusting language. A man came into one of these clubs with a child in his arms and said to one of these women: 'Come, lass, for I cannot keep this bairn quiet, and the other I have left crying at home.'

SOURCE 7 From Lord Shaftesbury's diary, 1842

7 June Brought forward my motion – the success has been wonderful.
July Accounts from all parts of the country are full of promise. The handloom weavers [who were unemployed] rejoice in the banning of females, as they themselves will go down the mines and take their places.

SOURCE 8 Extracts from Parliamentary reports

1833 The crowding together of the young of both sexes, and the hot atmosphere of most mills [24° C] conspire to produce a very early development of sexual appetites.
1843 When the men come up at night [from the mines] they change their clothes in this hovel and the pit girls, who are generally in their teens, are mixing with them and become very immoral and obscene.

SOURCE 9 Written by a modern historian, Jane Rendall, in 1990

Both social reformers and most male trade unionists were opposed to the extension of women's work, especially where it might conflict with the interests of male workers. Both shared a view that an adult male worker should be able to support his wife and children from his earnings. In 1877 one trade union leader supported restrictions on women's work because women should be in their proper place at home, seeing after their homes and families.

1. List all the reasons that you can find for different people's support of Factory Reform.
2. Were any of these reasons not really to do with helping the women?
3. In Source 4 factory work is said to be worse than the conditions faced by slaves in the West Indies. Do you agree?

Activity

Prepare two speeches, one in favour of reforming women's working conditions and another against it.

Remember that there may be reasons why some women themselves would be against reform.

Why was slavery abolished?

MOST of the changes you have so far studied in this book were brought about by the middle and upper classes. On pages 82–101 we are going to look at ways in which the working classes changed things.

You will remember how important the slave trade was to Britain from pages 42–44 and how cruel a system slavery was from pages 70–74.

In 1807 the slave trade was abolished by the British Parliament. It became illegal to buy and sell slaves, but people could still *own* them. In 1833 Parliament finally abolished slavery itself, both in Britain and throughout the British Empire.

Why, when the slave trade and the plantations in the West Indies seemed to be making so much money, were they abolished?

Sources 1 and 2 give two opinions.

> **SOURCE 1** The view of an English historian writing in 1869
>
> 66 *The crusade of England against slavery may be regarded as one of the most virtuous acts recorded in the history of nations.* 99

> **SOURCE 2** The view of a West Indian historian writing in 1938
>
> 66 *Those who see in the abolition of slavery the awakening conscience of mankind should spend a few minutes asking themselves why it is that man's conscience, which has slept peacefully for so many centuries, should awake just at the time that men began to see the unprofitableness of slavery.* 99

---

1. Explain how the two historians in Sources 1 and 2 differ about why slavery was abolished.

Until recently most books have given the impression that the slaves were freed only because of white campaigners in England. But on pages 82–85 we are going to look at evidence which suggests that a range of factors may have been important.

Some historians say that:

- Black slaves, both in Britain and in the West Indies, were the ones who brought an end to slavery, because by running away and rebelling they made it impossible for slavery to continue.
- In practice most slaves had become free in Britain long before 1833.
- Slavery was abolished because it was no longer making a profit.

See what you think.

Factor 1:
The white middle-class campaigners

Granville Sharp

A chance meeting started one of the greatest campaigners against slavery on his work. As Sharp left his house one day in 1765 he noticed a black youth queueing for free medical help. His head was badly swollen, he was nearly blind and he could hardly walk. His name was Jonathan Strong and he told Sharp that he had been brought to Britain as a slave and had been beaten up by his owner, so he had run away.

Sharp took Jonathan Strong to a hospital, where he gradually recovered. Two years later he was healthy and working as a messenger boy. But one day his old master saw him, had him captured and sold him. Strong would be taken back to Jamaica as a slave. Granville Sharp took the case to court, where the Lord Mayor of London ruled: 'The lad has not stolen anything, and is therefore at liberty to go away.'

Sharp had won this case. But what about all the other similar cases that the courts were waiting to hear? Sharp fought many of these cases on behalf of black people. He saved many of them from being sent back to the West Indies. Judges agreed that a master could not force a slave to go out of Britain. Sharp did not manage to get slavery or the slave trade abolished, but he had started the campaign against slavery.

Granville Sharp was also involved in other court cases, such as case of the slave ship *Zong* (see page 70). These cases were beginning to turn public opinion against slavery.

William Wilberforce

The campaign to abolish slavery was led by the Quakers, who believed that slavery was sinful and against Christian teachings.

In 1797 twelve opponents of slavery, including several Quakers, formed a group to fight for abolition. William Wilberforce is the best known of them. He was an MP and made many speeches in Parliament against the slave trade. Another member of the group, Thomas Clarkson, collected together all the information he could about the terrible conditions on the slave ships. He used this to persuade people of how awful the trade was. Huge petitions were collected and presented to Parliament.

Again and again the campaigners tried to get Parliament to abolish the slave trade. At last, in 1807, they were successful.

SOURCE 3 Josiah Wedgwood, the owner of Britain's most famous potteries, made thousands of plaques like this. He even sent a shipload to the USA. The caption reads 'Am I not a man and a brother?'

BARBARITIES in the WEST INDIES

SOURCE 6 An eighteenth-century cartoon referring to an incident when a sick slave who could not work was held in a tub of boiling sugar for three quarters of an hour

SOURCE 4 Extracts from a speech by Prime Minister William Pitt in a debate in the House of Commons in 1792 about the abolition of the slave trade

I know of no evil that ever has existed worse than the tearing of 70,000 or 80,000 persons annually from their native land. If we tempt the slave traders to sell their fellow creatures to us we may rest assured they will use every method – kidnapping, village breaking, bloodshed and misery – to supply their victims to us.

Think of 80,000 persons carried away out of their own country. Do you think nothing of their families which are left behind?

SOURCE 7 From a print distributed in the late eighteenth century

1. Look at Sources 5–7. Explain which of these pictures were drawn to support the abolitionists and which to oppose them. Give reasons.

▶ SOURCE 5 An eighteenth-century cartoon by James Gillray. The white man on the sofa is Wilberforce

WHY WAS SLAVERY ABOLISHED?

Factor 2:
The white working-class campaigners

In 1788 petitions began to flood into Parliament demanding the abolition of the slave trade. These petitions were from working-class people. In Manchester in 1788 over 10,000 working people signed a petition. Support grew: in 1792 over 20,000 Manchester people signed another petition (out of a population of 75,000). Huge meetings were held.

When the slave trade was abolished in 1807 these campaigns did not stop. They continued, with the aim of making slavery illegal and freeing all existing slaves. In 1814 one and a half million people signed petitions. In fact, more people signed these petitions than signed the famous CHARTIST petitions in the 1840s demanding reform of Parliament (see page 92).

---

1. Look at Sources 8 and 9. One was written by a rich nobleman in 1793 and the other is from a speech at a working-class meeting in Sheffield in 1794. Explain which is which.
2. Do the two sources agree about anything?

SOURCE 8

The idea of abolishing the slave trade is connected with the levelling system and the rights of man. And what is liberty and equality? Look at Haiti [where there had been a violent slave rebellion and the slaves had seized power] and see what the rights of man have done there.

SOURCE 9

Slavery is insulting to human nature. Its abolition will redeem the national honour, too long sullied by the trade of blood, and promote the cause of liberty. It will avenge peacefully ages of wrongs to our negro brothers.

Factor 3:
Black people's actions

In the eighteenth century many black slaves in Britain began to demand to be treated like ordinary servants. They demanded wages. Many others simply refused to be kept as slaves and ran away. Often the slave's owner went to court to get the slave back, but the legal position of slavery in Britain was never clear. Everyone knew that slaves could be kept in other parts of the British Empire, such as the West Indies. Everyone also knew that slaves could be traded around the world. But what happened if a slave was brought into Britain? There was no law that said slavery was legal in Britain and no law that said it was illegal. When cases of slaves claiming their freedom were brought to court in Britain the judges seemed to make a different decision every time!

Granville Sharp helped many of these slaves who were determined to remain free to fight their cases in the courts. Increasingly, the law courts did set them free. Soon it was not worth the trouble for slave owners to chase down their escaped slaves. By 1800 slaves were still being sold in Britain and being taken against their will to the West Indies, but most black people in Britain were free – through their own efforts.

SOURCE 10 A complaint about black slaves by a magistrate in 1768

They no sooner arrive here, than they put themselves on a footing with other servants, become intoxicated with liberty and begin to expect wages.

Olaudah Equiano

When he was just ten years old Olaudah Equiano was taken from Africa to Barbados as a slave. He worked as a servant to a ship's captain and so travelled widely. He stayed in London for some time, where he learned to read and became a Christian. He hoped he would be made free, but his master took him back to America and sold him. However, Equiano eventually bought his freedom and returned to England, where he married Susan Cullun from Ely.

In 1789 he wrote the story of his life. This was widely read and turned many people against slavery. He travelled the country speaking at meetings and worked closely with other ABOLITIONISTS like Granville Sharp. In fact it was Equiano who brought the case of the slave ship *Zong* to the public's attention. He died in 1797.

SOURCE 11
A portrait of Olaudah Equiano

Slave revolt!

The ideals of equality and liberty that were behind the French Revolution in 1789 also took root in the island of St Domingue, a French COLONY in the West Indies. The plantation owners did not like these ideals, and to avoid another revolution like the one in France they planned an alliance with Britain. The slaves knew this would mean that slavery would continue. The conditions for the slaves on St Domingue were among the worst in the West Indies. The death rate among the slaves was very high because of the dreadful treatment they received.

In 1791 the slaves rebelled, murdering white plantation owners and setting fire to the sugar cane fields. British troops tried to take control, but the slaves, brilliantly led by a slave called Toussaint L'Ouverture, defeated the British as well as the French.

Slavery was abolished, and in 1804 the island declared itself independent with the new name of Haiti. All over the West Indies, plantation owners lived in terror of these ideas spreading to their own slaves. Meanwhile, people in Britain who were against abolition used Haiti as an example of what would happen if everyone was given equality (see Source 8).

---

1. Choose one or more of the three possible endings to this sentence:
'The actions of black people . . .
- had no effect on the debate about slavery'
- helped to bring about the end of slavery'
- made people worried about the effects of abolishing slavery'.
  Explain your choice.

Factor 4:
Economics

From the 1770s onwards the West Indies were becoming less important to Britain. Cuba and Brazil could produce cheaper sugar. Many plantations in the West Indies were closed down. The demand for slaves fell. For example, in 1771 Barbados imported 2728 slaves, but in 1772 none were imported.

SOURCE 12 Written by the poet and travel writer William Beckford in 1790 about the situation in the West Indies

66 *Without an importation of slaves the crops will decline, and the population and the produce will soon be extinct and at an end.* 99

SOURCE 13 Written by the economist Adam Smith in 1776

66 *The experience of all ages and nations, I believe, demonstrates that the work done by slaves, though it appears to cost only their maintenance, is in the end the dearest of any. A person who can acquire no property can have no other interest but to eat as much and to labour as little as possible. Whatever work he does can be squeezed out of him by violence only.* 99

The slave trade was abolished in 1807. It then took another 27 years to get slavery itself abolished. It was a gradual process. First, Parliament passed laws to improve conditions on the plantations. However, the laws had little effect, and in 1831 slaves in Jamaica went on strike and set fire to the cane fields. In response, the plantation owners shot 100 slaves and hanged 300. This made many people realise that conditions could never be improved, and in 1833 slavery was finally abolished.

---

1. Write down these four statements as headings in your book:
- 'Slavery was abolished because of the actions of middle-class whites.'
- 'Slavery was abolished because of the actions of working-class whites.'
- 'Slavery was abolished because of the actions of blacks.'
- 'Slavery was abolished because the whites realised it was not making any money.'

   Under each heading write down all the evidence you can find on pages 82–85 to support that view.
2. Write an essay entitled 'Why were the slave trade and slavery abolished?' At the end of your essay explain which you think was the most important reason.
3. Look back at your answers to the questions on page 75. Does the story of the abolition of slavery change your view about whether the British were racist?

Activity

Work in pairs. One of you should design a poster campaigning against the slave trade. The other should design a poster campaigning against the principle of slavery itself.

Compare your posters. How are they different? How are they similar?

Trying to get the vote

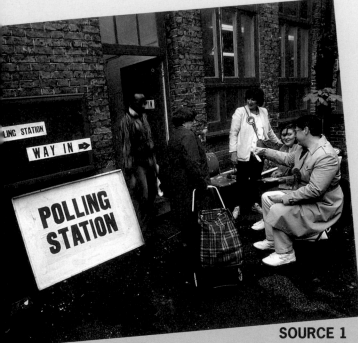

SOURCE 1
A polling station on election day in 1987

SOURCE 2
Political posters from 1992

1. List as many differences as you can between British democracy in the 1990s and the 1820s.
2. If you had to make criticisms of the voting system in the 1820s which five criticisms would you make?

Democracy in the 1990s

■ Everyone aged eighteen or over can vote, except for 'lunatics', lords and some criminals.

■ Everyone's vote is secret. Nobody has to tell anyone else how they have voted.

■ Britain is divided into 651 constituencies. These vary in size. For example, the Isle of Wight has 99,838 voters, while the Western Isles have 22,784 voters.

■ Each constituency sends one MP (Member of Parliament) to Parliament in London.

■ Each voter in a constituency votes for one person whom they want to be their MP, from a list of candidates. Most of these candidates are from a political party (Conservative, Labour, Liberal Democrat, Scottish Nationalist, etc.). The only candidates who stand much of a chance of being elected are those from the main parties. When most people vote they vote for the party not the person.

■ In each constituency the candidate who gets the most votes becomes an MP and sits in the House of Commons. MPs are paid a salary.

■ The party which has most MPs forms the government and its leader becomes Prime Minister.

■ There must be a General Election at least every five years.

■ Parliament consists of the House of Commons and the House of Lords. The House of Commons has much more power than the House of Lords.

■ Parliament passes new laws. These new laws must be passed by the House of Commons and the House of Lords. The House of Lords can make changes to Bills, but the House of Commons can refuse to accept them.

Democracy in the 1820s

■ Nobody under 21 can vote. No women at all are allowed to vote.

In the counties any man who owns property worth 40 shillings a year (the rent it would fetch if it was rented out) can vote.

In the boroughs the right to vote varies from place to place. In some boroughs, such as Westminster, nearly all the men can vote, in others very few can vote.

■ Voting is not secret. In fact, voters have to announce to everyone whom they are voting for.

■ The country is divided into constituencies. There are two types of constituency: counties and boroughs. Most counties send two MPs to Parliament. Within the counties there are boroughs (towns and villages) which are allowed to elect their own MPs. Most boroughs send two MPs to Parliament.

■ Only men can become MPs and they have to own a lot of property to be allowed to stand. Most candidates belong to one of the two main parties, the WHIGS and the TORIES.

■ In many constituencies there is no contest. The local landowner is so influential (for example, because the voters are his tenants) that he is able to control the elections, and so no one bothers to stand against his candidates (see Source 5).

■ In constituencies where there is a contest, threats and bribery are often used on the voters (see Source 4).

■ The candidate who gets the most votes becomes an MP in the House of Commons. MPs are not paid a salary.

■ There has to be a General Election at least every seven years.

■ Parliament consists of the House of Commons and the House of Lords. Laws have to be passed by both Houses, but the House of Lords is more important. The Prime Minister usually comes from the House of Lords.

SOURCE 3
An eighteenth-century picture by William Hogarth. It is called *The Election* and shows people being brought to vote

SOURCE 4 A nineteenth-century cartoon showing people supporting a Parliamentary candidate as he distributes '50,000 reasons for being elected'

SOURCE 5 Sir Philip Francis, MP for Appleby, describes how he was elected in 1784

❝ *I was elected by one voter to represent this borough in Parliament. There was no other candidate and no opposition.* ❞

TRYING TO GET THE VOTE

Was reform needed?

You may think that the way elections were run in the early nineteenth century needed to be reformed. But many people at the time thought no change was needed. Even people who did want some reform did not want to give everybody the vote. The cartoons on this page show three sides of the argument that was going on around 1830.

Middle-class industrialist

It is time to make some changes. Over the last 100 years Britain has been transformed. Cotton mills, iron foundries and factories of all sorts have grown up. Britain's wealth now comes from industry and trade, not from farming. Yet large towns like Leeds, Manchester and Liverpool, with hundreds of thousands of people, do not have their own MPs. 'Rotten boroughs' like Dunwich, Old Sarum and Bramber, with no people at all, each have two MPs!

At the moment the House of Commons is full of landowners, who know nothing about industry. We need to elect INDUSTRIALISTS and manufacturers as MPs so that Britain's industrial future can be planned properly.

We do not want a revolution. All we want is to give more of the middle classes the vote and to let some of the prosperous middle classes into Parliament as MPs. Let's take the seats from the rotten boroughs and give them to the towns with large populations.

Tory landowner

There is nothing wrong with the electoral system. It is the best in the world and could not be made better. This system has made Britain the richest and most powerful country in the world, and everybody has benefited from this.

It doesn't matter that most people do not have the vote. Why should they vote? To have a say in the running of the country you should have a stake in it – you should own some land. Britain's wealth comes from the land. It is the land which feeds everyone. We own and look after the land. We all come from old rich families that have been involved in running the country for generations. We have been born and educated to rule. People who have no permanent stake in the country might not be so bothered about how well the country is governed.

You might think that the present ideas for reform are not dangerous because they don't give the vote to everyone, but don't be fooled! Once the first reform has been passed others will follow!

Look at what happened in France when they tried to give more people a say in government. It ended in chaos! We do not want that to happen here. DEMOCRACY will mean the rule of the mob and the destruction of property.

Working-class radical

The ordinary people are suffering yet again! Because of the bad harvests and the slump in trade many ordinary people are out of work and starving. If they are in work their wages have been cut. Who is looking after us? No one. Certainly not the government, which only looks after the rich landowners. We must be given the vote so that we can elect a government which will pass reforms to help us live decent lives.

SOURCE 6 Written by William Cobbett in his *Weekly Political Register*

It will be asked, will the reform of Parliament give the labouring man a cow or a pig, will it put bread and cheese into his satchel instead of infernal cold potatoes, will it give him a bottle of beer to carry to the field instead of making him lie down on his belly and drink out of the brook? Will it put an end to the harnessing of men and women by a hired overseer to draw carts like beasts of burden?

The enemies of reform jeeringly ask us, whether reform would do all these things for us; and I answer, 'IT WOULD DO THEM ALL.'

SOURCE 9 From a speech made by an MP in the early nineteenth century

I am unwilling to open a door which I see no chance of closing. This is the first step to a series of changes which will directly affect property and totally change the character of this country. It will be fatal to our liberty, our security and our peace.

SOURCE 10 From a speech made by Henry Brougham, MP for Yorkshire, in 1830

Nothing can be more suitable than that the manufacturing and commercial interests of this great country should have a representative of their own choice to do their business in Parliament. We don't live in the days of barons, thank God, we live in the days of Leeds, of Bradford, of Halifax and of Huddersfield – we live in the days when men are industrious.

SOURCE 7 A cartoon from 1819 commenting on Parliamentary reform

SOURCE 11 A cartoon from 1793 showing Tom Paine, an early campaigner for political reform. Paine had been a corset maker and here he is shown forcing Britannia into a new shape. The tree is the British oak

SOURCE 8 A cartoon published in 1832 entitled *Old Sarum*

1. For each of Sources 6–11 on this page, explain which of the speakers on page 88 would most agree with it.

Activity

Divide into groups.

As a group, decide which of the three points of view on page 88 you wish to work on. Design a campaign in the style of 1830, with posters, letters to the press, events and speeches, to get your ideas across to the public.

TRYING TO GET THE VOTE

Why did the government agree to reforms?

At this time the country was ruled by the WHIGS. Like the TORIES, the Whigs were mostly rich landowners. They feared possible revolution and they did not want democracy. However, many Whigs, including the Prime Minister, Earl Grey, were sure that unless some electoral reforms were passed there might well be a revolution. The Tories, on the other hand, thought that reform would start the slide into a revolution. Who was right?

The early 1830s were a time of great hardship for most ordinary people. Harvests were bad, so food prices rose. There was widespread unemployment. Many ordinary people saw electoral reform as their great hope for a better life. Demonstrations demanding reform happened all over the country. One of the biggest reform organisations was the Birmingham Political Union, formed in 1829. By 1830, 100,000 people were attending its meetings.

In 1830 a General Election ended in a Tory victory, with the Duke of Wellington as Prime Minister. But many new MPs were in favour of reform. The timeline below shows what happened next.

SOURCE 12 Two contemporary views of the riots in Bristol, October 1831

A

B

1. How do the two pictures in Source 12 differ in their impressions of the riot? Make sure you give at least five reasons for your answer.
2. Suggest possible reasons why they differ.

SOURCE 13 An account written by a modern historian

> The whole of Bristol was on the verge of destruction: the mansion house, the custom house, excise office and bishop's palace were plundered and set on fire, the toll gates pulled down, the prisons burst open with sledge-hammers and the prisoners set free. During the whole of Sunday the mob were the unresisted masters of the city. Forty-two offices and houses were destroyed. The number of rioters killed or wounded was 110. Of the sixteen that died, three died from the shots or sword cuts of the army, the rest died from excessive drinking.

November 1830 The Duke of Wellington's government loses its support in Parliament because Wellington refuses to introduce parliamentary reforms. The Whig leader, Earl Grey, becomes Prime Minister

March 1831 The First Reform Bill is introduced into Parliament for debate, but there is much opposition

April 1831 Earl Grey decides that another General Election is necessary to increase his support in the House of Commons. In the General Election the Whigs win a majority of 130

June 1831 A second Reform Bill is passed by the House of Commons

October 1831 The House of Lords rejects the Reform Bill. Riots break out in Bristol, Leeds, Nottingham and many other places

December 1831 A third Reform Bill is passed by the Commons

April 1832 The Bill is held up in the Lords. Earl Grey resigns. Riots break out again

May 1832 Earl Grey returns as Prime Minister

June 1832 The Reform Bill is passed by both Commons and Lords

3. Which of the versions of the riots in Source 12 is supported most by Source 13? Make at least five points in your answer.
4. Use Sources 12 and 13 to explain why it is important for historians to use as much source material as possible when they study events like the Bristol riots.
5. Look at the timeline. How important were the riots in bringing about reform?

Was the Reform Act great?

The 1832 Reform Act is usually called the Great Reform Act by historians. Most argue that although it did not lead to many immediate changes the flood gates had opened, and more reforms were bound to follow.

Look at the evidence below and see if you agree.

■ In the counties a few more people were given the vote.

■ In the boroughs the vote was given to every man occupying property worth £10 a year.

■ Altogether, about 250,000 extra people now had the vote. One in five men, or one in ten of all adults, had the vote.

■ 56 rotten boroughs lost their MPs. These were given to the large industrial towns in the North.

■ There were still 73 rotten boroughs after 1832.

■ The number of constituencies where a contest actually took place decreased after 1832. In 1832 228 constituencies were contested, in 1841 only 168 were contested.

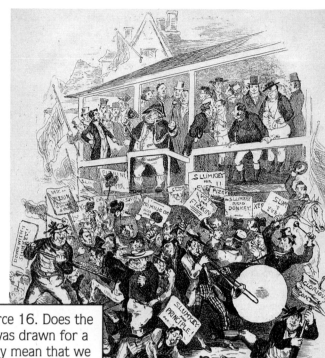

SOURCE 16
A cartoon from *The Pickwick Papers*, a novel by Charles Dickens, published in 1837

1. Look at Source 16. Does the fact that it was drawn for a fictional story mean that we cannot trust it?
2. Using all the sources, explain whether or not you agree that the 1832 Reform Act did not immediately bring about great change.

SOURCE 14 The money spent by MP John Hobhouse to bribe voters in Nottingham

1834	*£2,000 – he won*
1837	*£4,000 – he won*
1841	*£6,000 – he won*
1843	*Nil – he lost*

SOURCE 15 A contemporary description of the 1835 election in Wolverhampton

Everybody was told that if he did not vote for Colonel Anson, he should have it; if they voted for him they were greeted with loud cheers, if they voted for Sir F. Goodricke, they were hissed, jostled and spat on. One voter had an immense quantity of horse manure thrown all over him. Dead rooks and other missiles were thrown.

What happened later

Before the Reform Act the electoral system had remained the same for hundreds of years. In the 50 years after the 1832 Act, however, the reforms shown in Source 17 took place.

Even by the end of the nineteenth century less than half the adult population was allowed to vote!

1. Using all the evidence on these two pages, do you think the 1832 Reform Act deserves to be called 'Great'? It might help to consider these points:
■ Did it lead to immediate changes?
■ Did it open the flood gates for a torrent of reform later in the nineteenth century?
■ Did it open the way for a trickle of reform?

SOURCE 17 Electoral reforms, 1832–84

Date		Percentage of the population who could vote
1831		*2.7 per cent*
1832	*Reform Act*	*4.4 (one in five adult men, no women)*
1867	*Reform Act*	*8.5 (one in three adult men, no women)*
1872	*Voting by secret ballot*	
1884	*Reform Act*	*16.6 (two in three adult men, no women)*

Were the Chartists revolutionaries?

The Six Points
OF THE
PEOPLE'S CHARTER

1. A VOTE for every man twenty-one years of age, of sound mind, and not undergoing punishment for crime.
2. THE BALLOT.—To protect the elector in the exercise of his vote.
3. NO PROPERTY QUALIFICATION for Members of Parliament— this enabling the constituencies to return the man of their choice, be he rich or poor
4. PAYMENT OF MEMBERS, thus enabling an honest tradesman, working man, or other person to serve a constituency, when taken from his business to attend to the interests of the country.
5. EQUAL CONSTITUENCIES, securing the same amount of representation for the same number of electors, instead of allowing small constituencies to swamp the vote of large ones.
6. ANNUAL PARLIAMENTS, thus presenting the most effectual check to bribery and intimidation, since though a constituency might be bought once in seven years (even with the ballot), no purse could buy a constituency (under a system of universal suffrage) in each ensuing twelvemonth; and since members, when elected for a year only, would not be able to defy and betray their constituents as now.

SOURCE 1
A handbill handed out in the streets around Britain in 1838

SOURCE 2 The Chartists taking their petition to Parliament in 1842

SOURCE 3 A cartoon about the Chartists' petition, called *A Charter Party*, drawn in 1843

Look at Source 1. These demands for reform were being made just six years after the 1832 Reform Act. Look carefully at what the handbill is demanding. Remember what you have already learned about the system of voting at this time and about the Reform Act.

1. Who do you think was making these demands:
   - the working classes
   - the middle classes
   - the landowning classes?
2. Take three of the demands and explain why the group you have chosen was making these demands.
3. Explain why one of the other two groups would not be making these demands.

---

1. Look at Source 3. Which of these sentences best describes what the cartoonist is trying to say in his cartoon?
   - 'Chartists and MPs held a party.'
   - 'The doors to Parliament are very small.'
   - 'The demands of the Chartists were so radical that they scared the MPs.'

The Chartist petitions

The 1832 Reform Act was a disappointment to the working classes. They had taken part in demonstrations for reform, but they did not benefit from the Reform Act. In 1836 London artisans formed the London Working Men's Association, which was led by William Lovett. They drew up a petition, or Charter, including the six demands shown in Source 1. Over a million and a quarter people signed the petition (it was three miles long!). But when it was presented to Parliament in 1839 the MPs ignored it.

In 1842 another of the CHARTIST leaders, Feargus O'Connor, organised a second petition. This one gained over three million signatures. But again, Parliament ignored it.

In 1848 Feargus O'Connor organised another petition. This one had over six million signatures! The Chartists now planned to hold a mass meeting of half a million people on Kennington Common in London. They would then all march to Parliament to present their demands.

The government was so worried that 8000 soldiers under the command of the Duke of Wellington were brought into London. But the demonstration was a flop. It rained heavily and only 20,000 Chartists turned up. Sources 4–6 show various views of the same event.

When the petition was studied carefully some very suspicious signatures were found, including 'Queen Victoria', 'the Duke of Wellington', 'Longnose' and 'No Cheese'.

Chartism was finished.

◄ **SOURCE 6** A cartoon from *Punch* magazine showing the meeting on Kennington Common. The cartoonist has shown the Duke of Wellington nine times in the picture!

2. Do Sources 4 and 6 give similar impressions of the meeting? Explain your answer.
3. Is the photograph in Source 5 more useful to the historian than Sources 4 and 6?

Why did so many people support Chartism?

It is no coincidence that the Chartist movement began in 1836 – just four years after the Reform Act, two years after the Poor Law was changed, and two years after the Grand National Consolidated Trade Union collapsed. The economic situation in Britain was getting worse and many workers were desperate.

However, as you will see, people differed widely in their reasons for supporting Chartism and in what they wanted to achieve.

SOURCE 7 Written in 1839 by General Charles Napier about the causes of Chartism in Nottingham

66 *The streets of this town are horrible. The poor starving people go about by twenties and forties. The mayor agrees with me in all my opinions as to the accursed new Poor Law . . . Its guardians guard nothing, they cause outrageous misery.* 99

SOURCE 8 A government report on a Chartist prisoner, 1840

66 *Name and age: Charles Davies, aged 26*
Married or Single: Married, no family
Education:
  Very limited but has considerably improved himself and is a man of talent and energy.
Condition in Life:
  Has been unable to get work for two years because he has taken an active part in campaigning for higher wages.
General notes:
  He says only political power will achieve higher wages for the working man. If wages were what they ought to be no one would be interested in the vote. 99

SOURCE 4 A contemporary drawing of the 1848 meeting on Kennington Common

SOURCE 5 A photograph of the meeting on Kennington Common

WERE THE CHARTISTS REVOLUTIONARIES?

In 1842 industrial depression hit the north of England. Mill owners had to reduce the workers' wages, and strikes broke out. Chartists made sure that the factories had to stop by removing parts from the steam boilers.

SOURCE 9 From the *Leeds Mercury*, 1842

All this, they claim, is to force the government to reform the constitution. Our conviction is that the real cause of the present trouble is long-continued, widespread distress [poverty].

The Chartists included printers and newsagents, shopkeepers and tradesmen, weavers and tailors, shoemakers and cordwainers. One of the Chartist leaders in London was William Cuffay, the son of an African slave. Chartism also had a special appeal for home based workers whose jobs were being taken by the factory workers.

Women played an active part in Chartism, although it is difficult to work out what the attitude of male Chartists was to this. Some Chartist leaders, for example, complained about women factory workers taking men's jobs, and the movement never demanded the vote for women. All the same, women formed many Chartist clubs – particularly in the North of England – and about one third of those who signed the petitions were women.

SOURCE 10 From Feargus O'Connor's paper the *Northern Star*

Where are we to find employment for men put out of work by machines? On the land! We wish man to have a life of independence on the land. He should have enough land to give him a living – to feed, clothe, shelter and educate his family. Improvements he makes, he will benefit from.

In 1845 Feargus O'Connor set up the Chartered Land Plan, with the aim of moving unemployed factory workers to the countryside. There were soon 70,000 members, who each paid small weekly subscriptions which together totalled £3200 per week. With this money O'Connor bought five estates (Source 11 shows plans for the estate in Hertfordshire). The idea was that all members would move to these estates, but after five years only 250 had been settled. They were nearly all town workers and they failed as farmers. In 1851 the whole scheme was wound up.

SOURCE 11 A picture of O'Connorville, one of the new communities planned by Feargus O'Connor

SOURCE 12 A description of Feargus O'Connor by another Chartist

Six feet in height, stout and athletic, with a sort of aristocratic bearing. He inspired the masses with a solemn awe. He was the universal idol.

1. Why do you think so many people joined the Land Plan? Use Sources 10, 11 and 12 to support your answer.
2. Was the Land Plan 'revolutionary' – i.e. trying to do something completely new – or was it trying to return to a way of life from the past?

Historians disagree over whether the Chartist movement was really about politics or economics. Source 13 is what one Chartist leader, Joseph Stephens, said in 1838.

SOURCE 13

If any man is asked why he wanted the vote he would answer so he could shelter himself and his family, have a good dinner on the table, and have as much wages as would keep him in plenty.

3. In your own words explain how Joseph Stephens (Source 13) thinks that getting the vote will help the working man.
4. Using Sources 1–13 make a list of all the aims of the Chartists.
5. Sort your list of aims into the following categories: political, economic and social.

Activity

It is 1846. You are a government official. You have to write a report on why the Chartists are attracting so much support. Write a report of no more than 100 words.

Were the Chartists violent? The case of Newport

In 1839 there was a riot in Newport, South Wales. The trouble centred around Henry Vincent, a Chartist leader, who was being held prisoner by the authorities. When the Chartists marched into the town to demand his release, troops were waiting for them in the Westgate Hotel. The incident ended in violence, with many people killed. Whose fault was this?

1. Compare Sources 14 and 15. Which is more reliable?

A

SOURCE 14 From the evidence of Edward Patton, a carpenter, during the trial of John Frost, the Chartists' leader, at Newport

66 *The 200 or 300 people I saw were armed with sticks with iron points. I did not see many guns. I never saw anything done to the windows of the Westgate Inn. I did not hear a crash of windows. They drew up in front of the Westgate. They asked for the prisoners. They came close to the door. Then a rush was made. Then I heard firing, and took to my heels. I was 25 yards from the Westgate when I heard a very loud voice say, 'No, never.' I could not say when the firing began. It is likely enough the firing began from the Westgate Inn.* 99

▲ ▶ **SOURCE 16** Two contemporary engravings of events at Newport

B

SOURCE 15 Written by R.G. Gammage in his *History of the Chartist Movement*, 1854. Gammage was a Chartist, but he was opposed to the use of violent methods

66 *A company of soldiers was stationed at the Westgate Hotel. The crowd marched there loudly cheering. The police fled into the hotel for safety. The soldiers were stationed at the windows, through which some of the crowd fired. The soldiers returned the fire. In about twenty minutes ten of the Chartists were killed on the spot, and 50 others wounded.* 99

Activity

Work in two groups.

Group A. Decide which of Sources 14–16 suggest that the violence at Newport was the fault of the Chartists. Find as many reasons as you can. Design a government poster condemning the Chartists.

Group B. Decide which of Sources 14–16 suggest that the violence of Newport was the fault of the authorities. Find as many reasons as you can. Design a Chartist poster blaming the government

The Rebecca Riots

In 1839, the same year as the CHARTIST uprising at Newport, some very different disturbances began in another part of South Wales. They were known as the Rebecca Riots. They took place mainly in rural areas, where most of the people were farmers with smallholdings (where they grew only the food they needed to live on). Many of these farmers were near to starvation because of the had harvest, but their troubles did not end there.

■ Landowners were combining smallholdings into larger farms. They offered these to whoever could pay the highest rent. Many poor families lost their farms.

■ The new Poor Law introduced in 1834 stopped money payments to the poor. Instead, poor people were sent to workhouses, which were so unpleasant that many people starved rather than be sent there.

■ In 1836 a law was passed which said that tithes (taxes paid to the Church) had to be paid in money not goods. The amount to be paid was fixed by the vicar. In South Wales tithes went up.

■ Some roads in South Wales were owned by TURNPIKE TRUSTS, which charged tolls to road users. The trusts were run by outsiders who were simply interested in making as much money as possible. These trusts were very unpopular with the farmers who had to use their roads a lot.

> **1.** Can you think of three reasons why farmers would need to use the roads a lot?

Trouble at the turnpikes

The farmers used lime to fertilise their land. As you can see from Source 1, they fetched the lime from quarries at the edge of the South Wales coalfield. Long strings of carts carried the lime westwards along the turnpike roads. These carts did much damage to the roads.

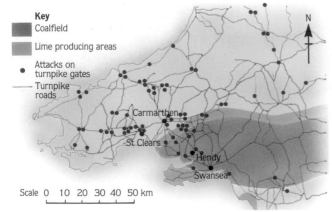

SOURCE 1 Toll roads in South Wales and the centres of the riots, 1838–44

In 1838 toll gates were put up for the first time on the main roads used by the lime carts. On the night of 13 May the gate at Efail-wen was destroyed. The trust rebuilt it. On 6 June a mob of about 400 people smashed the gate with large sledge-hammers and dismantled the toll house. They were all in disguise. Some of them had blacked their faces. Others wore women's dresses.

Other attacks followed. The attackers called their leader 'Becca'. He was probably a man called Thomas Rees. He had had difficulty finding women's clothing large enough to fit him until he borrowed those of a woman called 'Big Rebecca', who lived nearby.

SOURCE 2 A contemporary cartoon of the Rebecca Rioters

SOURCE 3 *Rebecca and her daughters assembling to destroy a Turnpike Gate*, a contemporary print

> **1.** What are the differences and similarities between Sources 2 and 3?
> **2.** What different impressions do Sources 2 and 3 give of Rebecca?
> **3.** Which one do you think is the more realistic?

On 23 July 1839 the trust agreed to take the gates down. The trouble died down. Then, in October 1842, the Whiteland Trust built a new gate on a lime road near St Clears. The gate was destroyed. The trouble spread quickly, and by March 1843 every single gate in South Wales owned by the Whiteland Trust was down.

In May there was an attack on a toll gate in the town of Carmarthen. 'Rebecca' told the farmers not to pay any more tolls at this gate. Some of the farmers who refused to pay were taken to court and sentenced to hard labour. 'Rebecca' ordered everyone to attend a meeting in Carmarthen on 19 June. When the farmers arrived in the town they attacked the workhouse, but the authorities were ready with troops and the rioters were arrested or chased away.

Opponents of the turnpike trusts were now organising public meetings all over South Wales to consider the best way of restoring peace. The biggest was held in August 1843 on Mynydd Sylen (see Source 4).

> **SOURCE 4** From *Yr Amserau*, a Welsh language newspaper
>
> 66 *Mr Hugh Williams read out a petition to be sent to the Queen. It included a list of the country's complaints, such as toll gates, the new Poor Law, the change in the method of paying tithes. They also asked for the government to be sacked and a new one to bring in measures to restore the prosperity of the kingdom.* 99

Despite these attempts to find peaceful solutions, the violence got worse. The movement was now becoming more sinister. 'Rebecca' sent letters to vicars threatening to mutilate them if they collected tithes. The man in charge of Newcastle Emlyn workhouse received a letter in red ink headed 'the Vengeance of Blood', telling him to leave the workhouse.

In September 1843 rioters burned down a toll house at the Hendy Toll Gate, which was run by 75-year-old Sarah Williams (see Source 5).

> **SOURCE 5** Evidence given by Margaret Thomas, who lived near Hendy Gate
>
> 66 *I told Sarah to carry her things to our house. She went back to the toll house and took her furniture out on the road. I heard the sound of four or five guns and Sarah came towards my house. She sank down at my door. We took her into the house, but she did not speak a word. She died in about two minutes. I did not see anything except a little blood on her forehead.* 99

At the inquest on Sarah's death the jury of local people came to this verdict: 'Sarah Williams died from the effusion of blood into the chest which caused suffocation, but from what cause is to this jury unknown.'

The death shocked many local people. The authorities now began to deal with the rioters more harshly. In October three men were sentenced to transportation (to be sent to Australia). At the same time the government set up an enquiry into the causes of the troubles. Local people were interviewed and a report was published in March 1844 (see Source 6).

'Rebecca' had made her last appearance. Farmers were now replacing the gates she had broken down and were even volunteering for the special police force which was set up.

> **SOURCE 6** Some of the recommendations of the government report
>
> 66
> ■ *Farmers should not have to keep paying tolls for return journeys. One payment should last for seven miles without another having to be paid.*
> ■ *The toll on lime should be halved.*
> ■ *Other tolls were fixed at the following rates: horse 1½d; horse and cart 4d; twenty sheep or cattle 10d; two-wheeled steam carriage 12d.* 99

> 1. Were the people involved in the Rebecca Riots the same kind of people as those in the Chartist movement?
> 2. Write down six causes of the Rebecca Riots.
> 3. Which of these were long-term causes and which were triggers?
> 4. Write out three reasons why the riots stopped.
> 5. Which of these three reasons do you think was the main one?
> 6. Do you think 'Rebecca' and her followers were successful?
> 7. Do you think 'Rebecca' was right to use the methods she did?
> 8. Why do you think the Rebecca Rioters were more successful than the Chartists?

Women lead the way

IN 1888 a SOCIALIST called Annie Besant interviewed some women who worked at the Bryant and May factory in the East End of London. The factory produced matches and matchboxes. She was shocked by the working conditions and pay: the women could be hit or fined by the foreman, and some were paid only one penny per hour.

Annie Besant published her findings in an article called *White Slavery in London*. As you would expect, Bryant and May were not very pleased. The women who had spoken to Besant were sacked, and the others were ordered to sign a document saying that conditions in the factory were good.

With Besant's help, however, the women formed a union and went on strike. Many newspapers and members of the public took the side of the match workers and within three weeks the company gave in. The fines were stopped and working conditions were improved.

SOURCE 3
A photograph of some of the workers at the factory

SOURCE 1 A summary of conditions in the factory, as reported by Annie Besant

> ■ *Ventilation in the factory had been destroyed by building an extra storey.*
> ■ *Phosphorus fumes from the matches caused 'phossy jaw', a form of bone cancer. [Working with phosphorus had been banned in the USA because it was so dangerous.]*
> ■ *Meal breaks were taken in the work area, so the women ate the phosphorus along with their food. This led to loss of teeth and baldness.*
> ■ *The work was winter work only. In the summer the women had to find other work if they could.*
> ■ *Women were fined for talking, going to the toilet or dropping matches.*
> ■ *The hours were 6.30 a.m. to 6.00 p.m. There were two short meal breaks.*
> ■ *The pay was $2\frac{1}{4}$d for making 144 boxes. For making matches it was about $2\frac{1}{4}$d an hour. The women earned about four shillings a week.*

SOURCE 4 A photograph of the match factory in the 1890s

▶ **SOURCE 2** A contemporary drawing of the match workers

98

SOURCE 5 From a statement by Bryant and May in June 1888, during the strike

Certain people have the idea that this firm, so far from being of use to the locality, does much to oppress labourers. This is a baseless rumour.

The appearance of the factory and the people who work in it are each suggesting of hard work, good order and a fair day's wages being earned for a fair day's work.

Our work people were thoroughly happy with us until the socialistic influence of outside agitators started to disturb their minds. I have no doubt that they have been influenced by the twaddle of Mrs Besant and other socialists.

SOURCE 6 From an article in *The Times*, June 1888

The pity is that the matchgirls have not taken their own course but have been egged on to strike by irresponsible advisers. No effort has been spared by these pests of the modern industrialised world to bring the quarrel to a head.

The matchgirls have expressed their determination to hold out and they stick together well. The arrangements for strike pay have been made with great thoroughness. Not one of them gets less than four shillings.

1. Compare Sources 2 and 4. Is the photograph more reliable than the drawing for telling us what working conditions in the factory were really like?
2. Look at the photograph of the match workers in Source 3. Would you say they are happy, well dressed and well paid? Make sure you refer to the evidence in the photograph.
3. Is *The Times* (Source 6) for or against the strikers?
4. Who do you think was to blame for the strike: Bryant and May, Annie Besant or the match workers? Give reasons for your answer.

The success of the match workers' strike set off a wave of strikes in other industries.

SOURCE 7 From *The Magnificent Journey* by the historian Francis Williams, written in 1954

It did not take long for the condemned and angry workers of the East End to learn the lesson. If the matchgirls could win without national organisation so could others.

The following year the London dockers followed the match workers' example. Conditions in the docks were very bad. The dockers' jobs were not secure. They were employed by the hour whenever a ship came in. Wages were also very low.

In August 1889 the dockers went on strike. The strike quickly paralysed the docks. But the dockers themselves also suffered great hardship, as they had no union to provide strike pay. They relied on donations from the public and the churches. But they had many people on their side, including powerful newspapers such as *The Times*. And at the moment when it seemed as if hunger was about to drive many striking dockers back to work, they received a massive donation from supporters in Australia. The strike went on.

After four weeks' bitter struggle, on 10 September 1889 the employers agreed to almost all of the dockers' demands for better wages and more secure employment.

SOURCE 8 The dockers' leaders organised daily processions of dockers into the City of London to listen to speeches and to raise public support. This is a contemporary painting of one of the processions. Thousands of Londoners turned out to watch these processions. Eye-witnesses commented how disciplined the dockers were

Activity

It is August 1889. Write a letter from Annie Besant to the dockers' leader Ben Tillet. Tell him why the match workers' strike was successful and whether the dockers can learn lessons from it.

Popular protest movements

YOU have seen how the lives of ordinary working people in Britain were affected by changes in industry. Whether people were better off or worse off after these changes is a matter of opinion. But for most people it was still a struggle to keep themselves and their family alive. As you have seen, housing conditions were often appalling, and conditions at work were hard. Bad harvests meant that food prices rose and people starved. A slump in trade meant that workers lost their jobs and again their families starved. What could ordinary working people do to improve their lives?

Between 1750 and 1900, people who were trying to improve their situation grouped together in many different movements and organisations. You have already studied some of these in detail on pages 92–99. We have summarised some of the others in Source 1, together with some important events from the time. In the boxes below you can see a summary of the different methods these protest groups used, and the different aims they had at different times.

Movements

Abolitionists campaign to get the slave trade abolished ——————

Luddites attack machines being used in the new factories

Peterloo: in Manchester a peaceful meeting to support parliamentary —— reforms ends in violence, with 11 people killed and 400 wounded by soldiers

Captain Swing riots: farm workers burn ricks, barns and machines ——————

Riots demanding parliamentary reform in Bristol and other cities ——————

Grand National Consolidated Trade Union set up. Soon has 800,000 —— members

Tolpuddle Martyrs: farm workers arrested for joining GNCTU and —— transported to Australia for seven years

GNCTU collapses ————————————————

Chartists begin to organise petitions for reform of Parliament ——————

Chartist demonstrations: some violent, some peaceful ——————

Rebecca Riots: attacks on toll gates in South Wales ——————

Chartism loses support ————————————————

Co-operative movement started in Rochdale. Workers join together to buy —— goods which they sell at prices lower than normal shops. Profits shared between members

New Model Unions formed by skilled workers: members pay a weekly —— subscription and in return are paid sickness and old-age benefits. These skilled workers are well paid. Their unions aim to work with and not against the employers

Unskilled workers began to form mass unions. They are poorly paid so are —— more willing to go on strike for better pay and conditions

Match workers' strike ————————————————
London dock strike ————————————————
Independent Labour Party set up to get workers elected into Parliament——

Co-operative Movement has over 1,500,000 members ——————

Aims
■ Better conditions: e.g. better working conditions, better living conditions, lower taxes or tolls.
■ Political power: gaining influence over MPs in Parliament.
■ Revolution: overthrowing the existing system of government and replacing it with something new.

Methods
■ Peaceful protest: e.g. marches, speeches and petitions.
■ Violent protest: e.g. attacking people or property.
■ Self help: e.g. organising your movement so that people help themselves and don't depend on others.

1. Make a table with four columns headed 'Movement', 'Date', 'Methods' and 'Aims'.
2. Fill this table in from the timeline in Source 1.
3. Did the aims and methods of working-class movements gradually change in one continuous direction, or was there a variety of aims and methods throughout the period? Using the table you have just made, write two paragraphs in answer to this question.
4. Sometimes the movements used peaceful methods, and at other times they used violent methods. Why did they do this?

Date	Other events
1776	The American Revolution ends British rule
1789	The French Revolution overthrows the French government
	Both these events cause fear in the British government of a revolution in Britain
1760–1830	
1799–1800	Combination Acts passed making trade unions illegal
1811–12	In the textile industry machines are replacing skilled workers, who lose their jobs
1815	War against the French ends. Soldiers and workers in iron industries unemployed. Food prices high
1819	Six Acts passed, large public meetings banned
1824	Trade unions made legal
1830	Low wages for farm workers because of new threshing machines
1830–32	Reform Act passed in 1832 but working classes not given the vote
1830	
1834	
1834	
1836	
1839–48	Unemployment, widespread hunger
1840s	
1848	Economic conditions improve
1844	
1850s	
1867	Male workers in towns get the vote
1880s	
1884	Male workers in the countryside get the vote
1888	
1889	
1892	
1900	

SOURCE 1 Popular protest movements, 1750–1900

SOURCE 3
A contemporary sketch of machine breakers

SOURCE 4 The emblem of the Associated Shipwrights' Society, a new model union for skilled workers

SOURCE 2 A contemporary engraving of rick burning in Kent in the 1830s

The two faces of London

The imperial capital

IN 1900 London was regarded as the greatest city in the world. It was certainly the largest. In 1801 one million people lived there; by 1901 there were seven million. London was also at the heart of the British Empire, the largest in the world. Many people thought that London represented the pinnacle of human achievement and everything that was best about life. See if you agree with them.

To a visitor in 1900 London must have been an incredible sight. Many of its great buildings had recently been completed, including the Houses of Parliament (Source 2), most of the main bridges over the River Thames, and great museums such as the Natural History Museum in Kensington. There were also magnificent new railway stations, such as St Pancras and Paddington. They were the size of cathedrals and just as grand. St Pancras (Source 3) was built in the popular Gothic style. This deliberately copied the architecture of medieval churches.

Developments in transport had changed the face of London forever. As the railways grew, London grew with them (see Source 4). Lower middle-class workers (such as clerks or shop workers) could now live on the outskirts of the city, in suburbs, where cheap housing was built (see Source 1). The government made the railway offer low fares to workers so that they could afford to travel into London to work. The first underground railway was opened in 1863 (see Source 6) and two more were opened by 1900. People also travelled in from the suburbs to shop in the massive new department stores.

London's industry was also changing. In 1851, 86 per cent of workplaces had less than ten workers. By 1900 these small workshops were being replaced by factories. Source 8 lists the industries in one small area of London. New industries making new products such as electrical goods or motor vehicles were also appearing.

The entertainment and leisure industry was growing, too. By 1900 London had more than 80 theatres and 90 music halls. The first cinemas had opened. Film studios had been set up in Ealing.

Regent's Park Zoo had opened in 1847, and Twickenham Rugby Stadium in 1860. The first cricket 'test' matches were played at Lord's cricket ground in the 1880s. Football clubs sprang up all around London. The new stadium at Crystal Palace could hold 100,000 spectators.

▼ **SOURCE 2** The Houses of Parliament, built in the Gothic style in 1872

▼ **SOURCE 1**
Housing built in 1875 for the lower middle classes in the growing suburb of Peckham

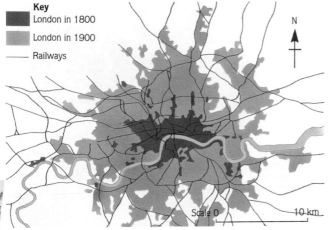

SOURCE 8 Industries in West Ham in 1900

Leather cloth works
Distillery
Iron works and shipyard
Docks and warehouses
Guano works
Sugar factory and refinery
Alizarin works
Marmalade factory
India rubber works
Gutta percha works

SOURCE 3 St Pancras Station and Hotel. The railway companies built hotels for their passengers above their main-line stations

SOURCE 6 The Metropolitan Railway, London's first underground railway, opened in 1863. It was steam-powered until it was electrified in 1905

1. Do some research to find out what guano, alizarin and gutta percha are.

Activity

It is 1900. Some of you are in charge of attracting tourists to London. Some of you are in charge of attracting people to live and work in London. Use the information and sources on this page to design two brochures. How should the two brochures be similar and how should they be different?

Key
London in 1800
London in 1900
— Railways

N

Scale 0 _____ 10 km

SOURCE 4 The growth of London 1800–1900

◀ **SOURCE 5** Bethnal Green before and after a
▼ slum clearance scheme completed in 1900

SOURCE 7 The Theatre Royal, Drury Lane, one of the oldest and grandest of London's 80 theatres

THE TWO FACES OF LONDON

No. 24 In the parlour to the left, a man, a labourer, a wife and two children. She strong, and clean in person. Both drank at times.

To the right lived Mrs O'Brien and her two boys. The husband is in hospital, leaving his wife in great poverty. Nothing in the house but a market basket, reversed to serve as a table at which the children would kneel, and a bundle of something in the corner to serve as a bed.

On the first floor the man is a sweep who lived with and abused a woman to death. He so knocked her about she was never free from bruises. His sons by another woman, as soon as they grew up, did the same and her own child died. The man spent all his pay on drink. Some weeks ago she came back from hospital, her head bound up, her arms black and blue. A few weeks later she was on her bed unconscious, with blackened eyes and face all bruised. She is now dead. There was no prosecution.

No. 26 The third floor. A man and a woman about 26 years old, who earned their living by making toys in the form of mice, which run round a wooden plate by the manipulation of a wire beneath. He making, and she selling. The room was fairly clean. No bedstead but a bundle rolled in the corner to sleep upon. One chair and a broken table at which they work and eat. In this way these people lived year after year.

General notes
These houses contain cellars, parlours, and first, second and third floors, mostly two rooms on a floor. Few of the familes who live here occupy more than one room.

The stairs at the end of the passage turn down as well as up. The kitchen parlour (like the first floor room) occupies the whole width of the house. There is usually a back kitchen with a wash house and scullery. The people who own the house usually only use the kitchens and let out the other floors.

The little yard at the back is just large enough for a dustbin and closet and water tap – all serving six or seven families. The water is drawn from a cistern that is always full of rubbish, sometimes a dead cat.

SOURCE 9 An artist's reconstruction of Shelton Street

Living in the East End

In 1880 Charles Booth, a rich businessman, moved to London to open a branch of his shipping business. He was very impressed by the aspects of London mentioned on pages 102–103, but he was appalled by the slums he saw in the East End of London, near to the docks.

He decided to tell everyone in Britain about the terrible conditions he saw. His team of assistants visited every house in the area and in 1889 he published his report. Here is what he found in one street, Shelton Street.

> 1. From the general notes draw a plan of the ground floor of one of these houses, and label it.

SOURCE 10 A family living in one room in the 1890s

No. 20 In one of the parlours lived Burton and his wife. He was 60 years of age and was a scavenger. They had not a chair to sit on, and the room was swarming with vermin.

No. 4 In the ground floor room lived Mr and Mrs Shane and their four children. The eldest was fourteen. Mr Shane took cold from exposure and was groaning in bed for nine months before he finally died. Mrs Shane earns a living by selling watercress. This family was tidier than some, but the woman was given to drink at times. An older son was in prison.

On the first floor was a family of six, costermongers. They hire their barrows and buy early in the morning at Covent Garden, bring home what they buy, sort it over and then go out to sell it.

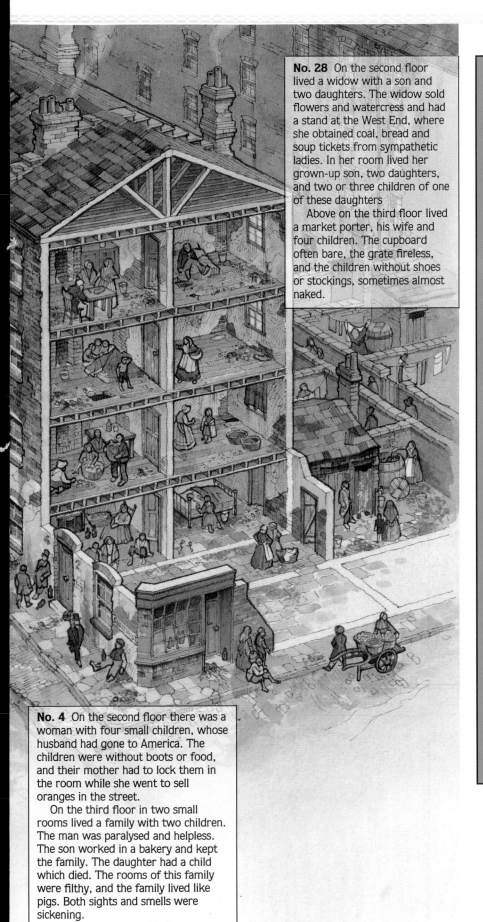

No. 28 On the second floor lived a widow with a son and two daughters. The widow sold flowers and watercress and had a stand at the West End, where she obtained coal, bread and soup tickets from sympathetic ladies. In her room lived her grown-up son, two daughters, and two or three children of one of these daughters

Above on the third floor lived a market porter, his wife and four children. The cupboard often bare, the grate fireless, and the children without shoes or stockings, sometimes almost naked.

No. 4 On the second floor there was a woman with four small children, whose husband had gone to America. The children were without boots or food, and their mother had to lock them in the room while she went to sell oranges in the street.

On the third floor in two small rooms lived a family with two children. The man was paralysed and helpless. The son worked in a bakery and kept the family. The daughter had a child which died. The rooms of this family were filthy, and the family lived like pigs. Both sights and smells were sickening.

Activity

It is 1881. You have been appointed as a researcher on the CENSUS for that year. You must report on the people living in Shelton Street. You have rough notes on each household as in Source 9.

1. Your teacher will give you a census form to complete for this street. It has the following headings: Address and floor; Name; Gender; Age; Married/Single; Occupation. Some of the information is not available – e.g. some names and ages – so you will have to leave those columns blank.

2. There are a number of references to deaths. Your teacher will give you another form to complete, with as much detail as you can, for each death. It has the following headings: Address and floor; Name; Gender; Age at death; Cause of death.

3. Now you have organised all this information, write a report about the people in this street under the following headings: occupations, standard of living, health and hygiene, and size of families.

4. Choose any two of these people. Write five questions you would want to ask them to find out more about their lives. What are the most important things you want to know?

Images of the Victorians

How the Victorians saw themselves

SOURCE 1 *Iron and Coal* by William Bell Scott, painted in 1861. It shows workers at an iron works in Newcastle

SOURCE 3
An illustration for Charles Dickens' novel *Oliver Twist*, 1837. Oliver is in the workhouse. He is asking for more food

SOURCE 4 A cartoon about 'sweated labour' by George Cruikshank, published in the 1840s

SOURCE 2 From the *Illustrated London News*, 1897. The centre panel shows changes during the 60 years of Victoria's reign. Around the outside are great British scientists, engineers and inventors

SOURCE 5 A Victorian Christmas card

SOURCE 6 *Pitmen Playing at Quoits* by Henry Perlee Parker, painted in the 1840s

How other people have seen the Victorians

SOURCE 7 An advertisement by the Empire Marketing Board, 1931. It uses pictures of Victorian families to sell tea and salmon

SOURCE 10 A poster advertising the film of *Oliver Twist*

SOURCE 8 A Christmas card published in the 1990s

SOURCE 11 Characters from the film *Scrooge*, made in the 1970s

SOURCE 9 A biscuit tin made in 1980

1. Look at Sources 1–6, which all come from Victorian times.
a) Which ones show the Victorians as proud of themselves?
b) Which ones show the Victorians' criticisms of themselves?
2. From your knowledge of the period, which two of Sources 1–6 best represent Victorian society?
3. Compare Sources 3 and 10. How do they differ?
4. Sources 7–11 come from the twentieth century. What attitude to Victorian times do they show: is it sentimental, or critical, or both?
5. Why do you think the modern sources take this view of Victorian times?
6. Choose five pictures from pages 2–105 which you would add to this collection to give what you think is a more accurate impression of life in Victorian Britain. Explain your answer.

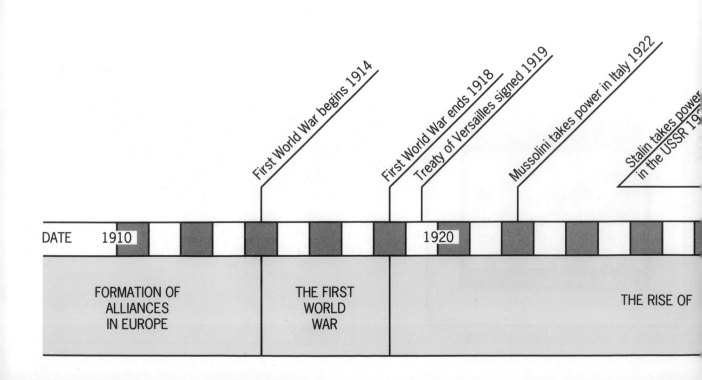

First World War begins 1914

First World War ends 1918

Treaty of Versailles signed 1919

Mussolini takes power in Italy 1922

Stalin takes power
in the USSR 19...

DATE   1910   1920

FORMATION OF   THE FIRST   THE RISE OF
ALLIANCES   WORLD
IN EUROPE   WAR

THE ERA OF THE SECOND WORLD WAR

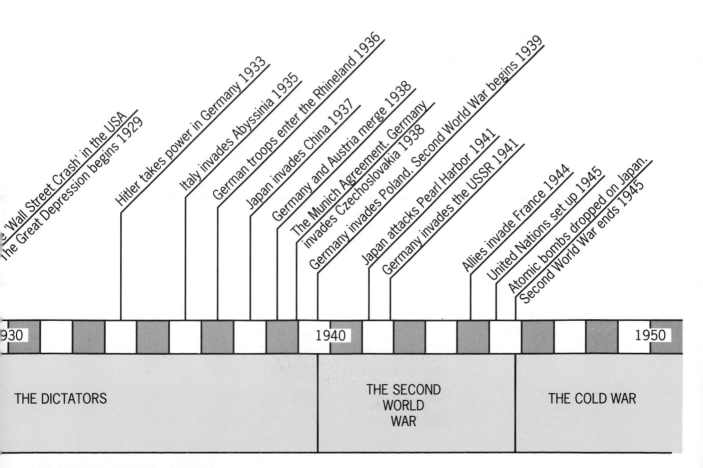

The 'Wall Street Crash' in the USA
The Great Depression begins 1929

Hitler takes power in Germany 1933

Italy invades Abyssinia 1935

German troops enter the Rhineland 1936

Japan invades China 1937

Germany and Austria merge 1938

The Munich Agreement. Germany invades Czechoslovakia 1938

Germany invades Poland. Second World War begins 1939

Japan attacks Pearl Harbor 1941

Germany invades the USSR 1941

Allies invade France 1944

United Nations set up 1945

Atomic bombs dropped on Japan. Second World War ends 1945

1930		1940		1950

THE DICTATORS	THE SECOND WORLD WAR	THE COLD WAR

The stage is set for war

To be a great nation you must colonise

In 1900 nearly everyone would have agreed with this statement made by a French politician. A large empire was important not only for trade but also for prestige.

In 1800 France and Britain both had large empires, and during the nineteenth century these continued to grow. In the 1870s Italy and Germany became united countries for the first time. They too wanted overseas empires. The result was that in the years up to 1900 competition between the European powers grew more intense. There was a scramble for territory, especially in Africa. By 1914 large parts of the world were controlled by the various European powers (see Source 1).

This competition for COLONIES caused several disputes. For example, in 1906 and 1911 Germany and France quarrelled about Morocco. But none of these disputes led to a war.

> **1.** Study Source 1. Which two countries expanded their empires most between 1870 and 1914?

SOURCE 1 European countries' empires in 1914

	Population (millions)	Population of overseas colonies (millions)	Area of overseas colonies (million km²)
Britain	40.8	390.0	27.0
France	39.6	63.0	11.0
Germany	63.0	15.0	2.5
Austria	50.0	—	—
Russia	139.0	—	—
Italy	35.0	2.0	2.0

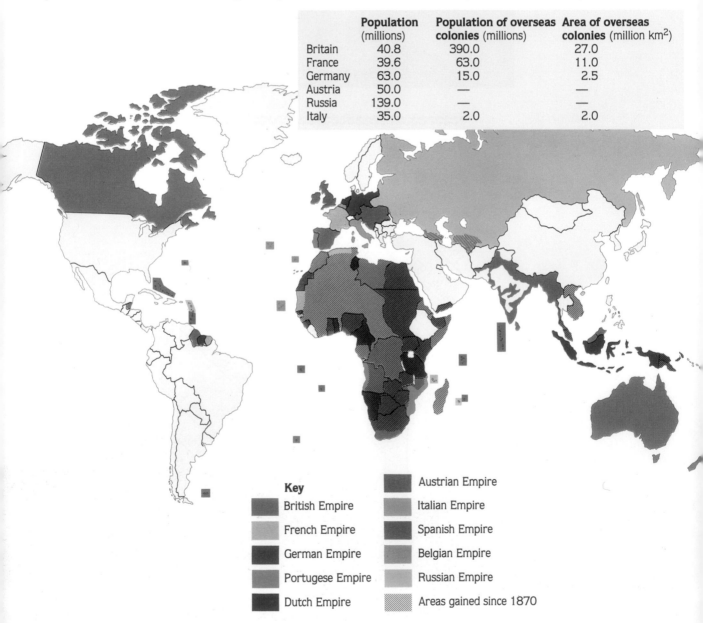

Key

- British Empire
- French Empire
- German Empire
- Portugese Empire
- Dutch Empire
- Austrian Empire
- Italian Empire
- Spanish Empire
- Belgian Empire
- Russian Empire
- Areas gained since 1870

Our future lies upon the ocean

This is what Wilhelm II, Emperor of Germany, said in 1898. Germany was very keen to become an imperial power (a country whose power was based upon its empire). In order to do this, it was building up its navy very rapidly.

In 1900 Britain's navy was still by far the largest in the world. It had to be, to protect the British Empire. But Britain was beginning to realise that it did not have enough resources to protect its vast Empire. In particular, Britain was very worried about the growing size of the German navy.

The British were determined that their navy should remain the largest. Soon a race to build new battleships developed between Germany and Britain. In 1906, Britain launched HMS *Dreadnought*, a new type of battleship which was stronger and faster than any ship built before. Soon Germany began to build 'Dreadnoughts' as well.

SOURCE 2 A photograph of a British Dreadnought, the warship HMS *Barham*

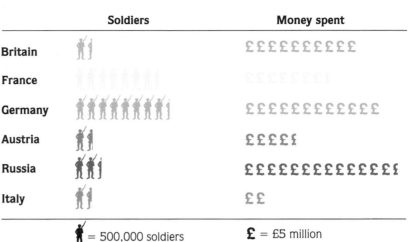

	Soldiers	Money spent
Britain	🪖🪖	£££££££££
France	🪖🪖🪖🪖🪖	££££££££
Germany	🪖🪖🪖🪖🪖🪖🪖🪖	££££££££££££
Austria	🪖🪖	££££
Russia	🪖🪖🪖	££££££££££££££
Italy	🪖🪖	££

🪖 = 500,000 soldiers   £ = £5 million

SOURCE 3 European military spending and size of armies, 1913–14

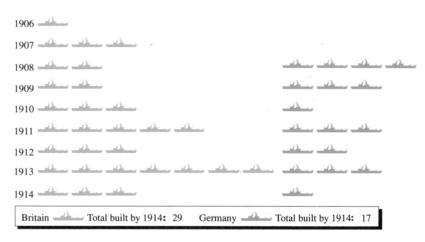

Britain ⚓ Total built by 1914: 29   Germany ⚓ Total built by 1914: 17

SOURCE 4 Numbers of Dreadnoughts built each year by Britain and Germany, 1906–14

Fast modern turbine engines

Thick armour plating

Guns on rotating turrets can fire shells over six miles in any direction

THE STAGE IS SET FOR WAR

By 1907 Europe was divided into two armed camps or alliances. Source 5 shows you how this happened.

Many people would have agreed with *The Times* newspaper's comment above. They thought that as long as the two alliances were equal in strength they would not risk attacking each other, and so peace would be kept.

The division of the great powers into two balanced groups will check ambition and outbreaks of race hatred.

SOURCE 5 How Europe was divided into two armed camps

Suspicion between the two alliances grew. The Germans were so certain that they were being surrounded ready for an attack that in 1905 German army generals drew up the Schlieffen Plan. They planned to attack and defeat France quickly, by going through neutral Belgium, avoiding France's defences. They would then turn and fight the Russians who, the Germans believed, would take time getting their army ready to fight.

---

1. Look at Source 5. Make a list of the countries in the two alliances. Then make it into a chart with three columns headed 'Soldiers', 'Battleships' and 'Population'. Using all the information on pages 110–112 fill in the figures for each country in 1914.
2. Which alliance was the stronger in 1914?

1870
In 1870 Germany became a united country. It had ambitions to become a great power like Britain.

The Germans were worried that France might attack them to win back Alsace and Lorraine (two rich industrial areas which the Germans had recently won from France in a war).

Meanwhile, the vast Austrian Empire was in danger of falling apart. Some areas of the Empire were trying to become independent with the support of Russia. Austria needed a strong ally.

1879
Austria and Germany formed an alliance. They promised to help each other if either country had to go to war.

1882
Italy saw that it would benefit from joining Austria and Germany, so in 1882 the TRIPLE ALLIANCE was formed.

1870
In 1870 France lost land in Alsace and Lorraine to Germany. It feared more attacks from Germany, so it built up its forces on its borders with Germany.

1893
France formed an alliance with Russia. Russia had borders with both Germany and Austria. France and Russia promised to help each other if either of them was attacked.

1904
In the past France had always been Britain's main rival. But Britain had become increasingly worried about growing German power. In 1904 Britain and France reached an agreement that patched up their old quarrels.

1907
Britain and Russia reached a similar agreement and the TRIPLE ENTENTE was formed.

The British said that they had formed the Triple Entente to prevent Germany taking over all of Europe.

Germany said that the Triple Entente had been formed to surround and threaten Germany.

28 June 1914 – the spark!

You might think, from what you have read so far, that Europe was close to war. War was certainly a possibility, but a spark was needed to set it off. You could think of the events so far as the building of a bonfire which still needed somebody to set it alight.

On 28 June 1914 the spark came. Archduke Franz Ferdinand, heir to the Austrian throne, was visiting Sarajevo in Bosnia (see Source 6). Many people in this far corner of the Austrian Empire were Serbs who wanted Bosnia to leave the Austrian Empire and join with neighbouring Serbia, which ruled itself. As the Archduke's car drove along the riverside in Sarajevo the Archduke and his wife were shot dead by a Serb in the crowd.

As Source 7 shows, this event started a chain reaction which drew all of Europe into a terrible war just one month later.

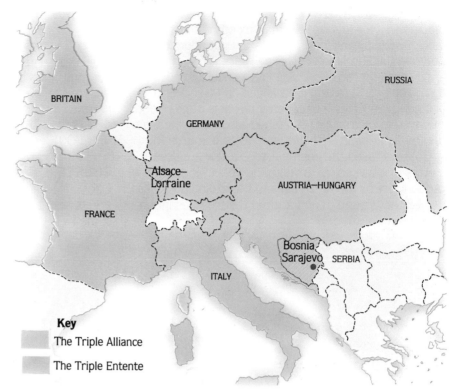

Key

The Triple Alliance

The Triple Entente

SOURCE 6 Europe in 1914

SOURCE 7 The main events leading to the First World War

	28 July Austria blames the assassination on the Serbian government and uses it as an excuse to attack Serbia
	29 July Russia has promised to protect Serbia against any Austrian attack and begins to prepare its army
	**1 August** Germany hears about the Russian preparations and declares war on Russia
	2 August Britain mobilises its fleet of warships
	**3 August** Germany declares war on France. This is either because Germany is worried about a French attack, or because the Schlieffen Plan says France has to be attacked before Russia
	4 August German soldiers march into Belgium. Britain and Belgium declare war on Germany
	6 August Austria declares war on Russia
	12 August Britain and France declare war on Austria

Activity

Work in groups. Your group is a special commission appointed to decide who or what was to blame for the outbreak of the First World War. Give each of the following a score out of ten (1 means no responsibility):

- Britain
- Germany
- France
- Austria
- the Serbs
- Russia

When the group has completed the chart, each person should answer these questions.

1. Was any one country to blame for the War, or were several countries to blame, or was the War no one's fault?
2. Did the alliance system help prevent war, or did it drag countries into war?
3. Were there other factors which helped to cause the War?
4. What was the most important cause of the War?

A new kind of warfare

THE First World War was the most terrible war the world had ever known. German troops did not quickly sweep through France. They got bogged down in Belgium and northern France. The British and French on the other side were unable to push them back to Germany. Both sides dug trenches to protect themselves from enemy machine guns. Soon this system of trenches stretched across Europe from the English Channel to Switzerland (see Source 2).

Soldiers faced the enemy across a few hundred metres of churned up ground known as 'No Man's Land'. Most of the time rain and the exploding shells turned the ground in and around the trenches into a huge ocean of mud.

Each side's trenches were so heavily defended that it was impossible to attack them successfully. As men charged across 'No Man's Land' they were killed in their thousands by the enemy machine guns. Even so, for four years both sides sent wave after wave of men to their deaths. The positions of the trenches hardly altered. In the Battle of the Somme in 1916, 420,000 British troops, 195,000 French troops and 400,000 German troops were killed or wounded.

SOURCE 1 *The Harvest of Battle*, painted in 1919 by C.R.W. Nevinson, who was one of the official war artists sent by the government to record the fighting in the First World War

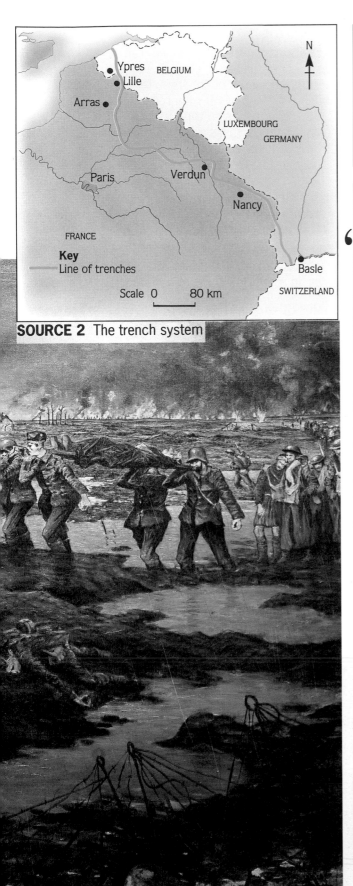

SOURCE 2 The trench system

1. Study Sources 1 and 2. Use them to help you write a description of what fighting conditions were like during the First World War.
2. Why do you think the painting is called *The Harvest of Battle*?
3. How reliable do you think Source 1 is for telling us about conditions in the First World War?

SOURCE 3 Soldiers killed during the First World War

Germany	1,950,000
Russia	1,700,000
France	1,500,000
Austria	1,050,000
Britain (and Empire)	1,000,000
Italy	533,000
USA	116,000

In 1917 the War was still in a state of stalemate. Neither side could win. But neither side was ready to make peace. Then in April 1917 the USA joined the War on Britain's side, and in March 1917 there was a revolution in Russia. In March 1918 the new COMMUNIST government made peace with Germany.

.The Germans now launched a final enormous attack on France, before many American troops arrived. But they could not break through. Back in Germany, people had had enough of the War, and food shortages were so bad that they were starving. So Britain and its allies took the opportunity to counter-attack. They began to push the German army back. The German Emperor, Kaiser Wilhelm, fled from the country and the government which replaced him asked for an armistice (cease fire). On 11 November 1918 the War was over.

Activity

After the War, many people vowed that there should never be a war in Europe again. Use the information on pages 110–115 to produce a leaflet encouraging political leaders to avoid another war. You should be able to find some photographs of the War in your school library, which will give you an idea of how to illustrate the leaflet.

Write three paragraphs for the leaflet, explaining:
■ how terrible war is
■ how Germany should be treated in the peace talks
■ how countries can avoid another war in the future.

Was the Treaty of Versailles a mistake? Part One

The aims

In 1919 a peace treaty was drawn up at Versailles, near Paris. Most of the decisions were taken by the leaders of the 'Big Three': Woodrow Wilson, the American President, David Lloyd George, the British Prime Minister, and Georges Clemenceau, the French Prime Minister. Nobody from Germany or Austria was allowed to take part in the negotiations.

Each of the Big Three had its own ideas about what it wanted to achieve.

The USA

The USA had suffered a great deal less than Europe in the War. Wilson believed that punishing Germany would only make Germany want revenge. This would mean more trouble in the future. Wilson suggested Fourteen Points which he felt would bring world peace. He wanted countries such as Poland and Czechoslovakia, which were neighbours of Germany, to become strong and independent. He wanted France to feel safe against another German attack. And he wanted to set up a League of Nations – an organisation to protect world peace.

France

Much of the War had taken place in France. The damage to France was staggering: 750,000 homes and 23,000 factories had been destroyed. One and a half million young French men had died. Clemenceau wanted to punish Germany for this, and he wanted compensation as well. He also wanted to make sure France was safe from another attack.

Britain

Lloyd George wanted to make a fair settlement. He agreed with many of Wilson's Fourteen Points. But the British public were demanding that Germany be harshly punished.

On 28 June 1919 the Treaty of Versailles was signed.

SOURCE 1
The signing of the Treaty in the Hall of Mirrors, Versailles, painted by William Orpen

The terms

In the boxes on these pages you can see the main terms of the Treaty.

The Germans thought these terms were very unfair, but the two German representatives knew that if they refused to sign the Allies would start the War again. Many Germans never forgave the new German government for this.

As you can see, it was not long before some of the problems caused by the terms of the Treaty were becoming clear.

Who is to blame for the War?

Terms
Germany accepted all the blame for starting the War in a 'war guilt' clause.

Consequences
The Germans bitterly resented being blamed for the War. They felt they were being blamed because they had lost. The leader of the German representatives said, 'An admission that we alone are guilty is a lie.'

---

1. In 1955, a British historian wrote, 'As for the "war guilt" clause, it is difficult to see what were the objections to it. To state that Germany was responsible for starting the War is to state historical fact.' Do you agree?

What to do about German military strength

Terms
■ The German army was cut to 100,000 men. Only volunteers could join the army; conscription was not allowed.
■ The navy could have only six battleships.
■ Germany was not allowed to build any submarines, planes or tanks.
■ Germany was not allowed to keep any troops in the Rhineland (the area of Germany that bordered on France). Allied troops would be stationed there for fifteen years.

Consequences
■ German soldiers and sailors bitterly resented this. They wanted to rebuild their forces.
■ Instead of keeping a massive army Germany built a small, very professional army which could quickly train extra troops if needed.
■ While they were in the Rhineland Allied troops did help keep France safe.

Key

Germany in 1919

Land lost by Germany

Former Austrian Empire

SOURCE 2 Europe after the Treaty of Versailles

Should land be taken away from Germany and Austria?

Terms

■ Germany lost land to France, Belgium, Denmark, Poland and the League of Nations
■ By a treaty in September 1919, the Austrian Empire was broken up into independent nations. Austria was forbidden to unite with Germany.

Consequences

The plan was that the new countries created in Eastern Europe would be a buffer around Germany. But when Germany began to build up its strength again after the War, the new countries were too small and weak to stand up to Germany.

It became a matter of pride for Germany to recover its European lands, especially because these contained many Germans who wanted to be a part of Germany.

What to do about Germany's overseas Empire

Terms

All of Germany's colonies were taken away and given to the Allies.

Consequences

Germany was no longer distracted by looking after an overseas Empire. It could concentrate on its position in Europe.

How to settle future disputes between countries without going to war

Terms

The League of Nations was set up. It was designed to give countries a chance to talk over their problems rather than fight over them. The League had no armed forces of its own.

Consquences

■ Without its own armed forces there was a danger of the League becoming just a 'talking shop' which wouldn't be able to make countries take notice of what it said.
■ The USA never joined the League of Nations, which severely weakened it. Germany was not a member until 1926, and Russia not until 1934.

Who will pay for the War damage?

Terms

In 1921 the Allies decided that Germany should pay £6600 million REPARATIONS in gold and goods.

Consequences

Germany found it impossible to pay the reparations. The USA had to lend huge amounts of money to Germany to help it to pay.

---

1. For each of the terms of the Treaty listed in the boxes on these pages, say whether you think the main aim was:
   ■ to punish Germany and get revenge
   ■ to weaken Germany so that it could not threaten other countries in Europe
   ■ to reward or compensate the Allies
   ■ to preserve world peace.
   Explain your choice for each one.
2. Do you think that the Treaty was
   ■ fair
   ■ too harsh on Germany
   ■ not harsh enough on Germany?

The Treaty of Versailles had many different consequences. Some of them were expected, some were unexpected. Some were short-term, some were long-term. On pages 136–137 we return to the Treaty of Versailles and see how it affected the way events developed in Germany and Europe during the 1920s and 1930s.

The rise of the dictators

YOU will remember how, before the First World War, the big powers were divided into two rival alliances. In the 1930s new divisions were forming, this time between DEMOCRACIES and DICTATORSHIPS.

You have already seen (on page 86 in Unit A) how Britain is run as a democracy. The main features of a democracy are:

■ Everybody (in Britain everyone over the age of 18) can vote and help choose the government.

■ Voters have a choice between several political parties.

■ A government is in power for a limited period (in Britain five years). After that there must be another election.

■ Everybody, including the government, must obey the law of the land.

■ Freedoms, such as the right to criticise the government or to protest against it, to belong to trade unions, and to follow any religion, are highly valued and in some democracies are protected by the law.

Powerful countries such as the USA, Britain and France followed this system in the 1930s, but many other countries had rejected it, as you can see from Source 1. Many countries had abandoned democracy and turned to dictatorship. Some countries, such as Germany and Italy, had FASCIST dictatorships. The USSR (previously the Russian Empire), had a COMMUNIST dictatorship.

> 1. As we investigate the story of three of these dictatorships, look for:
>   ■ the features of a dictatorship and how it is different from a democracy
>   ■ how economic problems helped the rise of the dictators.

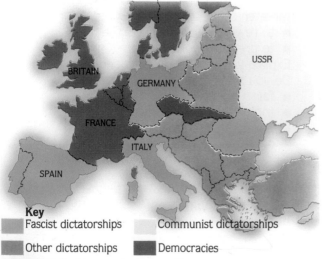

Key
- Fascist dictatorships
- Communist dictatorships
- Other dictatorships
- Democracies

SOURCE 1 Europe between the wars

Case study 1: the USSR

Russia was a vast country. But at the beginning of the twentieth century it was very backward. The vast majority of its people were peasants, and they were very poor. There was little industry.

Russia was governed by Tsar (Emperor) Nicholas. He was not elected, but kept himself in power by harsh laws. He had spies, or secret police, to discover opponents and get rid of them, usually by sending them to labour camps.

Russia's involvement in the First World War only made things worse. Nearly two million Russian soldiers were killed, and the army suffered heavy defeats. There was a severe shortage of food, and people were starving. In 1917 there were two revolutions, which brought the COMMUNISTS, led by Lenin, to power. Russia, together with the smaller states it controlled, was renamed the Union of Soviet Socialist Republics (USSR). In 1924 Lenin died and within a few years he was replaced by Joseph Stalin.

The Communists ran the USSR as a dictatorship:

■ No other parties were allowed to exist. Opponents were executed or sent to labour camps. Stalin sent about eight million people to labour camps, where many died.

■ No one was allowed to have any open religious beliefs. Pictures and statues of Stalin were put up everywhere to encourage people to obey and almost worship him.

■ All industry was taken over by the STATE. Industry grew very quickly in the 1920s and 1930s. The Communists also improved state education and health care for ordinary SOVIET people.

■ Individual peasants were no longer allowed to own their own farms. Instead, they worked with other peasants in collective farms owned by the state. Peasants who objected were executed or sent to farm in remote northern regions. Well-off peasants, called *kulaks*, were killed in their thousands. But feeding the Soviet people was still a problem. In a terrible famine in 1932–33 five million peasants died.

All the other countries in Europe were worried about what had happened in Russia. They did not want similar Communist revolutions to take place elsewhere. The USSR became isolated and Stalin feared that it might be attacked.

SOURCE 2 A photograph of a Russian peasant family in 1921

SOURCE 3 A cartoon 'travel poster' published in the 1930s. The man on the right is Stalin. He is saying, 'Visit the USSR's pyramids'

1. Look at the family in Source 2. Do you think they benefited from Communist rule?
2. Look at Source 3. What is the artist saying about the USSR?
3. Source 3 was published in France by a Russian artist who had left Russia. Do you think he could have published his cartoon in the USSR if he had wanted?
4. Do you think people in Britain in 1917 would be worried about what was happening in Russia? (Your knowledge of Britain in the nineteenth century should help you to answer this question.)

Case study 2: Italy

Although Italy had been on the winning side in the First World War and many of its soldiers had been killed, it gained very little from the Treaty of Versailles. The Italians felt cheated.

In 1919 they were suffering from unemployment and high food prices, and many people were going hungry. There were strikes and demonstrations. Many rich people were worried that there might be a Communist revolution as there had been in Russia. They wanted a strong leader who could bring back order to the country. Many began to support Mussolini, the leader of the FASCIST Party. His followers beat up Communists and other opponents. Mussolini promised to bring back strong government if he was in charge.

In 1922 thousands of Mussolini's followers announced that they were going to march on Rome. Fearing chaos and street battles, the King made Mussolini Prime Minister. Gradually Mussolini took over completely. He was soon a dictator.

Opponents of the Fascists were beaten up or imprisoned and other political parties were abolished. Workers were not allowed to go on strike. Mussolini made Roman Catholicism the official religion of Italy and so gained the support of the Pope.

Mussolini also made great improvements in Italy's economy: he built new roads, he developed farming and industry, and he built huge dams to provide electricity. He said that his next aim was to build a great new Italian Empire to rival the Roman Empire thousands of years before.

SOURCE 4 A six-year-old boy's membership card of the Fascist youth movement. The card says 'In the name of God and Italy I swear to obey the orders of Mussolini and to serve the cause of the Fascist Revolution with all my strength and, if necessary, my blood.'

1. Find two similarities and two differences between the dictatorships in the USSR and Italy.

THE RISE OF THE DICTATORS

Case study 3: Germany – why did Hitler rise to power?

As you saw on page 115, in November 1918 Kaiser Wilhelm of Germany fled to Holland and a new government took over. Immediately it had great problems. It was criticised by many people for agreeing to the Treaty of Versailles. But worse was to come. Germany, already exhausted by the War, had to suffer bad harvests and rapid INFLATION. The German currency became almost worthless – by 1923 people needed wheelbarrows to carry their wages home, but all they could buy with the money was a cup of coffee.

To make matters worse, Germany was having to pay massive REPARATIONS to the ALLIES, and had lost some of its best coal and iron fields to France under the Treaty of Versailles. In 1923, when Germany stopped paying reparations to France, French troops marched into the Ruhr district of Germany and seized more of Germany's coalfields. Soon many thousands of Germans were unemployed and terribly poor.

At this point a politician called Adolf Hitler appeared on the scene. He had invented his own version of Fascism, called Nazism. He used all the troubles that the German government faced to win support for his own Nazi Party.

In 1923 he thought the time was right for his party to take over government in Germany. He attempted to seize power by a *putsch* (a violent uprising), but it failed and he ended up in prison. While in prison he wrote down his political ideas in his book *Mein Kampf* ('My Struggle'). When he was released from prison in 1924 he began to rebuild the Nazi Party.

But it was in 1929 that large numbers of people began to join the Party.

The reason for this increase in Hitler's popularity was that by 1929 Germany's economic problems were being made even worse by the collapse in world trade. During the late 1920s American businesses were booming. The USA was at the centre of the world economy. Businesses in other countries did well, too. Then, in 1929, confidence collapsed. The price of SHARES on the New York stock market crashed, and many businesses went bankrupt.

SOURCE 6 German children playing with worthless banknotes, a photograph taken in 1923

SOURCE 5 Adolf Hitler in 1923

Thousands of shareholders were ruined and there was a huge increase in unemployment. The amount of trade between America and other countries decreased and soon the rest of the world was pulled into a serious slump. This is known as the Great Depression.

Because of the economic problems Germany already had, and because of the reparations it still owed, the effects of the Depression were most dramatic there. As the economic situation got worse, support for Hitler's Nazi Party grew.

By July 1932 the Nazis were the largest party in the Reichstag (the German parliament), although they didn't have an overall majority. No other party was able to rule successfully or do anything about the economic crisis, and so in 1933 the President of Germany, Hindenburg, appointed Hitler as Chancellor (a similar position to that of Prime Minister in Britain).

Why did the German people support Hitler's Nazi Party? The following sources will give you some clues.

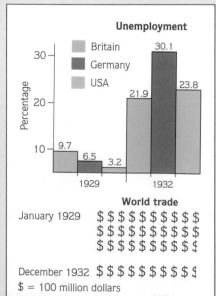

SOURCE 7 Unemployment and world trade, 1929–32

SOURCE 8 A camp built in a Berlin park in 1931 by unemployed men who had been evicted from their homes

SOURCE 9 A description by Albert Speer, a leading Nazi, of how he felt after hearing a speech by Hitler in 1931

66 *Here it seemed to me was hope. Here were new ideals, a new understanding, new tasks. The dangers of Communism could be stopped, Hitler persuaded us, and instead of hopeless unemployment Germany could move towards economic recovery.*

It must have been at this time that my mother saw a parade of Storm Troopers [Hitler's private army]. The sight of such discipline in a time of chaos, and the impression of energy and hope, seems to have won her over. 99

SOURCE 11 A summary of some of the ideas in *Mein Kampf*, which Hitler wrote while he was in prison

66 ■ *The Treaty of Versailles must be cancelled and land taken from Germany must be returned.*
■ *All the people of German blood (including many living in neighbouring countries such as Czechoslovakia or Austria) must be allowed to live in a Greater Germany.*
■ *We demand land and colonies to feed our people and to house surplus population.*
■ *We demand a strong central government led by a single strong leader, a Fuehrer.*
■ *The Germans are the 'Master Race'. They must keep themselves pure. Only those of German blood may be citizens. No Jews may be members of the nation. It was the Jews who helped bring about Germany's defeat in the First World War. They must be destroyed.* 99

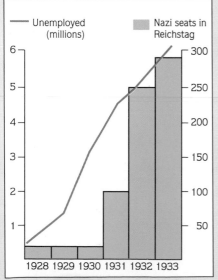

SOURCE 10 Unemployment in Germany, 1928–33, and seats won by the Nazis in the Reichstag, 1928–32

SOURCE 12 Written by Victor Schiff in 1934. He was a leading German politician who had to flee from Germany when Hitler came to power

66 *Hitler owes his rise to power to the World Economic Crisis: to the despair of the unemployed working classes, to the university educated youth for whom there is no future, to the middle-class businessman and craftsman heading for bankruptcy and to the farmers threatened with a fall in food prices.* 99

1. What reasons might each of the following people have had for voting for Hitler:
   ■ an unemployed person
   ■ a German army officer
   ■ a middle-class businessman or woman
   ■ a young person who had just left university?
   Use Sources 8–12 to support your answer.
2. Which do you think was the more important reason for Hitler's popularity: the Depression or the Treaty of Versailles?

THE RISE OF THE DICTATORS

What was life like in Nazi Germany?

Once in power, Hitler moved quickly. He soon made the Reichstag give him the power to pass laws without consulting it. All opposition parties were banned, as were trade unions. The Gestapo (secret police) was used to round up opponents, such as Communists, who were imprisoned in 'concentration camps'. The Nazis took over control of the press and radio, and they controlled what was taught in schools. Jews were persecuted. To start with, the Nazis made laws to limit their freedom, and encouraged attacks on Jewish homes and businesses. Gradually the persecution increased, until in 1941 the Nazis started to send Jews to 'extermination camps'. Between 1941 and 1945 six million Jews were murdered.

In 1933 Hitler and the Pope signed a Concordat. The Pope recognised Hitler's government and Hitler said he would allow the Catholic Church in Germany to be independent

Under Hitler, German industry was improved so that the country could make everything it needed. This provided jobs for everyone and unemployment soon fell. The army, navy and airforce were also built up very rapidly. Hitler did not bother to keep his REARMAMENT plans a secret, even though they were against the Treaty of Versailles. He held a huge meeting in 1935 which he called 'The Proclamation of Freedom to Rearm Rally'.

Sources 13–18 show you the kind of country that Hitler created.

SOURCE 14
A display by the army and airforce in 1938

SOURCE 15
An American cartoon published in 1936

"In these three years I have restored honor and freedom to the German people!"

SOURCE 13
A photograph of political opponents of the Nazis (Communists and trade unionists) being rounded up during the election campaign of 1933

---

1. Do you think Hitler made Germany a better or a worse place to live in?

SOURCE 18
The opening of one of the new motorways built by the unemployed

SOURCE 17
A Nazi poster of 1937 showing what the Nazis thought the ideal family should be like

1. Look back at the list of features of a democracy on page 118. Compare those features with the way the dictators in Germany, Italy and the USSR ran their countries. Make a list of all the differences.

Activity

You are an adviser to the British government in 1935. You have to write a report for it on whether you think the rise of the dictators in Europe in any way threatens peace.

Divide your report into three sections (your teacher will give you a form to fill in if you want it):

■ background information on the three dictators – Stalin, Mussolini and Hitler
■ whether the dictators have anything in common. Do you think they are likely to make alliances with each other?
■ whether anything about the dictators suggests they will be a threat to peace.

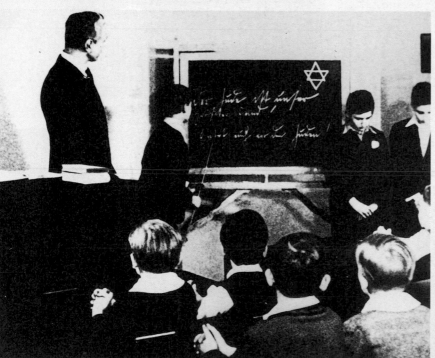

SOURCE 16 A photograph of a classroom in a German school in 1935. The two boys made to stand at the front are Jewish. On the blackboard is written 'The Jews are our greatest enemy! Beware of the Jews!'

Hitler's war

HITLER came to power in 1933. Just six years later Germany was fighting a war which lasted for six years and involved countries all over the world.

One British historian, a few years after the end of the War, wrote: 'The Second World War was Hitler's personal war, in that he intended it, he prepared for it, he chose the moment for launching it.'

What evidence is there to support this view? We are going to look first at what Hitler wrote and said, and then at what he did. See if you agree with the view that Hitler deliberately planned and started the War.

What Hitler wrote and said

SOURCE 1 Three of the main demands from the Nazi Party programme, dating from before the attempted *putsch* in 1923

66■ *We demand the union of all Germans to form a Greater Germany.*
■ *We demand the cancellation of the Treaty of Versailles.*
■ *We demand land and colonies to feed our people and settle our surplus population.* 99

SOURCE 2 Two extracts from *Mein Kampf*, written by Hitler in 1924–25

66■ *The reunion of Germany and Austria is our life task.*
■ *Germany has an annual increase of nearly 900,000 people. The securing of new land for this excess population has a great many advantages. Such a policy must be carried out in Europe. We must turn our gaze to the land in the East. When we speak of new land we mean Russia and her border states.* 99

SOURCE 4 From speeches by Hitler in the late 1920s and early 1930s

66■ *Instead of everlasting struggle, the world preaches everlasting peace . . . There will never be a solution to the German problem until we return to the idea of struggle . . .*
■ *I aimed from the start to become a destroyer of Communism. I am going to achieve this task.*
■ *Perhaps the best way to use my power is fighting for new trade for Germany, but probably better is the conquest of living space in the East and ruthlessly making everything there German.* 99

SOURCE 5 An extract from the *Hossbach Memorandum*. Hossbach was Hitler's Adjutant (assistant) in 1937, when Hitler addressed the heads of the German army, navy and airforce. Hossbach made rough notes during the meeting, then wrote them up in his Memorandum a few days later

66*Hitler asked that this be regarded, in the event of his death, as his last will and testament.*

The aim of German foreign policy was to defend Germany and to enlarge it. It was therefore a question of space. The question for Germany was: where could it achieve the greatest gain at the lowest cost? He was determined to solve Germany's problem of space by 1943–45 at the latest. For the improvement of our position our first objective must be to overthrow Czechoslovakia and Austria. Hitler believed that Britain and France had already written off the Czechs. 99

SOURCE 3 A photograph of Hitler at a Nazi rally

SOURCE 6 An extract from Hitler's last will and testament, which he wrote just before he committed suicide in May 1945

"*It is not true that I wanted war in 1939. It was brought about by those international statesmen working for Jewish interests. After my experiences of the First World War, I never wished for a second war against England.*"

6. Match up each caption in the box with the correct part of the map in Source 7.
7. From what you have learned about Hitler's aims from his speeches and writings, which of these areas do you think he would try and conquer? Give a reason for each of your choices.

1. Study Sources 1–6. Make a list of all Hitler's aims.
2. Did Hitler have any consistent aims between the early 1920s and 1937? If so, what were they?
3. Do you think he was prepared to fight a war to achieve these aims?
4. Does Hitler contradict himself in Sources 5 and 6?
5. Which is more reliable, Source 5 or Source 6?

Captions

The Rhineland The Treaty of Versailles banned German troops here

Austria Hitler was Austrian. There were eight million German speakers in Austria. Versailles banned Austria and Germany from uniting

The Sudetenland The richest part of Czechoslovakia. It included good farming land and important raw materials and industries. Three million Germans lived there. It had been part of the Austrian Empire until 1919

The Polish Corridor This was given to Poland in 1919 to give it access to the sea. It cut Germany in two. There were many Germans living there

France France had been an enemy of Germany for many years. Hitler wanted revenge for Germany's defeat in the First World War

The USSR The USSR was a Communist country. Hitler hated Communism. He regarded the Soviet people as inferior

SOURCE 7 Europe in the 1930s

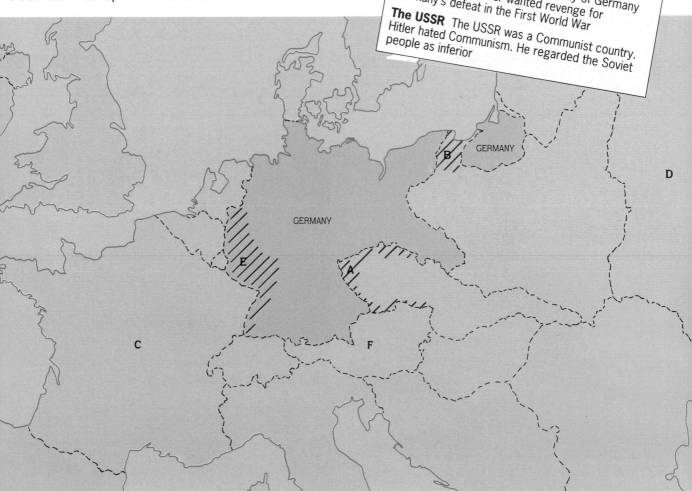

What Hitler did: rearmament

1933 Within three days of becoming leader of Germany Hitler told his military commanders that rearming Germany was his first priority. This would be done in secret

1935 Hitler no longer bothered to keep rearmament a secret. He organised a massive rally in Berlin in 1935 to proclaim Germany's rearmament plans (see Source 8).

Britain signed a Naval Agreement with Germany, allowing Germany to increase the size of its navy to 35 percent of the size of the British navy

1936 Hitler introduced CONSCRIPTION. Many factories were converted to producing armaments (weapons)

1937 Hitler used the Spanish Civil War as an opportunity to test out his new tanks and aircraft in active combat

1938 Hitler took personal command of the armed forces

1939 War against Britain and France began. At this stage Germany had fewer tanks than Britain and was producing tanks at a slower rate. Germany also had only three months' supply of aircraft fuel

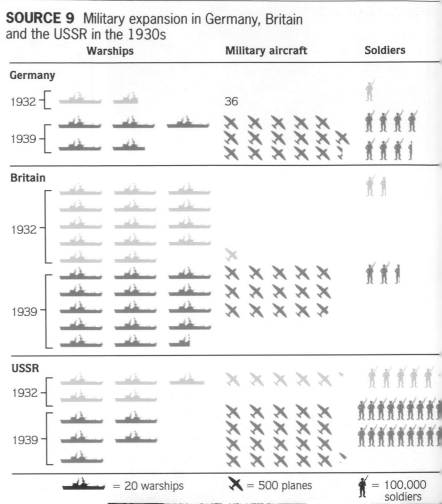

SOURCE 9 Military expansion in Germany, Britain and the USSR in the 1930s

Warships / Military aircraft / Soldiers

Germany — 1932, 1939
Britain — 1932, 1939
USSR — 1932, 1939

= 20 warships = 500 planes = 100,000 soldiers

SOURCE 8 The Proclamation of Freedom to Rearm Rally in Berlin, 1935

SOURCE 10 German tanks in 1935

Activity

Write notes for a speech by Hitler in 1939 describing German rearmament and why German people should be proud of it.

What Hitler did: foreign policy

Step 1: German troops enter the Rhineland
March 1936
The German army marched into the Rhineland. Hitler had only 30,000 fully equipped troops.
Reason given
The USSR and France had just signed a Mutual Assistance Treaty, so Germany was surrounded and needed protection.
Europe's response
The British refused to do anything and the French would not act alone. In any case, Hitler promised that all he wanted now was peace.

Hitler said to his advisers, 'The 48 hours after the march into the Rhineland in 1936 were the most nerve-racking of my life. If the French had opposed us then we would have had to withdraw. Our forces were not strong enough even to put up a moderate resistance.'

November 1936
Hitler made alliances with both Italy and Japan

1936

1937

SOURCE 11 An American cartoon published in March 1936, after the USSR and France signed their Mutual Assistance Treaty

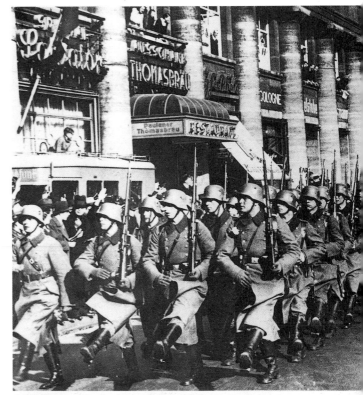

SOURCE 12 A photograph of German troops marching into the city of Cologne in 1936

---

1. What do you think the cartoonist of Source 11 is saying about the French–Soviet Pact?

127

1938

Step 2: Austria and Germany united
March 1938
Hitler sent the German army into Austria. Austria became part of Germany.

Reason given
To restore order in Austria. In fact, it was the Austrian Nazi Party that caused the disorder, by stirring up fights and demonstrations. Hitler bullied the Austrian leader Schuschnigg into giving all the important jobs in the government to Nazis. Hitler then forced Schuschnigg to resign. He was replaced by a Nazi, who asked Hitler to send in the German army to restore order. Hitler said that the Austrians supported the move. In a vote 99.75 per cent of Austrians then voted to be united with Germany.

Europe's response
Schuschnigg asked Britain, France and Italy for help, but they refused.

SOURCE 13 A photograph of German troops marching into Austria, March 1938

SOURCE 15 A cartoon published in April 1938. The caption reads: 'I have been waiting for this since 1918 and now it has come in one blow.'

SOURCE 14 A cartoon published in February 1938. The figure on the left is saying, 'All right, Adolf, I never heard a shot.'

1. Who do you think each of the figures in the cartoon in Source 14 represents?
2. Compare Sources 14 and 15. One of these cartoons was published in Britain, and the other in Germany. Explain which is which.

Step 3: Germany takes the Sudetenland
September 1938
On 12 September 1938 Hitler announced that the Germans were prepared to invade the Sudetenland region of Czechoslovakia, to protect the Germans there.

Reason given
Hitler claimed the Czech government was mistreating the three million Germans living in the Sudetenland. German speakers formed the majority of the population there.

The Sudeten Nazi Party stirred up trouble and organised pro-German demonstrations demanding to become a part of Germany.

Europe's response
The French had promised to help Czechoslovakia, and began to prepare for war.

Chamberlain, the British Prime Minister, was worried that there would be war if Germany did not get what it wanted. He persuaded Czechoslovakia to give up parts of the Sudetenland. He met Hitler in Germany on 15 and 22 September.

Then at a third meeting on 29 September in Munich (the Munich Conference) Chamberlain and the French agreed that Hitler should have the Sudetenland. Hitler promised that the rest of Czechoslovakia was safe. This is known as the 'Munich Agreement'. Chamberlain was sure he had prevented war. He came back to a hero's welcome.

October 1938
As agreed with Britain and France Hitler's troops marched into the Sudetenland on 1 October 1938.

SOURCE 17 A German cartoon published in October 1938. It shows German attitudes during the crisis over Czechoslovakia. On 12 September Hitler made his speech about invading the Sudetenland. On 21 September Czechoslovakia reached an agreement with Britain and France, but the Germans did not yet know what the agreement was. On 26 September President Roosevelt of the USA warned Hitler against using force to settle disputes in Europe. On 1 October German troops entered the Sudetenland

SOURCE 16 A British cartoon published in September 1938. It shows the British Prime Minister Neville Chamberlain trying to steer the world towards peace

3. Study Sources 16 and 17. Do these cartoons show that neither the British nor the Germans wanted war?

HITLER'S WAR

1939

Step 4: Germany invades Czechoslovakia
March 1939
Hitler invaded the rest of Czechoslovakia.
Europe's response
Britain and France did nothing. It was clear, however, that if Hitler continued his invasions then Poland would be next. Britain and France promised to help Poland if it was invaded by Hitler.

August 1939
Hitler realised that he would not be able to invade Poland without getting the USSR on his side. In August 1939 he signed the Nazi–Soviet Pact with Stalin. They agreed not to attack each other. They also secretly agreed to divide Poland up between them.

SOURCE 18 A photograph of Czech civilians and policemen watching as German troops enter their country

1. Look at Source 18. What is the attitude of the Czechs towards the Germans?
2. Compare it to the attitude of the people in Sources 12 and 13. Why do you think their reactions differ?
3. Look at Source 19. What is the attitude of the artist towards the Pact?
4. Explain why you think he has this attitude.

SOMEONE IS TAKING
SOMEONE FOR A WALK

◀ **SOURCE 19** A British cartoon published in November 1939 about the Nazi–Soviet Pact

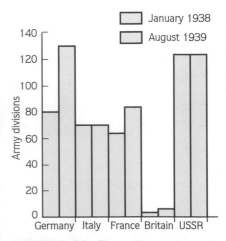

SOURCE 20 The military strength of the main European powers in January 1938 and August 1939

Step 5: Germany invades Poland
September 1939
In 1939 Hitler began to demand the port of Danzig and the 'Polish Corridor' from Poland. On 1 September his troops invaded Poland.
Reason given
Hitler said that it had been wrong to take these away from Germany at Versailles, and it was wrong to divide Germany into two.
Europe's response
On 3 September Britain and France declared war on Germany.

Activity
Working in groups, do a study of Hitler's methods. Was there a pattern to his actions? This is how one historian has described Hitler's methods:
'He usually began his conquests cautiously. He had to go carefully, because he always pretended to be much stronger than he really was. He would wait for chances and encourage Nazis to stir up trouble in the country to be conquered; this would give him an excuse for action. He often had doubts, but when he finally decided to act he was fast and decisive.'

In your groups, compare this description with what happened between 1933 and 1939, as described on pages 124–131. Each person in the group can concentrate on one sentence of the description. You could then put the whole answer together as a display headed 'Hitler's methods', using illustrations from Sources 1–21.

HERE'S SOME MISTAKE, IT WAS YOUR SMALL BROTHER I SENT FOR".

SOURCE 21 A British cartoon published three days after Britain and France declared war on Germany. Hitler is in his study. He has summoned the younger brother of Mars (the god of war). But Mars, the great war-god, appears instead. He towers over Hitler

5. Look at Source 21. What point is the cartoonist making?
6. Do you agree with him?
7. You have studied many cartoons on pages 118–131. Discuss in class how cartoons are useful to the historian, and what the problems are in using them. Each person should choose which they think is the 'cleverest' cartoon on these pages.

Hitler's war?
It is clear that Hitler bears much of the responsibility for starting the War. Clearly he had broken the terms of the Treaty of Versailles.

1. Look back at the terms of the Treaty on pages 116–117. Study the events shown on the timeline on pages 127–131. Make a list of all the times that Hitler broke the terms of the Treaty of Versailles between 1933 and 1939.
2. It is clear that Hitler was determined to conquer land and was prepared to fight for it. But do you think he was really planning to fight Britain and France? You will need to think about two things:
   ■ Was he strong enough to do so? (Look back at Source 9 on page 126 and Source 20 on page 130 which give details of Hitler's military strength in 1939.)
   ■ Did he want to? (Look back at pages 124–125.)
3. Do you think Hitler was the only person responsible for the War? You may feel that there were times when action by Britain and France could have stopped Hitler. Can you find any examples?

On the next few pages we are going to consider whether there were factors other than Hitler's actions which helped cause the Second World War.

Was Appeasement a mistake?

LOOK back at the list of examples you made of Hitler breaking the terms of the Treaty of Versailles (question 1 on page 131). It should be a long list. Why did Hitler get away with it?

The POLICY of Britain and France towards Germany during the 1930s is usually called Appeasement. This means keeping someone happy by letting them have what they want. Some historians have since criticised this policy, but at the time there were only a few people, like the MP Winston Churchill, who opposed it.

Arguments for Appeasement

■ Germany deserved a fair deal

By the 1930s many people in Britain accepted that the Treaty of Versailles was too harsh. If justice was to be done, Germany should have back the land and the people it had lost in 1919. Why shouldn't Germans be governed by Germany? If this was done Germany might be content and settle down.

■ Fear of another world war

Most people in the 1930s could still remember the terrible effects of the First World War, just over ten years before. People were determined never to allow such a dreadful war to happen again. Many people would agree to almost anything to avoid such a war. They certainly did not think that it was worth driving the world into war over a small, far-away country like Czechoslovakia.

■ Fear of Communism

In the Russian Revolution of 1917 the Tsar and his family had been murdered and a COMMUNIST government had taken over. This had led to many wealthy people losing their property and money, and many quite ordinary people, too. Private property was not allowed. Millions of people were murdered. You might think that there was not much difference between Hitler and Stalin, but many people at the time saw Hitler as the strong man of Europe, who had brought order and discipline to Germany and would stand up to Communism and make sure it didn't spread any further.

■ Britain needed time

Chamberlain was not a pacifist. He didn't believe in avoiding war at any cost. Although he believed the League of Nations (see page 117) should listen to Germany's complaints and try to find a solution, he also believed that Britain should get ready for war in case this was not successful. However, Britain had reduced the size of its armed forces after the First World War. It was pointless fighting Hitler if Germany had much stronger armed forces. Until Britain could rearm, it was best to appease Hitler.

REARMAMENT, like an athlete, has to peak at the right time. In the 1930s new types of weapons were being developed all the time, as well as new technology, such as radar and Spitfire aeroplanes. If a country poured its money into buying weapons too soon, it would end up with old-fashioned aircraft, or inferior guns or weapons.

In 1936 the British government introduced a four-year plan for rearmament. Between 1934 and 1939 the amount of money being spent on defence increased by four times; between 1938 and 1939 it doubled. Before the Munich Conference the government gave out gas masks to everybody in Britain, air raid shelters were dug, and metals, chemicals and aircraft were bought from the USA.

■ The British people had to want war

In 1938 not many British people thought it was worth fighting Germany over Czechoslovakia. British public opinion was not united behind the idea of war.

However, when Hitler broke the promise he made at the Munich Agreement, and then invaded Poland, British public opinion was united in favour of a war to stop him. The same was true in the British Empire. In 1938 countries like Australia and Canada would not have supported a war. In 1939 they did, and their contribution was a vital one.

Arguments against Appeasement

■ Appeasement encouraged Hitler to be aggressive

Every time that Hitler got away with acts of aggression, he became more sure that Britain and France would never act. There is evidence that he was very unsure and nervous about marching his soldiers into the Rhineland. To his surprise, nobody did anything. He could have been stopped there and then. From that time on Hitler's confidence grew. This encouraged him to make new demands for land.

■ Germany was growing stronger

Every time Germany took more land it grew stronger and more difficult to defeat. Sending soldiers into the Rhineland made it easier for Germany to defend itself. From Austria it gained soldiers, weapons, gold and great deposits of iron ore. From Czechoslovakia it gained soldiers, weapons, coal and armaments factories.

■ 'The Munich Agreement was a disaster'

This was what one of Chamberlain's greatest critics, the MP Winston Churchill, said. He believed it sacrificed Czechoslovakia and that Chamberlain was not really fighting for time to rearm and unite Britain, but was simply fooled by Hitler. In particular, Churchill felt that the time was not used well, since when war broke out Britain was still not ready.

■ Appeasement scared the USSR

Because Britain did not stand up to Hitler when he invaded Czechoslovakia, Stalin believed that Britain would not help the USSR either if Hitler invaded it. This persuaded Stalin that he might as well reach an agreement with Germany and the Nazi–Soviet Pact was signed. This allowed Hitler to invade Poland in 1939.

■ Hitler was determined to conquer Eastern Europe

In reality, Western politicians should have known what to expect from Hitler. From the start he made it clear in his speeches and writings that he wanted to conquer Eastern Europe. They should have known after the invasions of the Rhineland and the Sudetenland that his promises of peace were worthless.

John Bull. "I've known many Prime Ministers in my time, Sir, but never one who worked so hard for security in the face of such terrible odds."

A GREAT MEDIATOR

SOURCE 1
A cartoon from *Punch* magazine in 1938. The man on the left is Chamberlain. The man on the right is John Bull representing Britain

SOURCE 2 A cartoon from the *Evening Standard* newspaper, 4 October 1938. The title was 'our new defence'

Work in pairs.
1. Study Sources 1 and 2, and decide whether they support or oppose Appeasement.
2. Now study Sources 3–11 over the page. One of you should draw up a list of the sources you would use if you had to write a newspaper article supporting Appeasement. The other one should draw up a list of the sources you would use if you had to write a newspaper article criticising Appeasement.
3. For each of Sources 1–11 write at least a couple of sentences explaining why you have put it in that list.

WAS APPEASEMENT A MISTAKE?

For or against Appeasement?

SOURCE 3 Hitler's comment after sending soldiers into the Rhineland in 1936

> *The 48 hours after the march into the Rhineland were the most nerve-racking of my life. If the French had opposed us then we would have had to withdraw. Our forces were not strong enough even to put up a moderate resistance.*

SOURCE 4 From a speech by Hitler on 30 May 1938

> *I shall only decide to take action against Czechoslovakia if I am convinced that France will not march and that Britain will not intervene.*

SOURCE 5 Advice given to Chamberlain by his generals in 1938

> *From the military point of view time is in our favour. If war with Germany has to come, it would be better to fight her in six to twelve months' time.*

SOURCE 6 Results of public opinion polls in Britain in 1938

> *March 1938* Should Britain promise help to Czechoslovakia if Germany invades?
> Yes 33% : No 43%
> No opinion 24%
>
> *October 1938* Hitler says he has no more territorial ambitions in Europe. Do you believe him?
> Yes 7%   No 93%

SOURCE 7 From a speech by Chamberlain to Conservative Party members, 1938

> *When I think of those four terrible years [the First World War], and I think of the seven million young men who were killed, the thirteen million who were maimed and mutilated, I feel it was my duty to strain every nerve to avoid a repetition of the First World War.*

SOURCE 8 A photograph of Chamberlain as he returned from the Munich Conference, holding the agreement with Hitler. Chamberlain announced that it promised 'peace for our time'

"I HAVE SIGNED EVERYTHING": Mr. Chamberlain.

SOURCE 9 A cartoon from the *Daily Worker*, a British Communist newspaper, 1 October 1938

Activity

Imagine you have been asked the following questions in two opinion polls, one in October 1938 and one in November 1939:
- Does Germany want peace?
- Is Chamberlain's policy the right one?
- Should Britain risk war over problems in Europe?

Use a table like this to record your answers (tick one column for each year):

1938		1939	
Yes	No	Yes	No
Does Germany...			

How do your answers change between 1938 and 1939?

SOURCE 10 A British cartoon from 1938. Many British people felt that Czechoslovakia was a far-away country that had nothing to do with them

1. You have now read a great deal about Chamberlain's foreign policy. Explain why he followed the policy of Appeasement.
2. Do you think the policy of Appeasement was a mistake or not? Once you have decided, write an essay defending your point of view. These essays will be discussed in a class debate which your teacher will organise.

SOURCE 11 Digging air raid trenches in London in September 1938. People feared that a war would bring heavy bombing of civilians, as had happened in the Spanish Civil War

Was the Treaty of Versailles a mistake? Part Two

HITLER thought that the Treaty of Versailles was unfair to Germany. He was determined to undo its effects. But was he the only person who hated the Treaty? If there were other people who agreed with him, then perhaps there really was something wrong with the Treaty. Of course, we can look back now and see the trouble it seems to have caused, but did people at the time also see its faults?

As Sources 1–4 show, Versailles was unpopular with many German people. In fact, trying to change the terms of the Treaty was the POLICY of German governments long before Hitler came to power.

SOURCE 3 A German cartoon showing the Devil and his cronies gloating over the Treaty of Versailles. The figures are called Greed, Revenge and Lust for Power

SOURCE 1 From the German newspaper *Deutsche Zeitung* on the day of the signing of the Treaty

> Today in the Hall of Mirrors of Versailles the disgraceful Treaty is being signed. Do not forget it! The German people will press forward to reconquer the place among nations to which it is entitled. Then will come revenge for the shame of 1919.

SOURCE 2 Written in March 1933 by Bernhard von Bulow, German Secretary of State for Foreign Affairs. He was not a Nazi

> The aims of German foreign policy are set first and foremost by the Treaty of Versailles. The revision of this treaty is Germany's most pressing concern. The further task of exploiting opportunities which occur for Germany through the changes in Europe, has to take second place to the revision of Versailles.

SOURCE 4 A German cartoon published in 1919. The German mother is saying to her child, 'When we have paid 100,000,000,000 marks, then I shall be able to give you something to eat.'

Of course, this does not mean that the Treaty of Versailles itself actually caused the War. Hitler could have tried to negotiate changes peacefully. And as you can see from Sources 5–7, the Germans were not the only ones who thought the Treaty was unfair.

PEACE AND FUTURE CANNON FODDER

The Tiger: "_Curious! I seem to hear a child weeping!_"

SOURCE 5 A British cartoon published in May 1919. The figures on the right are the leaders of Britain, France, Italy and the USA leaving Versailles. 'Tiger' was the nickname of Clemenceau, the French Prime Minister

SOURCE 6 A British cartoon published in 1919. You can probably work out which figure represents Germany

1. Make a list of the criticisms of the Treaty of Versailles in Sources 1–7.
2. Add any criticisms of your own which are not mentioned in the sources.
3. From what you know about events leading to the Second World War, do you think these criticisms are fair?
4. Do you think it was possible for people in 1919 to look ahead and forecast what Versailles would lead to? Look carefully at the dates of these cartoons.
5. Do you think that Adolf Hitler was only interested in negotiating better terms for the peace than the Treaty of Versailles, or do you think his aims went further than that?

Did the USA and the USSR let Europe down?

DURING the years between the two World Wars, the USA and the USSR were, in theory, the strongest countries in the world. So we might expect that they would use their power to keep the peace and to stop Germany at an early stage. They did not do this. How much can they be blamed for the Second World War?

The USSR: the Nazi–Soviet Pact

For much of the 1920s and 1930s Stalin was more concerned with what was happening inside the USSR than what was happening outside. Stalin knew that the USSR was 100 years behind other industrialised countries. He put most of his efforts in this period into developing the USSR's industry and agriculture. The USSR did not even join the League of Nations until 1934. However, at the end of the 1930s the USSR did play an important and CONTROVERSIAL role.

In August 1939 Stalin and Hitler signed the Nazi–SOVIET Pact. They agreed not to attack each other. In secret they also agreed to divide up Poland between themselves. Western historians have argued that this agreement was very important, because it allowed Hitler to invade Poland. His biggest fear had been that if he invaded Poland he would have to fight a war with the USSR, at the same time as fighting Britain and France. The pact with the USSR meant he no longer had to worry about this. It looked as if Stalin, the great enemy of Fascism, had betrayed the rest of Europe.

Sources 1–5 give various views of the Pact.

SOURCE 1 A British cartoon published in September 1939

---

1. Judging by Sources 1 and 2, did the British view of the Pact change between 1939 and 1965?

SOURCE 2 Written by a British historian, R. Payne, in 1965

The secret part of the Pact was a diabolic document, for it ensured that Poland would be destroyed and that the War would extend across the whole earth. Germany and Russia were not in friendly alliance, Stalin and Hitler were conspirators giving aid and comfort to one another as they both prepared to plunge their knives into Poland.

SOURCE 3 Written by a Soviet historian, Kukushkin, in 1981

"*Why did Britain and France help Hitler to achieve his aims? By rejecting the idea of a united front proposed by the USSR, they played into the hands of Germany. They hoped to appease Hitler by giving him some Czech territory. They wanted to direct German aggression eastward against the USSR and the disgraceful Munich deal achieved this.*

As a result the USSR stood alone in the face of the growing Fascist threat. In this situation the USSR had to make a treaty of non-aggression with Germany. Some British historians tried to prove that this treaty helped to start the Second World War. The truth is it gave the USSR time to strengthen its defences."

2. Kukushkin (Source 3) and Payne (Source 2) disagree. Explain what they disagree about.
3. Do you think the reason for this disagreement is simply that one is from the USSR and the other from Britain?
4. Discuss in pairs which historian, Kukushkin or Payne, Sources 4 and 5 support.

SOURCE 5 A cartoon published in the USSR in 1939. The British and French are directing the Nazis towards the USSR and away from Western Europe (CCCP is Russian for the USSR)

5. Do you think the USSR was justified in signing the Nazi–Soviet Pact?

Source 3 suggests that the USSR was just looking for a breathing space during which to strengthen its defences. Yet on 17 September 1939 the Soviet army invaded the part of Poland it had agreed to take under the secret agreement with the Germans. Stalin described this as a 'local police action' to protect Russians who were living there from being mistreated by the Poles, and to prevent Germany from taking the whole of Poland. By the end of September, Poland was divided up between Germany and the USSR.

6. Do these new facts change your view of Stalin's motives?

Activity

You can be either a British or an American journalist. You have been asked to write an article about the Nazi–Soviet Pact. Write a headline and a short article for the front page of your newspaper and choose a cartoon from Sources 1, 4 and 5 to go with your article.

THERE'S ANOTHER SIDE TO IT

SOURCE 4 A British cartoon published in March 1937. Hitler is promising peace in Western Europe to the French and British. The figure on the right is the Soviet foreign minister

DID THE USA AND THE USSR LET EUROPE DOWN?

Was the USA isolationist?

President Woodrow Wilson of the USA was the most important person at the Versailles negotiations. The League of Nations was partly his idea. Yet when Wilson tried to get the American Congress (parliament) to approve American membership of the League, to everyone's surprise it refused. This has led historians to claim that the USA isolated itself from the world's problems and did nothing to prevent war in Europe until it was too late. Is this fair?

After the First World War the USA wanted to be free of Europe, with its disputes and wars. It certainly wanted to keep well clear of both Fascism and Communism. Many European countries were having problems paying their war debts back to the USA, but the USA refused to cancel the debts. It introduced high taxes on foreign imports. This made it harder for European countries to sell goods to America. The USA also limited the number of Europeans who were allowed to come and live in America.

However the USA did make huge loans to Germany to help it pay its REPARATIONS, and by 1924 it was sending officials to observe meetings of the League of Nations. The USA also attended conferences to try to limit the size of navies, and it even tried to get other countries to agree not to use war as part of their foreign policy.

But when Japan invaded Manchuria (in China) in 1931, the USA did nothing. Throughout the 1930s, as the storm clouds gathered in Europe, the USA resisted being dragged into conflict. In an opinion poll in September 1939, 94% of Americans said that the USA should *not* send its troops to Europe to fight Germany. Source 6 represented the views of most Americans at the time.

SOME DAY THE WORM WILL TURN

SOURCE 7 An American cartoon of 1936 suggesting what the people of Europe should say to the politicians who were leading Europe towards war

SOURCE 6 From a speech by American President Franklin D. Roosevelt in the late 1930s

"I have seen war. I have seen blood running from the wounded. I have seen men coughing out their gassed lungs. I have seen dead men in the mud. I have seen cities destroyed. I have seen children starving. I hate war. I have spent unnumbered hours planning how war may be kept from this nation."

1. Do you think that the USA was ISOLATIONIST?

Did America's isolationism matter?

From 1935 onwards, the USA passed several Neutrality Acts, which made it clear that it would not interfere in any conflict abroad. But did any of this matter? Even if America had been more involved in Europe, would this have stopped Hitler? Some historians believe that the League of Nations was seriously weakened because the USA, the richest and most powerful democratic country in the world, was not a member. The League certainly had a number of failures. Did America's absence encourage Hitler to use force and think he could get away with it? Sources 8–11 give several different views.

THE GAP IN THE BRIDGE.

SOURCE 9 A British cartoon from 1919

SOURCE 10 Hitler's view of the threat posed by the USA

What is America, but millionaires, beauty queens and Hollywood? America is led by an idiot. Because of its Neutrality Laws, America is not dangerous to us. America is hopelessly weak.

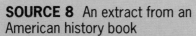
SOURCE 8 An extract from an American history book

The greatest achievement of Versailles was the League of Nations. Even though it was rejected by the American Congress, it is a milestone in the history of man's slow progress towards preventing war. For twenty years afterwards the American people fooled themselves that, because the League sat in far-off Geneva, it did not concern us. Yet without our political support it could not make its sanctions against Italy effective in the Abyssinian Crisis [when Italy invaded Abyssinia in 1935]. It took a Second World War, with its terrible cost, to bring the United States into the United Nations. If a nation can sit back in sackcloth and ashes, the United States should do so for its selfish rejection of the League.

SOURCE 11 An extract from *The Road to War* by R. Overy, written in 1989

In the mid 1930s the USA had no more than skeleton armed forces. The army had only 100,000 men. Other countries' armies were numbered in millions. Its morale was poor. Its weapons dated from the First World War. American soldiers were more at home with the horse than the tank. In September, the Air Corps and Navy had together only 800 combat aircraft; many were biplanes. Germany had 3600. Roosevelt had very little to threaten with.

1. According to Sources 8 and 9, how did the USA's absence weaken the League?
2. Do you think the USA could have stopped Hitler? Use Sources 8–11 to support your answer.

Activity

Divide into groups to prepare for a class debate. Some groups should argue that the USSR contributed more to the outbreak of war than the USA. Other groups should argue that the USA was more to blame than the USSR. Start by drawing up a list for each country of actions that helped contribute to the outbreak of war.

Why did the League of Nations fail?

YOU have already seen how the League of Nations was set up in 1919. Its main aim was clearly stated, as you can see in Source 1.

> **SOURCE 1** Article 16 of the Covenant of the League
>
> 66*Should any member of the League resort to war, all other members of the League shall immediately break off all trade and financial relations with it. The Council will recommend what effective military, naval, or air force the members of the League shall contribute to protecting the Covenant of the League.*99

SOURCE 2 A photograph of the League of Nations listening to the German ambassador's explanation of Hitler's invasion of the Rhineland, March 1936

1. From Sources 1 and 2 can you work out
   - the main aim of the League
   - the methods it used?

With the League of Nations there to keep the peace, why did the Second World War break out? Surely the League should have prevented it?

We are going to investigate why the League failed to prevent war, firstly by looking at the organisation of the League, and secondly by studying the League in action over a crisis in Abyssinia.

The organisation of the League

Most people would agree that to be successful a group such as the League needed to be:
- supported by the world's great powers
- able to act quickly and decisively
- able to make countries take notice of its decisions.

Yet from the start there were weaknesses in the organisation of the League that made it difficult for it to work well. Sources 3 and 4 provide evidence about the organisation.

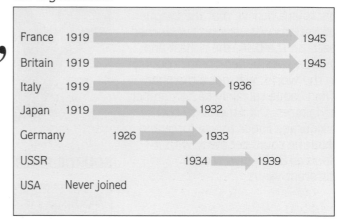

France	1919		1945
Britain	1919		1945
Italy	1919		1936
Japan	1919		1932
Germany		1926	1933
USSR		1934	1939
USA	Never joined		

SOURCE 3 Membership of the League, 1920–45

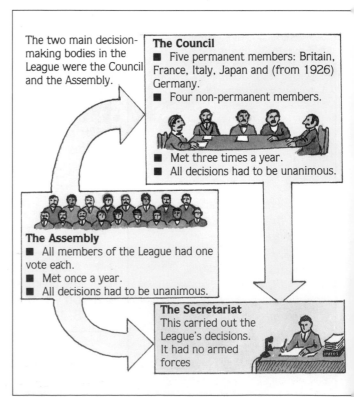

The two main decision-making bodies in the League were the Council and the Assembly.

The Council
- Five permanent members: Britain, France, Italy, Japan and (from 1926) Germany.
- Four non-permanent members.
- Met three times a year.
- All decisions had to be unanimous.

The Assembly
- All members of the League had one vote each.
- Met once a year.
- All decisions had to be unanimous.

The Secretariat
This carried out the League's decisions. It had no armed forces

SOURCE 4 How the League was organised

1. Look at Sources 3 and 4. How many weaknesses in the League can you find?

The League in action: Italy and Abyssinia

Mussolini, the FASCIST dictator of Italy, dreamed of building a new Roman Empire. He believed Italy could only be great if it had a large empire. As you can see from Source 5, Italy already had some COLONIES in Africa. It was very keen to get more. Its colonies bordered on Abyssinia, one of the few countries in Africa which had not been conquered by a European power.

In 1934 there was a skirmish (a minor battle) between Abyssinian and Italian troops at Wal-Wal in Abyssinia. The Abyssinian troops, who were on horseback, were routed (totally defeated) by the Italian armoured cars and aircraft.

Abyssinia and Italy were both members of the League of Nations. The Abyssinian Emperor Haile Selassie appealed to the League of Nations for help and Italy apologised. It might seem that the League had been successful. But would that be the end of the matter?

---

1. Do you think Mussolini would now forget his ambitions in Abyssinia, or would he invade despite the League of Nations? Using Sources 5–10, consider what kind of man Mussolini was and what his ambitions were. Then consider whether you think he would be likely to get away with it.

SOURCE 5 Italy's colonies in Africa in 1934

Key
- Italian colonies
- French colonies
- British colonies

SOURCE 6 From a statement by Mussolini outlining Italy's aims in Africa

" ... to rid ourselves of a constant threat to our African colonies and to get revenge for terrible insults committed by a barbarous state against our thousand-year-old civilisation. [In 1896 the Abyssinians had defeated an Italian army]. "

SOURCE 9 Some of Mussolini's beliefs and attitudes about warfare

Nothing has ever been won in history without bloodshed.

A day on the battlefield is worth 1000 years of peace.

Words are very fine things, but rifles, machines and warships are still finer things.

SOURCE 10 A description by an Italian writer of Mussolini's attitude to Italy's economic problems

" Dissatisfaction was rife [widespread] in poverty-stricken Italy. Mussolini himself admitted that the economic depression was at its very worst. He needed something to distract Italians away from the problems in Italy and give them something to cheer about. Mussolini believed that war was a way out of depression. "

SOURCE 7 A statement made by Mussolini in 1934 about Italy's role in Africa

" Italy could civilise Africa, and her position in the Mediterranean gave her the right and imposed this duty on her. We do not intend to control everything, but we do ask other powers that they should not block the expansion of Fascist Italy. "

SOURCE 8 British and French attitudes to Italy and Abyssinia

France
In 1935 France was so keen to remain friends with Italy that the French government sold its SHARES in the Abyssinian Railway to Italy and gave it part of French Somaliland.

France and Britain allowed Mussolini to move troops through the Suez Canal.

For several years Mussolini intercepted messages between the British and French embassies in Rome and their governments. He knew they were not willing to risk war over Abyssinia, and he knew British REARMAMENT had barely started.

Britain
Britain opposed Abyssinia's entry to the League of Nations in 1924 because it still allowed slavery. Abyssinia promised to end slavery, but broke its promise.

Early in 1935 the British Prime Minister said to the Italian ambassador about Abyssinia 'England is a lady; she likes things done discreetly, not in public. Be tactful and we will have no objections.'

In April 1935 Britain warned Italy not to attack Abyssinia.

In June 1935 Britain offered Italy part of British Somaliland if it left Abyssinia alone.

WHY DID THE LEAGUE OF NATIONS FAIL?

The invasion

In October 1935 the Italian army, with machine guns, aircraft, tanks and poison gas, defeated the Abyssinian army, which was armed with spears and out-of-date rifles.

SOURCE 11 A photograph of Italian forces in Abyssinia

SOURCE 12 A photograph of an Abyssinian village after an Italian attack

1. How might Mussolini have felt if he saw these pictures?
2. How might he justify his army's actions
   a) publicly, and b) privately?

The League's response

When the League found out about the invasion it could have reacted in a number of ways. It could have:
- thrown Italy out of the League
- stopped all trade with Italy
- stopped some trade with Italy
- sent armed forces to get Italy out of Abyssinia.

1. Put these possible actions in order of severity with the most severe first.
2. Which action do you think the League should choose?

To start with, Britain and France were slow to react. After pressure from public opinion, however, Britain and France persuaded the League to impose some economic SANCTIONS on Italy. Weapons and some other goods could not be sold to Italy. Italian goods could not be bought. But oil, steel, coal and iron were still sold to Italy.

The Italian invasion continued. In secret, France and Britain now began to negotiate with Italy. They hoped to give Italy what it wanted without causing too much international tension. Then, in March 1936, Germany invaded the Rhineland. Abyssinia was forgotten, and sanctions were lifted. Mussolini had got away with it!

Do you think the League could have acted differently? And if it had done, would it have been more successful in stopping the invasion? Look at Sources 13–15.

SOURCE 13 Part of a message from Mussolini to Hitler

66 *. . . if the League had extended economic sanctions to oil, I would have had to withdraw within a week.* 99

SOURCE 14 Written by Duff Cooper, who was British Secretary of State for War in 1935

66 *The British have such a horror of war that they will never support a policy which involves the slightest risk of it. They were very angry with Mussolini and very sorry for Abyssinia, but they were not willing to go to war.*

We had little to fear. Italy had no allies. If there had been a great leader in Britain he might have rallied [stirred up] the country, and if Britain had led, the smaller nations would have followed. 99

SOURCE 15 From a speech by the Soviet representative at the League of Nations in July 1936

"Four members of the League refused to apply any sanctions whatsoever. Seven did not stop selling arms, ten continued to sell goods to Italy, thirteen continued to buy Italian imports."

Activity

In groups, try to decide why the League failed. Was it because of:
- the organisation and membership of the League
- the lack of leadership from Britain and France
- other members of the League failing to act?

You might decide that it was a combination of all of these. If you do, which was the most important factor?

The consequences of the League's failure

Politicians at the time, and historians since, have had no doubts about how serious this failure was.

SOURCE 16 A German cartoon, May 1936. The League of Nations receives news from a messenger dressed as a Greek warrior: 'I am sorry to disturb your sleep, but I should like to tell you that you should no longer bother yourself about the Abyssinian business, the matter has been settled elsewhere.'

SOURCE 17 Written by Anthony Eden, Britain's representative at the League, after the War

"I have no doubts that Hitler was watching the Abyssinian struggle and that he was encouraged by our failure to stop Mussolini."

SOURCE 18 Written by the historian A.J.P. Taylor in 1966

"The real death of the League was in 1935. One day it was a powerful body imposing sanctions, the next day it was an empty sham, everyone scuttling from it as quickly as possible. Hitler watched."

THE MAN WHO TOOK THE LID OFF

SOURCE 19 A British cartoon published in October 1935. The figure taking the lid off is Mussolini

1. Are Sources 16 and 19 making the same point?

Activity

Work in pairs. Write two newspaper articles about the failure of the League, one for a British newspaper and one for a German newspaper.

1. In your own words, explain how important for future events in Europe the failure of the League over Abyssinia was.

The rise of Japan

ONE of the reasons why the USA did not get involved in Europe in the late 1930s was that it was worried about developments in another part of the world, East Asia. Both Britain and the USA had important trade links with China. In 1931 a major war broke out between China and Japan. To the USA, Japanese attempts to dominate East Asia were just as important as German attempts to dominate Europe.

Although most history books tell you that the Second World War started in 1939, with Hitler's invasion of Poland, there were in fact two separate wars being fought until 1941 – one in Europe and one in Asia. In 1941 they joined together when the USA entered both wars. Only then can we talk about a 'world' war.

By 1900 Japan was on its way to becoming a major power. It was rapidly building up its industry. It was a major trading nation, but depended on imports of RAW MATERIALS. To gain raw materials of its own it began to think about invading Manchuria (part of China: see Source 1). Manchuria had plenty of coal and iron and the people there would provide a market for Japanese goods. However, for the time being Japan simply increased its trade links with Manchuria.

In 1905 Japan won a war with Russia. As a result it gained control of Korea. It also sent soldiers to Manchuria to protect its business interests there.

The world economic crisis in 1929–33 hit Japan very hard because it earned all its money by exporting goods, which nobody could afford to buy.

Japan was soon in a desperate state. DEMOCRACY had only recently been introduced, and much of the power was still in the hands of the old aristocratic families. Many of these families also had close links with the army – some of the most powerful army officers belonged to them. In 1930 these army officers began to plot to overthrow the democratic government, and demanded that Japan should conquer Manchuria.

In 1931, without telling the Japanese government what it was going to do, the army acted. Japanese troops seized the whole of Manchuria. As an excuse, they said that Chinese troops had sabotaged the Southern Manchurian Railway, which Japan controlled.

This was just the kind of behaviour the League of Nations was meant to deal with. Its Council voted by thirteen to one for Japan to leave Manchuria. (Guess who voted against!) But decisions of the Council had to be unanimous and so nothing was done.

The League then sent Lord Lytton to investigate. Chinese witnesses whom he wanted to interview were murdered by the Japanese. Others had to send him information wrapped in bath towels, written on

SOURCE 1   Japanese expansion, 1900–41

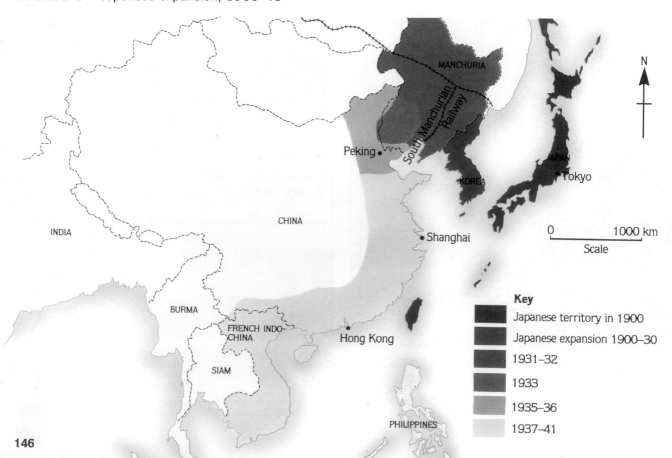

Key
Japanese territory in 1900
Japanese expansion 1900–30
1931–32
1933
1935–36
1937–41

menus and hidden in cakes. Lytton recommended that the Japanese should leave Manchuria. They refused, and left the League. Even though the USA was particularly worried about Japanese power, it did nothing.

This success in Manchuria meant that more Japanese people supported the idea of expanding into new territories. The newspapers began to praise the army, and demand that Japan should become the dominant power in the East. By 1932 the government was doing whatever the army wanted. The amount of money spent on the armed forces rose very rapidly. In 1930 the army had 250,000 men, in 1936 it had 400,000 and in 1937 it had 950,000.

The USA was now very concerned about events in East Asia. Its worries increased in 1936 when Japan signed a pact with Germany. Then, in 1937, Japan invaded China, and in 1941 it invaded Indo-China (see Source 1). The USA replied by banning trade with Japan. This hit Japan badly, as it depended on America for 80 per cent of its oil. The USA also announced that it was going to increase the size of its navy. If Japan was going to defeat the USA it had to act quickly, before the USA was ready. In December 1941 the Japanese airforce attacked the American naval base at Pearl Harbor, Hawaii, and the World War had begun.

SOURCE 3 A photograph of the Chinese city of Shanghai after a surprise bombing attack by Japanese aircraft in 1937. Scenes like this were soon common in Europe

1. Look at Source 2. Work out which country each figure represents.
2. What do Sources 2 and 4 tell you about relations between Japan and the West between 1933 and 1937?

SOURCE 4 A British cartoon from 1937. Britain and America are hiding in an air raid shelter while Japan attacks China

SOURCE 2 A German cartoon from 1933. The League of Nations, the figure on the left, is saying, 'Tut, Tut, Japsy, you should warn Auntie the next time you want to start a little war.'

1. As you were studying the events that led to war in Europe you will have noticed three features:
   ■ economic troubles putting democratic governments under threat
   ■ aggressive foreign policy
   ■ failure of the League of Nations.
   Are these same three features to be found in events in East Asia? Explain your answer.

How did the Second World War happen?

1. Using Source 1 to help you, make a list of all the causes of the Second World War.
2. Using a sheet you can get from your teacher:
a) explain how each cause contributed to the outbreak of war
b) show whether any of the causes were connected, and if so, how.
3. Would the War have broken out when it did if Hitler had been killed in the First World War?
4. Look at Sources 2 and 3. Why do you think historians disagree about whether Hitler caused the War?
5. Which of these two interpretations do you think is the best?

SOURCE 1 Causes of the Second World War

SOURCE 2 Adapted from an article written by a historian, Alan Bullock, in 1967

❝ *Hitler insisted that the future of the German people could only be secured by the conquest of living space in East Europe. It could only be won by force. Hitler first set down these views in* Mein Kampf *and repeated them in the* Hossbach Memorandum *in 1937. He held and expressed these views for over twenty years, and he set to work to put them into practice by attacking Poland and then Russia.* ❞

SOURCE 3 Adapted from a book written by a historian, A.J.P. Taylor, in 1963

❝ *Hitler had no concrete plan. He waited on events. It was Schuschnigg, not Hitler, who launched the Austrian crisis. It was Britain which took the lead in breaking up Czechoslovakia. It was the British in 1939 who gave Hitler the impression that they would not resist him over Poland. Others provided Hitler with the opportunities and he seized them. The blame for war can be put on the faults and failures of European statesmen and public.* ❞

1938

AUSTRIA

Now there will be peace.

CZECHOSLOVAKIA

Now there will be peace.

1939

POLAND

POLAND

Well, the Austrians are really Germans anyway.

Czechoslovakia's miles away. It's nothing to do with us.

BRITAIN & FRANCE DECLARE WAR ON GERMANY

Life's good here. Who cares what's going on in the rest of the world.

CHINA

PEARL HARBOUR

Activity

It is October 1939. War has broken out in Europe. In groups, design the front page of a newspaper putting forward one of the views in Sources 2 and 3.

The Second World War

THIS timeline shows the main events of the Second World War. In the next 50 pages we are going to examine some of these events in detail. These events are starred in the timeline. We will be investigating whether some of these events were so important that they were turning points in the War. We will also be looking at what life was like for soldiers and civilians during the War.

1. Look at these three headings:
   - 'Dark days for the Allies'
   - 'The tide turns'
   - 'Allied victory'

   Decide whereabouts on the timeline you would put these headings, mark them on your own copy and explain why you have put them there.

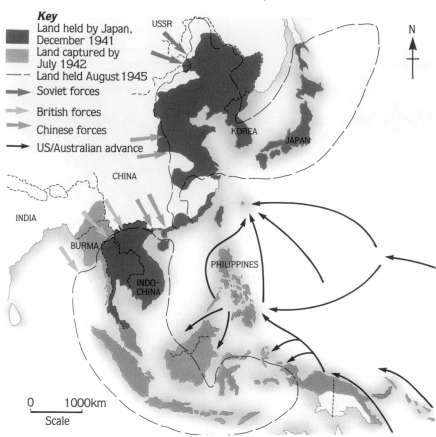

Key
- Land held by Japan, December 1941
- Land captured by July 1942
- --- Land held August 1945
- → Soviet forces
- → British forces
- → Chinese forces
- → US/Australian advance

USSR · KOREA · JAPAN · CHINA · INDIA · BURMA · INDO-CHINA · PHILIPPINES

N

0   1000km
Scale

SOURCE 2 The war in the Pacific, 1941–45

SOURCE 1 Numbers killed in the Second World War (selected countries, excluding concentration camps)

"
	Soldiers	Civilians
Australia	29,295	243
Britain	271,311	95,297
Canada	39,319	not known
France	205,000	173,000
Germany	3,300,000	800,000
India	36,092	79,498
Japan	1,380,000	933,000
Italy	279,820	93,000
USSR	13,600,000	7,720,000
USA	292,131	5,662
"

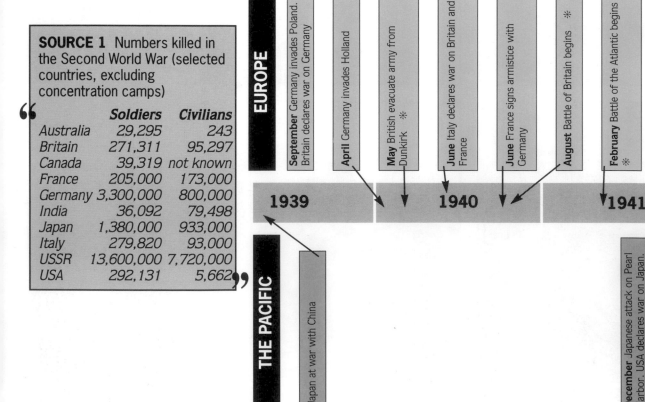

EUROPE

September Germany invades Poland. Britain declares war on Germany

April Germany invades Holland

May British evacuate army from Dunkirk ✳

June Italy declares war on Britain and France

June France signs armistice with Germany

August Battle of Britain begins ✳

February Battle of the Atlantic begins ✳

June Germany invades the USSR ✳

1939   **1940**   **1941**

THE PACIFIC

Japan at war with China

December Japanese attack on Pearl Harbor. USA declares war on Japan. Italy and Germany declare war on the USA. Japan invades Malaya and the Philippines ✳

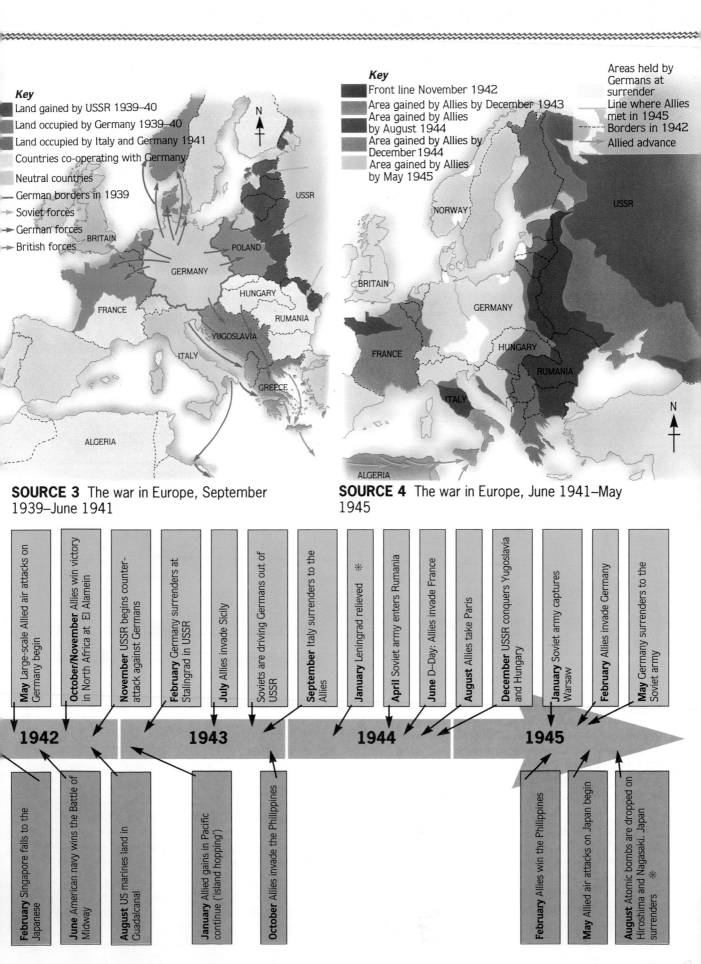

Key
- Land gained by USSR 1939–40
- Land occupied by Germany 1939–40
- Land occupied by Italy and Germany 1941
- Countries co-operating with Germany
- Neutral countries
- German borders in 1939
- Soviet forces
- German forces
- British forces

N

USSR

POLAND

BRITAIN

GERMANY

HUNGARY

FRANCE

RUMANIA

YUGOSLAVIA

ITALY

GREECE

ALGERIA

SOURCE 3 The war in Europe, September 1939–June 1941

Key
- Front line November 1942
- Area gained by Allies by December 1943
- Area gained by Allies by August 1944
- Area gained by Allies by December 1944
- Area gained by Allies by May 1945
- Areas held by Germans at surrender
- Line where Allies met in 1945
- Borders in 1942
- Allied advance

NORWAY

USSR

BRITAIN

GERMANY

FRANCE

HUNGARY

RUMANIA

ITALY

ALGERIA

N

SOURCE 4 The war in Europe, June 1941–May 1945

May Large-scale Allied air attacks on Germany begin

October/November Allies win victory in North Africa at El Alamein

November USSR begins counter-attack against Germans

February Germany surrenders at Stalingrad in USSR

July Allies invade Sicily

Soviets are driving Germans out of USSR

September Italy surrenders to the Allies

January Leningrad relieved ✷

April Soviet army enters Rumania

June D–Day: Allies invade France

August Allies take Paris

December USSR conquers Yugoslavia and Hungary

January Soviet army captures Warsaw

February Allies invade Germany

May Germany surrenders to the Soviet army

1942

1943

1944

1945

February Singapore falls to the Japanese

June American navy wins the Battle of Midway

August US marines land in Guadalcanal

January Allied gains in Pacific continue ('island hopping')

October Allies invade the Philippines

February Allies win the Philippines

May Allied air attacks on Japan begin

August Atomic bombs are dropped on Hiroshima and Nagasaki. Japan surrenders ✷

Living through the War: Part One

THE Second World War greatly affected the lives of British people. For six years civilians lived dangerous and disrupted lives, as you will see on the next six pages.

Waiting to be bombed

Britain was preparing for war well before it actually started. During recent wars in Spain and the Far East there had been awful bombing of towns and cities. The government expected the same to happen in this war and precautions were being taken months before the War began.

SOURCE 3 A photograph of a family practising wearing their gas masks in 1939

SOURCE 1 A photograph taken in February 1939. 'Anderson' bomb shelters are being delivered in London. The shelters were sunk into the ground in people's back gardens

SOURCE 2 'Black-out' instructions issued by the government in July 1939

> *Windows, skylights, glazed doors, or other openings which would show a light, will have to be screened in wartime with dark blinds or blankets, or brown paper pasted on the glass so that no light is visible from outside. You should now obtain any materials you may need for this purpose.*
>
> *All street lighting will be put out.*

On 1 September 1939, two days before war was finally declared, the black-out was introduced.

Everyone, however young, had to have a gas mask (see Source 3), and 38 million gas masks were issued. They had to be taken everywhere. Their smell of rubber and disinfectant made many people sick. Leaflets such as Source 4 were sent out to every house to explain what to do in a gas attack.

OFFICIAL INSTRUCTIONS ISSUED BY THE MINISTRY OF HOME SECURITY

GAS ATTACK

HOW TO PUT ON YOUR GAS MASK

Always keep your gas mask with you – day and night. Learn to put it on quickly. Practise wearing it.

1. Hold your breath. 2. Hold mask in front of face, with thumbs inside straps.
3. Thrust chin well forward into mask, pull straps over head as far as they will go.
4. Run finger round face-piece taking care head-straps are not twisted.

IF THE GAS RATTLES SOUND

1. Hold your breath. Put on mask wherever you are. Close window.

2. If out of doors, take off hat, put on your mask. Turn up collar.

3. Put on gloves or keep hands in pockets. Take cover in nearest building.

IF YOU GET GASSED

BY VAPOUR GAS Keep your gas mask on even if you feel discomfort
If discomfort continues go to First Aid Post

BY LIQUID or BLISTER GAS

1	2	3	4
Dab, but *don't rub* the splash with handkerchief. Then destroy handkerchief.	Rub No. 2 Ointment well into place. *(Buy a 6d. jar now from any chemist.)* In emergency chemists supply Bleach Cream free.	If you can't get Ointment or Cream within 5 minutes wash place with soap and warm water	Take off at once any garment splashed with gas.

SOURCE 4 One of the leaflets sent to every household in September 1939

1. Look at the instructions in Source 4. This leaflet frightened people so much that there was a sudden flood of marriages and people writing wills. Why do you think this was?
2. List the precautions taken by the government in 1939. Explain the reasons for each one.
3. Explain how civilians' lives were changed even before the War started.

Evacuation

Heavy bombing was expected in Britain's large industrial centres. The government thought that people would be safer in the country, so plans were drawn up to EVACUATE people from the cities.

Britain was divided into three zones:
- evacuation areas, where heavy bombing was expected
- reception areas – mostly country areas, safe from bombing. The evacuees would move here, and stay with local families
- neutral areas, which might suffer light attacks. Nobody would be evacuated from or into these areas.

---

1. On your own copy of Source 6, shade in where you think the evacuation areas, reception areas and neutral areas were.
2. About thirteen million people lived in the evacuation areas. But there was room in the reception areas for just 4.8 million people. The government said that certain groups of people should be moved first. Which groups of people would you have moved first?

On 1 September 1939, the day Germany invaded Poland, the evacuation of people from the large cities began. The government used posters, leaflets and messages on the radio to persuade parents how important evacuation was. Trains and buses were prepared.

Some people made their own evacuation arrangements and stayed with friends or relatives. Others went abroad to Canada and Australia.

SOURCE 5 Numbers of people evacuated by the government in September 1939

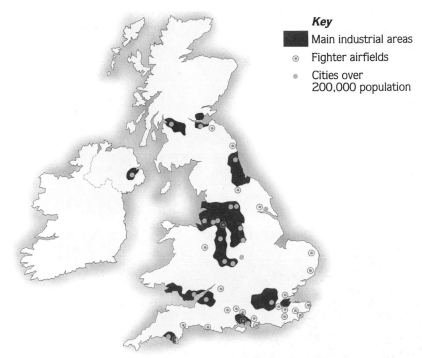

SOURCE 6 Industrial areas and centres of population

Key
- Main industrial areas
- ⊙ Fighter airfields
- • Cities over 200,000 population

Enormous numbers of people were evacuated. Altogether, nearly one and a half million people moved in September 1939. Most of these were moved in one weekend! The country's entire transport system was taken over for evacuation for four days.

Activity

Imagine you are going to be evacuated to another part of the country. Write out a list of the essential things you would need to take with you.

Your teacher will give you a list of what the evacuee children were told to take. Compare the two lists.

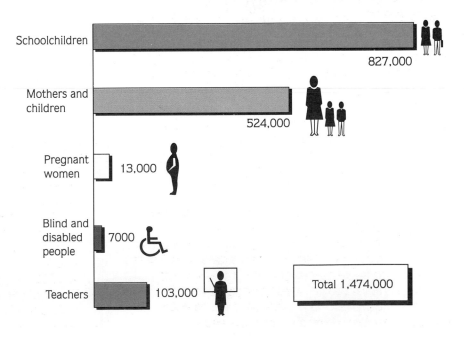

Schoolchildren — 827,000
Mothers and children — 524,000
Pregnant women — 13,000
Blind and disabled people — 7000
Teachers — 103,000

Total 1,474,000

LIVING THROUGH THE WAR: PART ONE

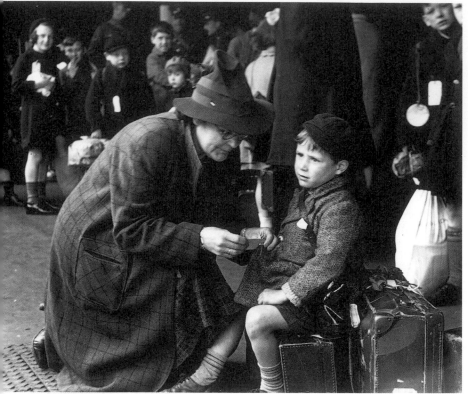

▲ SOURCE 7

1. Look at Source 7. Write down everything you can find out from this photograph about the boy and what is happening to him. Make sure you use all the clues in the picture to support your answer: for example, the label pinned to the boy's coat, his suitcase, the expression on his face, the line of children behind him.
2. Look at Source 8. These evacuee children have just arrived in the country.
a) Look at the expressions on their faces. Would you say they were worried, frightened or excited?
b) What do you think the woman is doing?

▼ SOURCE 8

SOURCE 9 Working-class children leaving their homes on their way to be evacuated to the country, 1 September 1939

When the evacuees reached the reception areas there were many problems. Quite often things were not very well organised. Villages expecting young children received hundreds of pregnant women instead. In other places the villagers inspected the evacuees and picked out the ones they wanted, leaving behind any they thought might be more difficult to look after. And both evacuees and hosts quickly had to adapt to a new way of life.

SOURCE 10 Middle-class girls from boarding schools being evacuated in May 1940

Just think about this from the evacuees' point of view for a moment:
■ The evacuees came from large busy cities and were not used to country life.
■ Many of the children were away from their homes and mothers for the first time.
■ Some were put into homes of a different social class from their own and had to learn to behave differently.

Now think about evacuation from the hosts' point of view:
■ Some of the children were very poor. They arrived badly clothed and were not used to keeping themselves clean. Some were very thin, or covered in lice.
■ Hosts found it difficult to cope with the behaviour of children very different from their own.
■ Many host families were soon short of money because the allowance they were given did not increase when food prices rose.
  Think what it would be like if a family of complete strangers came to live in your house. What changes would it make to your life?

3. Look at Source 9. These children are just about to leave for the country. Are they as worried as the children in Sources 7 and 8?
4. Look at Source 10. Compare the attitude of these girls towards being evacuated with the attitude of the children in Sources 7–9. Why do you think their attitudes are so different?

So as you can see, evacuation was not easy for anyone. Sources 11–17 give you an impression of evacuation from the point of view of a number of evacuees and their hosts.

SOURCE 11 One working-class evacuee remembers what happened when she and her younger brother arrived in the country

Villagers stood around watching us as we got out of the bus and went into the school. What followed was like an auction. Villagers came in to choose children. 'Mr and Mrs Jones would like a nice little boy.' Nobody wanted the awkward combination of a girl of eleven and such a small boy, from whom I had promised my mother never to be separated. We were left until the very last. The room was almost empty. I sat on my rucksack and cried.

SOURCE 12 A thirteen-year-old working-class boy from the East End of London remembers being evacuated to Buckinghamshire with his sister Rosie

Rosie whispered. She whispered for days. Everything was so clean in the room. We were even given flannels and toothbrushes. We'd never cleaned our teeth up till then. And hot water came from the tap. And there was a lavatory upstairs. And carpets. And clean sheets. This was all very odd. And rather scaring.

SOURCE 13 A photograph taken in 1940 of working-class and middle-class children evacuated to the country

SOURCE 14 A middle-class boy aged thirteen compares evacuation with his home life

After school we were expected to sweep out Mr Benson's butcher's shop and scrub down the marble slabs. . . I had never been asked to help my father in his bank.

Once a week we were bathed in a tin bath in front of the fire. We were stripped and scrubbed. Nanny might have approved of the scrubbing, but not of being bathed in the kitchen once a week.

Mrs Benson filled us up with thick slices of bread and margarine, just like the bread I used to see our maids eat for their tea.

Instead of having to play cricket in the garden, we went bird nesting.

One day we dammed up a stream. In the night it flooded the church and six houses.

SOURCE 15 Extracts from reports on evacuation made by Women's Institutes all over England

■ *The state of the children was such that the school had to be fumigated.*
■ *The children were filthy. We have never seen so many verminous children lacking any knowledge of clean habits. They had not had a bath for months.*
■ *One child was suffering from scabies, the majority had it in their hair, and the others had dirty septic sores all over their bodies.*
■ *Some of the children were sent in their ragged little garments. Most of the children were walking on the ground, their shoes had no soles and just uppers hanging together.*
■ *Many of the mothers and children were bed wetters.*

SOURCE 16 Some comments made by evacuees

a) By a mother to her six-year-old child
You dirty thing, messing up the lady's carpet. Go and do it in the corner.

b) By a child
They call this spring, Mum, and they have one down here every year.

c) By a child
The country is a funny place. They never tell you you can't have no more to eat.

SOURCE 19
A government poster published in 1940

SOURCE 17 Some comments made by people taking in evacuees

"a) By a rich woman
My six lads from London are making this dreary, lonely war not only tolerable, but often enjoyable.

b) By a middle-class woman
Some children from poor areas have become almost unrecognisable within a few weeks. One small girl was so chubby that she needed a larger size gas mask."

"Now I want you to promise me you're all going to be really good evacuees and not worry his Lordship"

SOURCE 18 A British cartoon from the *Sunday Express* newspaper

1. What point is Source 18 making about evacuation?
2. Source 14 tells you a lot about the kind of life the boy led before he was evacuated.
a) Write down five things it tells you.
b) How had his life changed?
3. You can also tell a lot from these sources about the home life of poor working-class evacuees.
a) Make a list of five features of working-class life in the cities, and say what evidence there is in Sources 11–18 for each feature.
b) Their lives were changed by evacuation, too. Which changes would they like most and which would they dislike most?
4. Who do you think enjoyed evacuation more: the evacuees or the host families?

Millions of people were evacuated in 1939. Yet from January 1940 onwards people began to return home to their families. No bombs had fallen, and families didn't see any reason for being split up any longer. And the stress of living in other people's homes was too much for them.

> 5. Look at Source 19. Does this poster prove that the government was successful in persuading people to evacuate their children?

Twelve months into the War, the bombing of British cities – 'the Blitz' (see page 164) – finally began. This triggered another wave of evacuation. However, this time not many people went to the country.

Four years later, in the second half of 1944, the Germans began to use flying bombs and massive 'V2' rockets launched from France to attack Britain. Once again, some people left the cities, but most did not stay in the country for very long.

Activity

Work in pairs.
One of you is a working-class child who has been evacuated in 1939, and the other a middle-class child. Write home to your parents telling them how you are, what you have been doing, and how your life has changed. Then compare the two letters. How do they differ? Why do you think there are these differences?

Dunkirk: triumph or disaster?

Blitzkrieg

THE Second World War was completely different from the First World War. It was a war of movement rather than a war of trenches. At the start of the War nothing could stop the German army. It took just a month for it to conquer Poland.

In May 1940 Hitler turned his attention to the West. France was his next target. As you can see in Source 1, the French had strong defences along the German border. Hitler simply went around them and invaded Holland, then Belgium, then France. Then he headed for the Channel. This all took less than two months! The speed was all part of the German tactics, called *Blitzkrieg* (lightning war).

The German advance was so quick that the British Expeditionary Force, along with parts of the French army, was caught by surprise and was pushed back to Dunkirk. The troops were trapped between the German army and the Channel. The only escape route was by sea.

At this point there was a real danger that the entire British army (over 300,000 troops) could be wiped out before the War had really got under way!

On 27 May the British government, now led by Winston Churchill, put into action a plan called 'Operation Dynamo'. The plan was to evacuate the troops to Britain by ship. As well as the ships of the Royal Navy, all sorts of craft were used, including pleasure steamers and fishing boats. Most of the soldiers were rescued.

Dunkirk is sometimes seen as a triumph and sometimes as a disaster. You can see from Sources 2–9 how people at the time viewed it.

SOURCE 1 The German advance of 1940

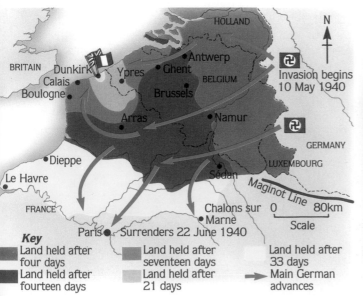

Key
- Land held after four days
- Land held after fourteen days
- Land held after seventeen days
- Land held after 21 days
- Land held after 33 days
- Main German advances

SOURCE 2
A *Daily Mirror* headline at the time

BLOODY MARVELLOUS!

SOURCE 3 A painting by Charles Cundall, who was sent by the British government to make an official painting of events on the beaches of Dunkirk

SOURCE 4 From a book published in England in July 1940

[At Dunkirk] a miracle was born. This land of Britain is rich in heroes. She had brave daring men in her Navy and Air Force as well as in her army. She had heroes in jerseys and sweaters and old rubber boots in all the fishing ports of Britain. That night when the word went round in all the south-east ports of Britain, there was not a man or a boy who knew how to handle a boat who was not prepared to give his own life to save some unknown son of his country who had faced, without flinching, the red hell of Flanders. For almost a week the epic went on. The little ships dodged their way up the waters and hauled over their sides the soldiers who waded waist deep to safety.

1. Look at Source 3 carefully. Describe in as much detail as you can what is happening.
2. How far is the account in Source 6 supported by the photograph in Source 7?
3. Which picture is more useful for telling you what happened on the beach at Dunkirk, Source 3 or Source 7?

SOURCE 5 From the BBC six o'clock radio news bulletin on 31 May. This was the first report about Dunkirk

All night and all day men of the undefeated British Expeditionary Force have been coming home. From interviews with the men it is clear they have come back in glory; that their morale is as high as ever, and that they are anxious to be back again 'To have a real crack at Jerry' [the Germans].

SOURCE 6 A first-hand account by a gunner officer, published in 1940

There were lines of men waiting in queues until boats arrived to transport them, a score [20] or so at a time, to the steamers and warships. The queues stood there fixed and regular, no bunching, no pushing . . .

Stepping over the bodies we marched onto the beach. A horrible stench of blood and mutilated flesh pervaded the place. There was no escape from it. We might have been walking through a slaughterhouse on a hot day.

SOURCE 7 A photograph taken on the beaches at Dunkirk

DUNKIRK: TRIUMPH OR DISASTER?

TO FIGHT ANOTHER DAY

SOURCE 8 A cartoon published in a British newspaper at the time of the evacuation. The name of the paddle steamer is the *Brighton Belle*

SOURCE 9 Written by a German fighter pilot in a letter home in 1940

❝*I hated Dunkirk. It was just cold-blooded killing. The beaches were jammed with soldiers. I went up and down spraying them with bullets.*❞

1. Why do you think the newspaper published Source 8 at that time?
2. According to Sources 4 and 8 how did civilians help at Dunkirk?
3. From Sources 2–9 decide which word best describes the events at Dunkirk: 'triumph' or 'disaster'? Give reasons for your answer.

Did you know?

There was not a single British reporter at Dunkirk. To write their articles the journalists had to depend on what they were told by the government. One government department said that the story of Dunkirk 'grips our imagination. It inspires our minds and it tears at our heart strings.' The evacuation had been going on for five days before any reports were allowed in Britain.

The government obviously wanted to keep everyone's morale high, and it succeeded. At the end of 1940 an opinion poll tried to measure how many British people thought Britain might lose the War. The number was so small it was impossible to measure.

1. How reliable do you think the accounts from the time (Sources 2–9) are in telling us what actually happened at Dunkirk? Are some accounts more reliable than others? Explain your answer.

Looking back

Sources 10–14 were written much later than Sources 2–9. They give a rather different verson of the events.

SOURCE 10 Written by General Sir Harold E. Franklyn, a divisional commander at Dunkirk, in 1962

The evacuation has been over-glamourised. Reports of 'merciless bombing' and 'the hell of Dunkirk' were quite ridiculous. I walked along the beaches on several occasions and never saw a corpse, there was very little shelling.

In every unit there are some men who have no stomach for a fight. There were instances of a few men embarking at Dunkirk when their battalions were still fighting near the canal.

SOURCE 11 In 1961 Richard Collier published a major work on Dunkirk. He had interviewed 1070 eye-witnesses and had access to official papers about Dunkirk that had not been seen before. His book includes accounts of these incidents

■ *a hotel cellar in Dunkirk packed with British and French troops singing, weeping and screaming drunk*
■ *groups of men, who had been deserted by their officers, prowling the town in a mood of savage violence*
■ *an officer shot through the head by another because it was the only way of preventing him from capsizing an already overloaded rowing boat*
■ *dispirited survivors newly arrived back in Britain, who, far from itching to return for another crack at the enemy, hurled their rifles from the train carrying them from Dover, according to a Kent police inspector.*

SOURCE 12 From a book called *Dunkirk, the Necessary Myth*, published in 1981

Before the secret was lifted most of the soldiers left from the beaches, mostly in craft manned by the Royal Navy, or by soldiers themselves. After the secret was lifted, when civilian volunteers began to come forward, 26,500 were rescued from the beaches. The contribution of civilian volunteers to the success of the Dunkirk evacuation was gallant; but it was not important in terms of numbers rescued.

SOURCE 13 From a book published in 1972, edited by a senior officer in the British army

Even though the troops had been evacuated from Dunkirk, Hitler had scored a crushing victory. 10,252 Germans had been killed, 42,523 wounded and 8467 were missing. However, Hitler announced that 1,212,000 Dutch, Belgian, French and British prisoners had been taken. In addition, he said that his armies had captured from the British 1200 field guns, 1250 anti-aircraft guns, 11,000 machine guns and 75,000 vehicles.

SOURCE 14 From a book published in 1989

By 4 June, 338,226 men had been evacuated, two thirds British, the rest French. German pressure on Dunkirk was relentless, but was restrained by brave and fierce resistance by the RAF, which flew 2739 sorties [expeditions against the Germans]. At least Britain had the core of an army left with which to prepare the defence of the UK.

1. Make a list of all the differences between the contemporary accounts (Sources 2–9) and the accounts written later (Sources 10–14). Are these differences of fact or opinion?
2. Why do you think there are these differences?
3. Do you think the British government was right to report Dunkirk as if it was a victory?
4. You have been asked to write an account of Dunkirk. Which sources would you use to show it was a) a triumph, and b) a disaster?
5. Historians still disagree about Dunkirk. Find two examples of disagreements.
6. Why do historians disagree about Dunkirk? Is it because:
   ■ the government controlled the reports at the time
   ■ new evidence is gradually emerging
   ■ historians' views change?
7. Do you think it will ever be possible to find out the 'truth' about Dunkirk?

The Battle of Britain: a turning point?

AFTER Dunkirk Hitler was master of Europe, except for Britain and the USSR. Preparations for 'Operation Sea Lion' (Hitler's cross-Channel invasion of Britain) now got under way. The first stage of this involved the German airforce, the *Luftwaffe*.

SOURCE 1 Directive No. 17 from Hitler, 1 August 1940

Top Secret

In order to establish the conditions necessary for the final conquest of England, I intend to continue the air and naval war against the English homeland more intensively.

■ *The German airforce is to overcome the British airforce as soon as possible.*

■ *The intensified air war may commence on or after 6 August.*

---

1. Why do you think it was so important for Operation Sea Lion that the *Luftwaffe* should overcome the Royal Air Force?

Hitler's idea was that German bombers would attack British airfields and destroy all the RAF's aircraft. The German bombers were protected by German fighter aircraft such as the Messerschmitt, which were supposed to shoot down any British fighter planes, such as Spitfires and Hurricanes, which attacked the bombers. As Source 2 shows, the Germans thought they had a good chance of destroying the British airforce.

SOURCE 2 A German Intelligence Report on the RAF, July 1940

The British aircraft industry produces about 180 to 330 fighters a month. It is believed this output will decrease.

Both the Hurricane and the Spitfire are inferior to the Messerschmitt. The Luftwaffe *is clearly superior to the RAF as regards equipment, strength, training, command and location of bases.*

In fact, the Spitfire and the Messerschmitt were more evenly matched than the Germans thought. But the rest of the German report was about right.

■ Many of the British pilots were reservists and part-timers. They had not received anything like the training the German pilots had. Many German pilots also had battle experience in Spain and Poland. Germany had been training 800 new pilots a month, Britain just 200.

■ The Germans had 824 fighters and 1017 bombers in service. Britain only had 591 fighters to set against them.

■ It took just five minutes for German aircraft to cross the Channel, but it took fifteen minutes for British planes to take off and reach the height necessary to intercept them.

The air war that raged during the summer of 1940 has become known as the Battle of Britain. Throughout August the number of German attacks increased. German planes dropped bombs on airfields, radar stations, factories, towns and ports all over Britain. The RAF lost large numbers of planes. British pilots were also growing very tired flying day after day. Source 3 shows how quickly pilots had to get back in the air after landing.

SOURCE 3 Procedures for a fighter pilot and his plane in between sorties against German bombers

However, the Germans had their problems, too. Their fighters could only carry enough fuel to fly over Britain for 30 minutes at a time. The German fighters were told to fly close together, which made it easier for the British to attack them. The British pilots soon realised that the important targets were the German bombers, not the fighters.

The Germans were losing more planes than the British (see Source 4). Even more important, while German production of fighter planes averaged 156 planes per month, the British switched their factories from producing bomber planes to producing fighter planes. They were making an average of 563 new planes per month from July to September.

SOURCE 4 British and German aircraft destroyed 1 July–31 October 1940

	British	German
1–15 July	51	108
16–31 July	69	117
1–15 August	156	259
16–31 August	249	332
1–15 September	268	323
16–30 September	133	213
1–15 October	100	147
16–31 October	90	161
Totals	**1116**	**1660**

On 7 September, in a surprise move, German bombers started to target London rather than the airfields. It seemed as if the Germans had abandoned their original aims.

As the autumn weather grew worse it soon became clear that the German airforce had failed to destroy the RAF in time for an invasion to take place. Ten days later, on September 17, the invasion plans were called off.

SOURCE 7 A Spitfire pilot recalls his experiences of the Battle of Britain

Throughout it all the radio is never silent – shouts, oaths, encouragements and terse commands. You single out an opponent. Jockey for position. All clear behind! The bullets from your eight guns go pumping into his belly. He begins to smoke. But the wicked tracer sparkles and flashes over the top of your own cockpit and you break into a tight turn. Now you have two enemies. The [Messerschmitt] 109 on your tail and your remorseless ever-present opponent 'G', the force of gravity. Over your shoulder you can still see the ugly, questing snout of the 109. You tighten the turn. The Spit [Spitfire] protests and shudders and when the blood drains from your eyes you 'grey out'. But you keep turning, for life itself is the stake. And now your blood feels like molten lead and runs from head to legs. You black out! And you ease the turn to recover in a grey, unreal world of spinning horizons. Cautiously you climb into the sun. You have lost too much height and your opponent has gone – disappeared. You are completely alone in your own bit of sky, bounded by the blue vault and the coloured drapery of earth below.

2. Which of Sources 5 and 6 would you have used in a British newspaper in August 1940? Explain why.
3. Who won the Battle of Britain? Why did they win?
4. Of the 3080 aircrew who took part in the Battle of Britain 520 were killed, yet many young men volunteered to be pilots. Why do you think they did this? Reading Source 7 will help you.

SOURCE 5 A photograph of British pilots between sorties, summer 1940

SOURCE 6 A photograph of a German bomber over the White Cliffs of Dover, summer 1940

Living through the War: Part Two

The Blitz begins

THE afternoon of 7 September 1940 was a glorious one. Many Londoners were enjoying the late summer sunshine when at 4.36 p.m. the air raid sirens started. Within minutes, wave after wave of German bombers appeared, showering London with bombs.

It was the terraced houses in the East End, near to the factories and docks, which suffered most. Many men, women and children were appallingly injured. Others were blown to pieces, so that nothing remained. Of some there was only a foot, a hand or a piece of raw flesh left. The 'all clear' didn't sound until 5.00 a.m. the next morning. The Blitz had begun.

During these first twelve hours 436 people were killed and 1600 severely injured. Two months of nightly bombing followed. Then the Germans turned their attention to other cities, such as Liverpool, Glasgow and Coventry. The Blitz did not end until May 1941. By that time 1,400,000 people in London had been made homeless. Across the country 43,000 people were killed.

During an air raid people relied on Civil Defence workers, who included the Auxiliary Fire Service, Air Raid Precautions (ARP) wardens and the First Aid Post, to do the most dangerous jobs. Many of these workers were unpaid part-timers with other jobs, and many were women.

The ARP wardens (one in six of whom were women) patrolled their areas once the air raid warning siren had gone. They called the emergency services, and as they were often the first at the scene they rescued people and helped put out fires.

SOURCE 1 An artist's reconstruction of the inside of an Anderson Shelter

SOURCE 2 A first-hand account of the Blitz, by a member of the First Aid Post, 14 September 1940

> *The church was a popular shelter. People felt that nowhere would they be safer than under the protection of the Church – so it was full when the bomb fell.*
>
> *The bomb had burst in the middle of the shelterers, mostly women and small children. The scene resembled a massacre with bodies, limbs, blood and flesh mingled with little hats, coats and shoes. The people were literally blown to pieces. The work of the ARP services was magnificent – by nine o'clock all the casualties were out.*
>
> *After a heavy raid there was the task of piecing the bodies together in preparation for burial. The stench was the worst thing about it – that, and having to realise that these frightful pieces of flesh had once been living breathing people. It became a grim and ghastly satisfaction when a body was reconstructed – but if one was too lavish in making one body almost whole then one would have sad gaps. There were always odd limbs which did not fit, and there were too many legs. Unless we kept a very firm grip on ourselves nausea was inevitable.*

1. How would you set about finding out how realistic this drawing is?

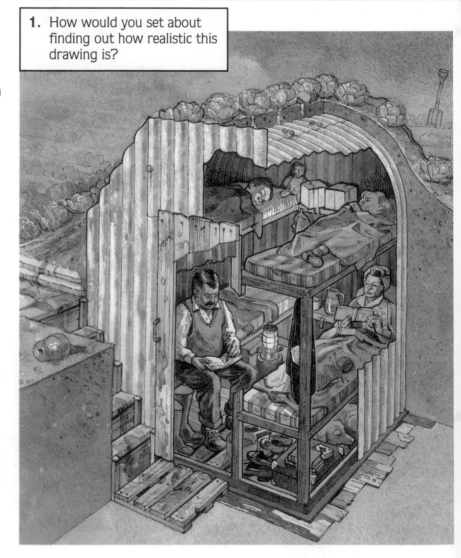

164

SOURCE 3
Civil Defence workers enter a bombed house

SOURCE 4 Ministry of Information records from November 1939 about where people would shelter if there was an air raid

Underground stations 4%
Public shelters 9%
Home shelters (Anderson Shelters) 27%
In own homes (often under the stairs or in ground floor rooms) 60%

2. In the early months of the War most people preferred to shelter at home with their family, as Source 4 shows. Do you think this changed once the Blitz began in September 1940?

To shelter from the bombing many Londoners bought platform tickets for the London Underground and then camped in the stations for the night. At first the government tried to ban this, but as there were not enough public shelters it eventually had to give in, and 70 stations were used as shelters. Everything was soon very organised, as Source 5 shows.

SOURCE 5 A first-hand description of sheltering in the Underground

By 4.00 p.m. all the platforms and passage space of the underground station are staked out, chiefly with blankets folded in long strips laid against the wall – for the trains are still running and the platforms in use. A woman or child guards places for about six people.

When the evening comes the rest of the family crowds in.

SOURCE 6 A Liverpool family's experience

When morning came we left the shelter and made our way home. There was no home. All that was left was a pile of bricks. We had nowhere to live except the shelter, and that was to be our home for six months.

SOURCE 7 An account of life during a period of heavy air raids, written by Alice Bridges, who lived in Birmingham

The one outstanding change in my home life is earlier hours at night. I used to sit up till midnight sewing and doing odd jobs, but since the air raids and the fact that the shelter is fixed as a bedroom we have had much more sleep.

Everyone I have met since our three-night bombardment has a strained expression, as much as to say, 'Will it be my turn next?' Most now shrug their shoulders and say, 'If there is a bomb with your name on it, it will get you, shelter or no shelter.'

I like to go straight down to the shelter if there is a warning. When I prepare a meal I lay it on the tray as I prepare it. When we are eating a meal I have the tray handy.

My husband's working hours are much fewer since the air raids. He comes home between seven and eight in the evening instead of eleven. The firm's night shift has been put on days because they will not pay for 'shelter time'.

In the shelter there is a divan bed. It is two feet wide, which just leaves room for J.'s little bed at the side, which consists of my padded deck chair put very low and levelled up with cushions and a footboard.

My husband has fixed a bullet-proof steel door which we can lock. The condensation is the biggest problem – my mattress soaks all the damp up. I have decided to change the mattresses every two days. Underneath the bed I keep a tin of emergency rations and my leather case, with all important papers in, and first aid.

Activity
Either: Design a leaflet giving advice from the government to someone sheltering in their own Anderson Shelter.
Or: Write down five entries from the diary of a Civil Defence Worker for September 1940.

LIVING THROUGH THE WAR: PART TWO

Morale

The aim of the Germans was clear. They wanted to bomb the British people into giving up. The British government realised this and knew that morale had to be kept high during this very difficult time. Newspapers were not allowed to show pictures of mutilated bodies and smashed houses. Reports and photographs concentrated on the heroism of the rescue services and everyone's determination to carry on as normally as possible, working together in good humour.

Activity

You are a government censor. It is your job to decide which of Sources 8–14 and 18 newspapers are allowed to publish.
1. Choose four which can be used. Write a caption to go with each one.
2. Choose four which you will ban and explain why.

SOURCE 8
Firemen fight a blaze at a hat factory in the East End of London, December 1940

SOURCE 11 An injured man talks to a civil defence worker in the ruins of his home, where his wife was killed, November 1944

SOURCE 9
The King and Queen visiting people sheltering in the London Underground, November 1940

SOURCE 10
A cartoon from the *Daily Express*, 1940. The caption read: After the raid – 'Is it all right now, Henry?' 'Yes, not even scratched.'

SOURCE 12 A photograph taken early one morning after a raid

SOURCE 13
A sketch by the sculptor Henry Moore of people sheltering in an Underground station

SOURCE 14 A photograph taken in London during the Blitz

SOURCE 15 A report from Coventry after a very heavy raid in 1940

> *There were more open signs of hysteria and terror than observed in the previous two months. The overwhelming feeling on Friday was the feeling of utter helplessness. The tremendous impact of the previous night had left many people speechless. On Friday evening (15 November), there were several signs of suppressed panic as darkness approached.*

SOURCE 16 From a letter from Humphrey Jennings to his wife, October 1940

> *What warmth – what courage! What determination. People singing in public shelters. WVS [Women's Voluntary Service] girls serving hot drinks to firefighters during raids. Everyone secretly delighted with the privilege of holding up Hitler. Certain of beating him.*

SOURCE 17 A report by local officials on conditions in the East End of London, September 1940

> *The whole story of the last weekend has been one of unplanned hysteria. The newspaper versions of life going on normally are grotesque. There was no bread, no electricity, no milk, no telephones. There is no humour or laughter.*

SOURCE 18 A painting by a British Communist painter, Clive Branson, showing the workers struggling through the Blitz

1. Read this statement, which summarises one popular view about the Blitz.
   ■ 'The Blitz brought out the best in the British. There was no panic. People carried on calmly and much as normal. The bombing made them more determined to defeat Hitler. Together, they laughed and joked their way through the Blitz'
   Now look at Sources 15–18. Do you agree?

2. Why do you think it is difficult for historians to know what life was really like during the Blitz?

LIVING THROUGH THE WAR: PART TWO

Working through the Blitz

CONSCRIPTION was introduced in 1939. All men aged between eighteen and 41 had to register with the government. The government decided whether they should go into the army or do other war work. Some male workers such as doctors and skilled workers in essential industries stayed in their jobs, but most men aged between eighteen and 40 went to do military service. This meant that much of the work in the factories, on the farms and in Civil Defence had to be done by women and retired people.

Single women between the ages of nineteen and 30 also had to register for war work. They worked in the Auxiliary Services, in the Land Army or in industry. Married women were not 'called up', because the government was worried about the effect it might have on their families, but many married women volunteered for war work anyway. Many women managed to look after their families *and* do war work.

Sources 19–28 show the wide range of work done by women.

SOURCE 20
An advertisement in a women's magazine

SOURCE 21 A government advertisement. The Auxiliary Territorial Service was the women's branch of the army

1. What attitudes about a woman's role do Sources 20 and 21 reveal?

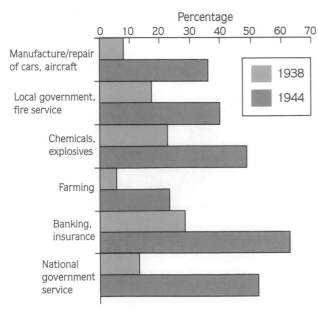

SOURCE 19 The proportion of workers in various occupations who were women in 1938 and 1944

SOURCE 22 Women workers in a munitions factory

SOURCE 23 From a speech by Clement Atlee, Deputy Prime Minister, in September 1942

The work the women are performing in munitions [weapons] factories has to be seen to be believed. Precision engineering jobs which a few years ago would have made a skilled turner's hair stand on end are performed with dead accuracy by girls who had no industrial experience.

SOURCE 26 Some women joined the Air Transport Auxiliary and flew newly built planes to air bases. This photograph shows an ATA pilot who has just delivered a Wellington bomber

SOURCE 24 Members of the Women's Land Army at work. In 1939 the Women's Land Army, which had been set up during the First World War, was started up again. Even before conscription to war work was introduced in 1941, 30,000 women had volunteered for it

SOURCE 27 An account by a Birmingham factory worker in the early 1940s

I'm going home to do an evening's scrubbing. First I've got to do my shopping on the way home. I have to queue for it. My two little boys are in school all day. They have their dinners there. I call for them at six o'clock. But I have to get the meal ready, and there's always some washing and mending to do every night.

SOURCE 25 Forty years after the War one woman remembered her work in the Land Army

The people were very resentful in the country, they didn't make it easy for you, we weren't really welcome. All we had in the Land Army digs [lodgings] were sausages, every day for nine months. The landlady used to cook them in water, they were horrible.

I was sent to a farm in Essex. There were four of us in a gang assigned to an old steam tractor with a threshing machine behind. Two of us switched the switch over and hooked the sacks on, the others threw the corn in the bin. It was very hard work. We had to go where the tackle was and sometimes we biked eight miles or so before beginning. Later I planted potatoes.

SOURCE 28 Written by a housewife in her diary in 1942

I thought of stacks of dirty dishes to tackle after tea, of furniture that was once polished every week, and now got done when I had the time. I wondered if people would ever get back to the old ways. I cannot see women who have done worthwhile things settling to trivial ways.

2. In what ways did women's lives change during the War?
3. Do you think women's lives improved or got worse during the War?
4. Do you think these changes would continue after the War ended?
5. Use the evidence from pages 152–157 and 164–169 to write an essay, or design a display entitled 'How important were women in the war effort on the Home Front?'

'Dad's Army'

On 14 May 1940 the government announced that it was setting up the Local Defence Volunteers, or 'Home Guard'. The Home Guards' job was to work in their local area to help defend Britain from attack. Men between the ages of seventeen and 65 could join, and the work was part-time and unpaid. On the first day, a quarter of a million men joined up. There is much disagreement about how useful they were. You may have seen the television programme *Dad's Army*, which shows them as accident-prone old men playing at soldiers and doing more harm than good to the war effort.

Here are some judgements by people at the time.

SOURCE 29
A cartoon by Giles from *Punch* magazine

" I want you men to imagine the enemy are approaching in large numbers, supported by tanks, flamethrowers, paratroops, etc., etc. . . ."

SOURCE 30 A description by a company commander in the 6th Cambridge Battalion of the weapons his men had

> Packets of pepper, short lengths of lead cabling and iron tubing.

SOURCE 31 From a speech by Prime Minister Winston Churchill in November 1940

> Such a force is of the highest value and importance. A country where every street and every village bristles with resolute armed men is a country which would not be able to be overthrown.

SOURCE 32 Written by a member of the Home Guard in 1944

> We of the Home Guard knew full well that in 1940 and 1941 we were the biggest bluff ever, and Hitler dared not call it.

1. What impression do Sources 29 and 30 give of the Home Guard?
2. Do Sources 31 and 32 give a similar impression to that given in Sources 29 and 30?
3. Some people claim that the impression the television programme *Dad's Army* gives of the Home Guard is completely wrong and has been created just to make people laugh. Do you agree?

Rationing

The other major change to people's lives was caused by RATIONING. This was introduced on 8 January 1940. It was needed because much of Britain's food and other goods like clothing came from overseas, but German U-boats (submarines) were sinking many of the supply ships crossing the Atlantic. Most people welcomed rationing because it was fair. Before it was introduced rich people could get whatever they wanted, if they paid enough money, but poorer people had trouble finding enough to eat.

SOURCE 33 Typical weekly food rations per person. The amounts varied from time to time, depending on the availability of items

> | | |
> |---|---|
> | Bacon | 6oz. |
> | Cheese | 4oz. |
> | Butter | 4oz. |
> | Eggs | 2 |
> | Milk | 1 pint |
> | Tea | 3oz. |
> | Sugar | 12oz. |
> | Sweets | 3oz. |
> | Dried milk | 4 pints a week |
> | Dried eggs | 12 every eight weeks |

There was also an extra allowance for luxury items such as rice, tinned fruit and cereals. Each person was given sixteen points every four weeks and could spend these points as they wished. Clothes rationing was introduced in May 1941. Everyone was given 66 coupons per year (see Source 35).

1. Keep a record of what you eat in a week and compare it with Sources 33 and 36.

NISTRY OF FOOD

OUR NEW RATION BOOK

HOW TO REGISTER WITH THE SHOPS

The new Ration Books are now being distributed. As soon as you receive your new Book you must fill in the particulars as explained below, and then take the Book to the shops for fresh Registration. It has been found possible to allow *immediate* Registration, and the sooner you register the better. This is what to do :—

1 On the pages of coupons for Rationed Foods (Meat, Bacon, Butter and Sugar) you must fill in your name and address (BLOCK LETTERS) in the space provided in the centre of each page.

2 At the foot of these pages are spaces marked 'Counterfoil'. Here you must write your name and address, the date, and the name and address of the shop where you wish to buy the particular food during the six months' period beginning July 8th.

3 Inside the front cover of your Ration Book you must write the names and addresses of the shops.

4 As soon as you have done this, take the Book to each of the shops with whom you intend to register, so that they may cut out their counterfoils.

EVERYONE MUST REGISTER FOR THE NEW PERIOD

The Ministry of Food is responsible both for the supply and quality of rationed foods. No retailer is, therefore, in a better position than another to secure supplies of rationed foods, nor can one retailer promise to provide a better quality than another.

SOURCE 34 Government instructions for using a ration book

SOURCE 35 The *Picture Post* newspaper advised its readers how they could spend their 66 clothing coupons wisely

66

1 dress or dressing-gown or jacket	*11*
2 pairs of shoes	*10*
6 pairs of stockings	*12*
1 nightdress, 1 lingerie set, 1 slip	*13*
2 pairs of gloves	*4*
1 jersey, 1 cardigan	*7*
In reserve – for apron, scarf, etc.	*8*
This makes up your coupon total	*66*

99

MONDAY

BREAKFAST (each day)—
Porridge or any breakfast cereal with fresh or stewed fruit, followed by bread and butter or toast and marmalade Eggs occasionally if means allow Milk to drink or milky tea.

DINNER —
Vegetable soup made with bone stock, or Jacket sausages (for the older ones). Raisin hasty dumplings with golden syrup

TEA-SUPPER —
Blackberry Bake. Wholemeal bread and butter. Cocoa.

TUESDAY

DINNER —
Mutton pie. Jacket potatoes. Baked or stewed apple.

TEA-SUPPER —
Macaroni cheese Bread and butter. Fresh fruit. Milk or tea.

WEDNESDAY

DINNER —
Braised flank of beef. (Beef should be boned and rolled, keeping bones for soup, and braised in large saucepan with vegetables round.) Chocolate blancmange.

TEA-SUPPER —
Scrambled eggs on toast. Stewed dried apricots. Milk drink.

THURSDAY

DINNER —
Baked marrow. (Stuff with remains of yesterday's beef, minced.) College pudding

TEA-SUPPER —
Mixed Vegetable Casserole. Oven-toasted bread and jam. Milky tea or fruit-juice drink.

FRIDAY

DINNER —
Bombay Rice Cabbage Golden Apples

TEA-SUPPER —
Vegetable Salad. (A mixture of any diced cooked vegetables – carrots, peas, potatoes, beetroot, – on lettuce.) Wholemeal Bread and Butter. Rice Pudding and Top Milk.

SATURDAY

DINNER —
Liver casserole. Mashed potaotoes. Greens. Milk jelly.

TEA-SUPPER —
Bread and Butter Pudding. Fresh or stewed Fruit.

SUNDAY

DINNER —
Boiled Beef, Carrots and Dumplings, Greens. Golden Sponge Pudding.

TEA-SUPPER _
Cheese and Tomato Sandwiches. Cake. Milk Drink.

SOURCE 36 A week's menus, from a government information leaflet

---

SOURCE 37 A government poster showing a popular slogan

Activity 1

Design a poster persuading people how important rationing is.

Work in groups.
1. Make a list of all the ways in which people's lives were changed during the War. You will need to refer to pages 152–157 and 164–171.
2. Draw a timeline for 1939–45 and mark on it when these changes or events affected people.
3. Decide which of the changes mainly affected children, which affected women and which affected men.
3. Decide which change was most inconvenient.
4. Decide which change would be welcomed the most.
5. Write four paragraphs comparing your life today with life during the War. Think about:
   ■ what the main differences are
   ■ whether you would like to have lived then
   ■ which things you would have found most difficult to live with
   ■ which things you would have enjoyed.

Activity 2

You are a housewife who is also a war worker. You have kept a diary during the first three years of the War. Write down six entries from 1939–41.

Hitler invades the USSR: the turning point?

Operation Barbarossa

In June 1941 the War was still going well for Hitler. Germany controlled most of continental Europe. The German army seemed impossible to defeat. Although Britain had successfully resisted the *Luftwaffe* in the Battle of Britain in August 1940, many people expected that Hitler would try to invade Britain again. However, in June 1941 Hitler invaded the USSR instead.

You will remember that Hitler had signed a Non-Aggression Pact with Stalin (see page 138), which meant that Germany could invade Poland safely in 1939. So why did Hitler invade the USSR? One likely reason was that he had failed to win the Battle of Britain, so decided to turn his attention elsewhere. But remember also that two of Hitler's central aims, which he had been talking about for many years, were to defeat Communism and to use land in the USSR as *lebensraum* (living space) for Germans. The Soviet people could be used for slave labour. He also knew that control of the huge wheatfields of the Ukraine region and the oilfields of the Caucasus region would further strengthen Germany.

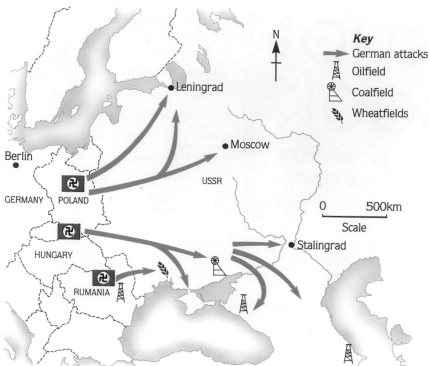

SOURCE 2 The German invasion plan

At the time, the invasion of the USSR seemed to be a reasonable gamble. The Soviet army appeared to be much weaker than the French army, which had been defeated in six weeks. Much Soviet equipment was believed to be out of date. Hitler also believed that many Soviet people would welcome the German army because it would be liberating them from Communism.

However, there were dangers. If the USSR held out, Germany could face war on two fronts. This is what the German army feared most. Hitler knew that there was a danger of the Soviet armies retreating deep into Russia, forcing his army to follow. This would make it almost impossible to get supplies to the German army. This had happened to the French Emperor Napoleon in 1812, and his army was wiped out by the freezing Russian winter. To avoid this, Hitler planned to surround the Soviet armies very quickly and crush them before the winter came.

> **3.** Why do you think Hitler attacked the USSR when he did?

Hitler sent over three million soldiers, 3580 tanks, 7184 guns, 1830 aircraft and 750,000 horses to the USSR. The Soviet army was caught by surprise and by October the Ukraine was conquered, Leningrad was surrounded, and the German army had reached the outskirts of Moscow.

> **SOURCE 1** Extracts from two letters Hitler wrote to his army
>
> **a) To his generals**
> *After the destruction of the Soviet Armed Forces, Germany will be master of Europe. The defence of this area will require considerably smaller forces than have been required until now. The newly conquered territories must be economically exploited.*
>
> **b) To his soldiers**
> *At last I can speak openly to you, my soldiers. This huge army is now going into action. It does so in order to save the European way of life from being destroyed.*

> **1.** Look at Source 1. What reasons does Hitler give for attacking the USSR?
> **2.** Explain what Hitler means by 'to save the European way of life'.

Tearing the heart out of the German army

As the Soviet army retreated it 'scorched the earth'. Anything that might be of use to the Germans was destroyed, including railways, buildings and crops. Whole factories were dismantled and rebuilt further east. In November the Russian winter arrived. It was a bitterly cold winter – temperatures dropped to 40 degrees below zero. It snowed and snowed. German sentries were found frozen to death at their posts.

Meanwhile, the people of Leningrad heroically held out under siege, in the most terrible conditions, for over two and a half years (see pages 174–175). With Russian troops fighting desperately, and in conditions they were used to, the German advance on Moscow was stopped. Gradually, between the winter of 1941 and 1944, the German army was forced back.

The war on the Eastern Front was crucial to the whole course of the Second World War in Europe. Throughout 1941–44 Stalin kept asking Britain and the USA to attack the Germans in order to take the pressure off the USSR, but they said they were not strong enough yet. However, as the USSR took the full force of the German army, Britain and the USA had time to build up their forces. Meanwhile, the strength of the German army was slowly drained away on the Eastern Front. Despite fighting 75 per cent of the German army, the USSR eventually won. Twenty million Soviet people died, but they stopped the German army.

For many historians it was the turning point of the War. The British Prime Minister, Winston Churchill, admitted that it was the Russians who 'tore the heart out of the German army'.

1. Look at Sources 5 and 6. What is the attitude of the British and Americans towards the USSR? Draw a cartoon of your own to show these attitudes.
2. Explain why the German invasion failed. Use all the evidence on this page to support your answer.

SOURCE 3 Dead German soldiers in temperatures of −40°C near Moscow, December 1941

SOURCE 4 A German general's memories of the Russian campaign

The Russian soldier values his own life no more than those of his comrades. He is immune to the most incredible hardships and does not even appear to notice them; he seems not to worry about bombs and shells.

Those arctic blasts that had taken us by surprise cut through our troops. In a couple of days there were 150,000 casualties from frostbite alone. A couple of days later our winter clothing arrived. Sixteen greatcoats and sixteen pairs of winter boots to be shared among a battalion of 88 men.

▶ **SOURCE 5** An American cartoon showing the Soviet giant, which is strong enough to push back the Nazi armies. The giant grows out of the united people and weapons of the USSR

RUSSIAN TREACHERY

▲ **SOURCE 6** A British cartoon, 9 July 1941

HITLER INVADES THE USSR: THE TURNING POINT?

The Siege of Leningrad, 1941–44

The city of Leningrad was surrounded by the Germans for over two and a half years. Almost no supplies could be brought in, so there was very little food. The Germans shelled the city continuously. The conditions suffered by the civilians and soldiers in the city were some of the worst faced by any people during the War. Nearly three million people lived in Leningrad, but one million died, mostly from starvation. This was more than the total number of American and British soldiers killed during the War.

> **SOURCE 7** From a speech by the chief city official to the people in August 1941
>
> *We have to teach the people in the shortest possible time how to fight: shooting, throwing grenades, street fighting, digging trenches, crawling. We must sign up children for auxiliary work: carrying shells and water, acting as messengers, and so on. We have to see that nobody is just an onlooker.*
>
> *The enemy is at the gates. It is a question of life and death.*

> **SOURCE 8** Hitler's orders to the German army in September 1941 concerning Leningrad
>
> *The Fuehrer has decided to wipe the city from the face of the earth.*
>
> *It is intended to blockade the city and destroy it by artillery fire and ceaseless bombardment from the air. If they want to surrender, they will be refused. We have no interest in keeping even part of the city's population.*

> **SOURCE 9** At the beginning of the siege there was only enough food for 35 days, so food had to be rationed. Here are the daily rations used while the food lasted (until November 1941)
>
> | | Labourer | Child aged 8 |
> |---|---|---|
> | Bread | 252g | 128g |
> | Fats | 19g | 17g |
> | Meat | 49g | 14g |
> | Cereals | 49g | 39g |
> | Sugar | 49g | 39g |
> | Total | 418g | 237g |
> | | = 1084 kCal | = 682 kCal |
> | Approximate daily need | 3500 kCal | 2800 kCal |

Soon the food ran out. From lack of food people's skin turned grey, their teeth fell out and their legs were covered in ulcers. The few cats, dogs and rats still alive were caught and eaten, sometimes raw. Teams of women and children searched for food in every corner of every building. Grains of food were scraped out of cracks and from beneath floorboards. Soap was made into jelly. Sausages were made from sheep's intestines, machine oil, horse flesh, pepper and leather dust. Cats' and sheep's intestines were flavoured with oil of cloves, then stewed and used in the place of milk.

People were so hungry and cold (in the winter it was fifteen degrees below zero and the electricity supply had been cut), that it was difficult to work. But they continued to build defences, bury the dead and dispose of the city's sewage. Women and children dug pits for human excrement. If one of them collapsed and fell in, they were left to be covered up by the excrement (see Source 10).

> **SOURCE 10** An eye-witness account
>
> *If this happened there was an immediate scrabbling in the filth for the dead person's ration card. Such were the indignities we suffered.*

> **SOURCE 11** An account written after the War by a child who survived
>
> *I watched my mother and father die. I knew perfectly well they were starving. But I wanted their bread more than I wanted them to stay alive. And they knew that. That's what I remember about the blockade: that feeling that you wanted your parents to die because you wanted their bread.*

SOURCE 12 A photograph of one of the dead being dragged through the city

SOURCE 13 A photograph of a palace in Leningrad in ruins

The temperature in the wards was usually about −2°C. The medical staff could barely stand on their feet through hunger, cold and overwork. The patients lay fully clothed, with coats and blankets and sometimes even mattresses piled on top of them. The walls were covered with frost. During the night the water froze in the buckets. The hunger had the effect of causing diarrhoea among the patients, many of whom from weakness were unable to use the bedpans. All the baths and bedpans were filled with excrement, all of which froze on the spot. Sheets on the beds were filthy. The only medicine available was sodium bromide [a disinfectant] and the doctors prescribed it to the patients under various names.

SOURCE 15
A British cartoon of 8 September 1941, at the start of the siege

In January 1944 the German army finally retreated. There was not much rejoicing. One girl's entry in her diary tells us this about her family: 'All died. Only Tanya remains.'

Activity

You are a teenager in Leningrad and you keep a diary. Make entries for these dates: August 1941, November 1941, November 1942, January 1944. Make sure you use the evidence in Sources 7–15. Try and explain how you feel and what your hopes and fears are, as well as what you are doing.

Which do you think was the hardest thing to bear – the hunger, the cold, the work, the deaths of friends and family, the filth, or the fear of the German army?

The Battle of the Atlantic: 'The only thing that ever frightened me'

NOT all the fighting in the Second World War was on land or in the air. Some historians argue that the crucial struggle took place at sea in the Battle of the Atlantic.

Britain depended on its merchant ships for an enormous quantity of imports – over 60 million tons a year. These imports included food, oil and RAW MATERIALS. In 1939 the Germans calculated that if they sank about 150 merchant ships every month for a year Britain would be forced to surrender. Admiral Raeder, head of the German navy, said in 1940, 'Britain's ability to maintain her supply lines is the decisive factor for the outcome of the War'. After the War Winston Churchill wrote, 'The only thing that ever really frightened me during the War was the U-boat peril.'

We are going to investigate why the Germans lost the Battle of the Atlantic, and what it was like for the men involved.

	Methods of sinking							
Year	U-boat	aircraft	mine	warship	merchant	E-boat	unknown	total
1939	114	10	79	15	0	0	4	222
1940	471	192	201	17	54	23	101	1059
1941	432	400	111	40	44	29	272	1328
1942	1159	145	51	31	30	23	222	1661
1943	463	76	37	0	5	6	10	597
1944	132	19	28	1	4	11	52	247
1945	56	6	28	0	0	5	10	105
Total	**2827**	**848**	**535**	**104**	**137**	**97**	**671**	**5219**

SOURCE 1 British merchant ships sunk, 1939–45

> 1. Using the figures in Source 1, see if you can write an account of the Battle of the Atlantic. Try to include your answers to these questions:
> a) What was the greatest threat to ALLIED ships, and was this always the greatest threat throughout the War?
> b) Did other methods of attack decrease or increase in importance as the War went on?
> c) Which year was the worst for the Allies?
> d) When did the threat to Allied shipping seem to be declining fast?
>   It will help if you write out answers to these questions first. Then write your account.

Now here is a brief account of the Battle of the Atlantic. Compare it to your answer to question 1.

Before the War the Germans did not realise how important submarines would be, and they cut back their building programme. When the War started they had only 57 submarines, which was 350 short of the number they needed to do the necessary damage to British merchant ships. So to start with the Germans used a balanced attack against Allied shipping: planes, mines and warships were also important.

The conquest of France in June 1940 gave Hitler the use of Atlantic ports for the first time. This allowed his U-boats and his aeroplanes to reach far into the Atlantic, where merchant ships were not usually escorted by Allied warships.

Gradually the Germans abandoned the balanced attack and relied mainly on U-boats. The U-boats started to 'hunt' in groups, known as wolf packs, which made it easier for them to sink ships.

1942 was the most successful year for the Germans, but after that their success declined and it was clear the Allies were winning the battle.

SOURCE 2 A photograph of an American escort ship during a storm

> 2. Look at Source 3. Which of these reasons did the Germans have control over, and which were outside their control?
> 3. Choose which you think are the three most important reasons for the Allies' success, and explain why.

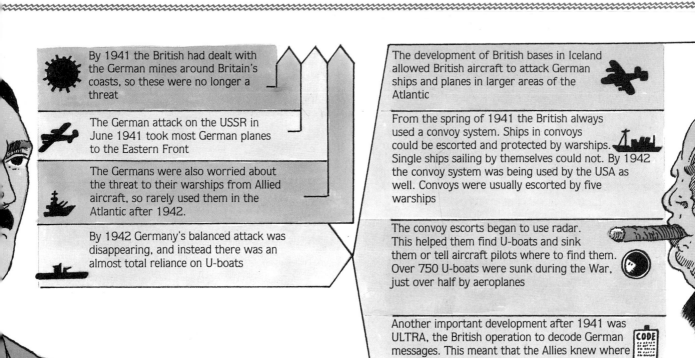

By 1941 the British had dealt with the German mines around Britain's coasts, so these were no longer a threat

The German attack on the USSR in June 1941 took most German planes to the Eastern Front

The Germans were also worried about the threat to their warships from Allied aircraft, so rarely used them in the Atlantic after 1942.

By 1942 Germany's balanced attack was disappearing, and instead there was an almost total reliance on U-boats

The development of British bases in Iceland allowed British aircraft to attack German ships and planes in larger areas of the Atlantic

From the spring of 1941 the British always used a convoy system. Ships in convoys could be escorted and protected by warships. Single ships sailing by themselves could not. By 1942 the convoy system was being used by the USA as well. Convoys were usually escorted by five warships

The convoy escorts began to use radar. This helped them find U-boats and sink them or tell aircraft pilots where to find them. Over 750 U-boats were sunk during the War, just over half by aeroplanes

Another important development after 1941 was ULTRA, the British operation to decode German messages. This meant that the Allies knew where the submarines were

Rationing in Britain reduced Britain's need for imports by more than half

Although the Germans sank 22 million tons of Allied shipping during the War, over the same period the Allies built 42 million tons of new ships

SOURCE 3 Some of the main reasons for the Allies' success

What was life like on board ship?

Being a sailor on a British merchant ship was very dangerous. About one quarter of the men – many of them African, Indian or Chinese – were killed. This is a higher proportion than for any of the 'fighting services'. The U-boats sank the merchant ships without warning them. Giving a warning would have given away the U-boat's position to the Allied warships and planes escorting the convoy. It was also impossible for the U-boats to pick up survivors.

The German sailors in the U-boats also lived very dangerous lives. They called their submarines 'steel coffins'. Out of 863 U-boats that sailed, 754 were sunk. Out of 39,000 men who went to sea in U-boats, over 27,000 died and 5,000 became prisoners of war.

The casualty rate on the warships escorting the merchant ships was much lower than for the merchant ships. But for all sailors the conditions were very difficult, as you can see from Sources 4–11.

SOURCE 4 A photograph of a U-boat near the American coast in 1941. The crew are looking for Allied ships using binoculars

THE BATTLE OF THE ATLANTIC: 'THE ONLY THING THAT EVER FRIGHTENED ME'

Sources 5 and 6 are accounts by men who served on merchant ships in the Atlantic.

SOURCE 5 R.T. Brown's account of his life aboard the *Volunteer*

❝There was a stir about 7.15 a.m. when the first person climbed from his hammock. There was no need to dress, as we slept in our clothes. The first one to rise made the tea. The bread, biscuit and jam was a help-yourself arrangement. The bread had to be vigorously shaken to be rid of the cockroaches.

During the morning those on duty went on watch, others cleaned the mess [living area] and prepared the midday meal. Into a large pot were put tinned stewing-steak, peas, beans and fresh potatoes and water. Those that were off duty caught up on lost sleep, as we very seldom had more than four hours at a stretch. Others sat around talking in undertones. If the weather was fine, it was time to get some fresh air on the upper deck. This was also time for washing – there were no baths or showers.

Supper was taken at 6.00. This was usually herrings or baked beans and bread.

SOURCE 6 An officer on the *New Westminster* describes what it was like in a storm

❝It was sheer unmitigated hell. Even getting food from galley [kitchen] to forecastle [at the front of the ship] was a tremendous job. The mess-decks were usually a shambles and the wear and tear on bodies and tempers was something I shall never forget.

SOURCE 8 An account of the sinking of the *Nariva* by an officer who was on duty at the time

❝*Nariva* was torpedoed with an ear-shattering roar and the deck bucked and heaved violently under my feet. A huge tower of black smoke, tons of water and debris was flung into the air just forward of the bridge.

The ship was taking water fast, the deck soon awash. The order was given to abandon ship and the lifeboats were launched.

We pulled away from the ship, but then saw another lifeboat released with a splash into the water and several men jump after it, where they clung desperately and shouted for help. We saw the raft drift slowly forward along the ship's side, and, to our horror, we watched helplessly as a great in-rush of water sucked the raft and its occupants into the hole blasted into the ship's side by the torpedo. Even now I can still hear the screams of the men inside the hull. But then they were swept out again, by which time we were much closer and could drag men to safety in our boat. One of them, as if in gratitude, became violently sick all over me.❞

1. According to Sources 5 and 6 what were the three biggest hardships on board?

SOURCE 7
The view through a U-boat periscope of a ship being hit by a torpedo

SOURCE 9 A painting by John Hamilton, showing a damaged U-boat surfacing during a night-time battle

SOURCE 10 A photograph of depth charges dropped by an aeroplane exploding around a U-boat caught on the surface

SOURCE 11 An account of the scenes on a U-boat during an attack, from *U-Boat War* by G. Buchheim, published in 1974

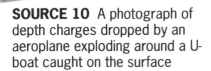

'Clear the Bridge! Flood and proceed at periscope depth.'

In the control room is a mind-boggling confusion of tangled cables, grey and red hand wheels, white dials, scales and indicators; the ventilators are switched off. At once an overpowering stench of fuel, sweat and bilge.

The First Officer is feeding the calculator data on the enemy ship's position: 'Port fifteen. Go to 40 feet please! Periscope still under water. Tubes one to four stand by for underwater firing. Flood tubes. Open torpedo doors!'

The soundman delivers his report: 'Propellor noise at 220 degrees – sound bearing steady – quite loud – no other noises.'

At last the commander ups the periscope. He is searching intently. Time ticks by without a word from him . . . then: '225 degrees – getting louder. There she goes. Range 12,000. We'll have to fire a spread. Dispersal at three degrees.' But he starts grumbling and cursing. The steamer has taken to zig-zagging. Could the crew have caught sight of our periscope?

He spins round in a circle for a look all the way round. You never know – there could be a destroyer lurking.

'Range 1500. Course twelve knots. Torpedoes to sixteen feet'. I can hear the calculator transmitting the new directions to the deadly eels. The tension is overwhelming. 'Tube one!'. A measured pause. 'Fire! Tube two – Fire!'

We surface. I have often asked myself what can they be feeling, the men aboard a doomed vessel, when our streaming tower emerges suddenly in an eddy of frothing water. Hatred? Horror? Paralysis?

2. Compare source 9 with Source 10. Do you think artists make events like this more exciting than they really are?

3. What do you think is the answer to the question asked at the end of Source 11?

4. Why do you think casualties were so high on both sides?

5. Where would you rather have served, in a U-boat, or in a surface ship?

6. After the War, Admiral Donitz, head of the German navy, was charged with WAR CRIMES because of the activities of his U-boats. Do you think he was guilty?

Activity

You have to make plans for ten merchant ships to sail from New York to Southampton. Using the map of the North Atlantic which your teacher will give you, make plans for the journey so that it is as safe as possible.

Why did the Japanese attack Pearl Harbor?

BY THE end of 1940 Britain was running short of money to pay for American supplies of food, RAW MATERIALS and weapons. So President Roosevelt decided to lend Britain what it needed, and in March 1941 the American Congress passed the LEND–LEASE Act. Some Americans were against this, because they thought it would drag the USA into the War. One American politician said, 'Lending war material is like lending chewing gum. You don't want it back!'

During the first half of 1941 the USA's involvement in the War increased. It repaired British warships. American ships gave the British navy information about the position of German U-boats. When Germany invaded the USSR in June 1941 Roosevelt extended Lend–Lease aid to the USSR. In September American warships began to help escort British convoys across the Atlantic. In October a German submarine sank one of the American warships. From then on the Americans armed their merchant ships. Germany and American were almost at war.

In Asia, meanwhile, the war between China and Japan was still raging. As you saw on pages 146–147, relations between Japan and America had been rapidly getting worse, with America demanding that Japan withdraw from China. So America was in danger of being dragged into this war as well.

Key
Land held by Jap
December 1941
Land captured b
July 1942

0   1000km
Scale

SOURCE 1 The war in the Far East 1941–42

The countdown to war

September 1940
Japan, Germany and Italy sign a defensive treaty.

July 1941
Japan invades French Indo-China. The USA stops sending oil to Japan. Japan depends on the USA for 80 per cent of its oil. It now has no oil for its industries.

October 1941
General Tojo becomes Prime Minister of Japan. The military are now in control.

November 1941
The USA demands that Japan withdraw from China and Indo-China and leave the alliance with Germany and Italy. In return the USA will discuss a new trade agreement with Japan. Japan sees this as a choice between giving in or war.

22 November 1941
The USA picks up Japanese radio messages saying 'something is going to happen' if the USA does not lift the ban on oil.

Night of 6–7 December 1941
A message to the Japanese embassy in the USA is intercepted: 'It is impossible to reach agreement through further negotiations.' The message is not passed on to anyone in authority.

7 December 1941
Japanese aircraft attack Pearl Harbor, an American naval base in Hawaii.

8 December 1941
The USA and Britain declare war on Japan.

11 December 1941
Germany declares war on the USA. The two wars in the West and the East are now joined. The War is now a World War.

The attack
In the early morning of 7 December, Japanese aircraft carriers were in position on the ocean about 200 miles north of Hawaii. The first wave of 183 planes took off for Pearl Harbor, where the American Pacific Fleet was at anchor.

In Hawaii it was a peaceful Sunday morning. On the ships some sailors were still asleep. Others were having breakfast or lounging on the deck. At 7.55 a.m. the Japanese planes struck. Screaming dive bombers swooped down, raining bombs on every ship in the harbour, and on airfields and barracks on land. In under two hours eighteen warships were sunk or crippled, three others were damaged, 177 planes were destroyed, most of them on the ground, and over 2300 men were dead. The Japanese lost 29 planes.

1. Which of Sources 2 and 3 is more useful as evidence about the attack on Pearl Harbor?

Causes and consequences

The attack on Pearl Harbor brought the Americans into the War. Looking back, we can see that the American role in the ALLIES' victory was crucial. So the attack may seem like a mistake by the Japanese. But did it seem like that at the time?

It is possible that the Japanese had decided that war with the USA was inevitable – after all, the Americans had been demanding that they withdraw from China for years. So perhaps the Japanese felt that they should make the first attack while the USA was still not really ready. If Japan could cripple the American navy in one blow, the USA could not fight back.

Japan had already invaded several countries in Asia; if it was able to conquer a few more it would be so strong no one would be able to defeat it. But to expand its Empire in South-East Asia it needed to get rid of the American navy first.

On the other hand, many Japanese soldiers and civilians thought of the USA as a land of film stars and gangsters. Its soft people would be no match for the Japanese armed forces. The Americans would probably not even have the courage to fight.

One other view put forward by some historians is that President Roosevelt deliberately provoked Japan into attacking because this was the only excuse for bringing the USA into the war against Hitler.

As you can see from Source 1, Japan conquered large amounts of land very rapidly after Pearl Harbor. It took American, British and Commonwealth troops a long time to win it back.

SOURCE 2
A photograph of the damage inflicted by Japanese planes

SOURCE 3
A painting of Pearl Harbor

Activity

Look at this list of possible causes for the Japanese attack on Pearl Harbor.
- Japan wanted to build a strong empire in Asia.
- Japan had appointed a war-like general as Prime Minister.
- The Japanese were stupid and had not thought through the consequences.
- Japan believed the Americans would not fight back.
- Japan believed a war with America was inevitable anyway and wished to strike first.
- Japan was already at war with China.
- America provoked Japan into war by imposing trade SANCTIONS and making impossible demands.
- Japan needed raw materials like oil. It could only get them by invading oilfields in South-East Asia.

1. From this list choose which you think are the five most important factors. Write a sentence for each one explaining how it helped cause the decision to attack.
2. Which of the factors in the list helped to trigger off the attack?
3. Are any of the reasons connected with each other? If so, explain how.
4. Now read the first three paragraphs on this page again. Do you think that even without Pearl Harbor America would soon have declared war on Japan, or did Pearl Harbor cause the outbreak of war?

Experiences of war

WHAT was life like during the War? This depended on who you were and where you were. Everyone's experience was different. You have already seen what life was like for some civilians, in the London Blitz and the Leningrad siege. For servicemen life could be equally grim, on the Atlantic convoys or in the freezing Russian winter. We are going to look briefly at a few other case studies to get a broader picture of the 'World' War. You will need to refer to the timeline on pages 150–151 to see how these case studies fit into the overall pattern of the War.

Case study 1: Japanese Americans

The attack on Pearl Harbor created such shock and outrage among Americans that there was total support for going to war. Many Germans and Japanese people were living in the USA. How would they be treated now that America was at war with their 'mother country'?

There was little persecution of German Americans, but Japanese Americans were treated very differently. There were about 112,000 Japanese living in California, on the West Coast of America. White Americans had always been suspicious of them, and there was a certain amount of racial prejudice against them. Americans now feared that they would be bombed by the Japanese and perhaps invaded, and that these Japanese Americans would help the enemy.

There was no evidence that any Japanese Americans were traitors. Nearly all of them had been born in the USA and they regarded themselves as loyal Americans. But they were forced to sell their homes and move to INTERNMENT camps which were built in the desert.

SOURCE 1
Location of case studies 1–5

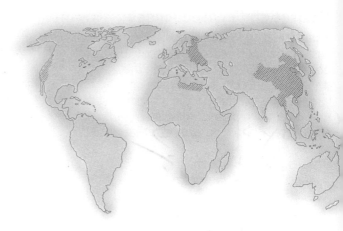

SOURCE 2
A Japanese American family on their way to an internment camp

SOURCE 3 An account by a student who was sent to a camp

❝Camp Minidoka was located in a semi-desert region. There were hundreds and hundreds of barracks to house 10,000 of us.

Our home was one large room, six by 7.5 metres. The only furnishings were an iron pot-belly stove and cots.

Our first day in camp we had a dust storm. We felt as if we were standing in a huge sand mixing machine. The summer sizzled on average 100 degrees. For the first few weeks I lay on my cot from morning till night, not daring to do more than go to the mess hall three times a day.❞

SOURCE 4 Written by an American historian in 1970

❝During January the climate of opinion in California turned harshly toward fear, suspicion, intolerance. Clamour arose for mass internment. This was because of the endless Japanese advance, combined with false alarms – stories of attacks on the coast, of secret broadcasting equipment. But the main reason for the demand to 'clean out the Japanese' was racism.❞

1. Why do you think Americans treated the Japanese Americans in this way?

Case study 2: Russia and the Ukraine

Sources 5 and 7 were written by German soldiers and show how they treated civilians in the Ukraine region of the USSR.

SOURCE 5

66 *Do you know how we behaved to the civilians? We behaved like devils out of hell. We left those poor villagers to starve to death, thousands and thousands of them. How can you win a war in this way?*

We shoot villagers on the slightest excuse. Just stick them up against the wall. We order the whole village out to watch. It's a vicious circle. We hate them and they hate us, and on and on it goes, everyone getting more inhuman.

The civilians were all ready to look on us as saviours. They had had years of oppression from the Communists. What did we do? Turn them into slaves under Hitler.

If the Russians should ever pay back one half of what we have done, you won't smile or sing again. 99

SOURCE 7

66 *We were quartered [living] in a house outside the town. Our dwelling for the night was a wooden house occupied by a Russian family of five children and old grandmother. We were bitten all night by vermin [fleas]. We opened our tins and made coffee, sharing what we had with the children and the old woman.*

The man of the house was a soldier and the mother had been taken away to dig trenches. The children all had the protruding bellies of long-term malnutrition. The reality is that after 22 years of Communist rule, a salted fish is the height of luxury. How this country depresses me. 99

1. What effect did the War have on the two German soldiers who wrote Sources 5 and 7?
2. What effect did the War have on the Soviet civilians, according to Sources 5–7?

Case study 3: The North African desert

Sources 8, 10 and 11 are three accounts by British soldiers of fighting against German armies in North Africa.

SOURCE 8

66 *Our life is dominated by the sun. At noon the desert is burning hot, the heat is like a solid wall. Mirages of shimmering blue cut off the horizon.*

Then there are the flies. Soon after sunrise they arrive in hordes from nowhere, then plague us all day, trying to land on our faces, in our eyes, ears and nostrils, and on our arms and necks. And once settled they bite hard. At the moment I'm spitting five of them away from my mouth.

Rations are cans of bully beef, tinned milk, tinned cheese and oranges. Fresh meat is unknown. The distribution of tea is a careful business, almost every leaf is counted. Each man has two gallons of water. 99

SOURCE 6 A photograph of a Russian orphan in the ruins of his town

SOURCE 9 German soldiers in North Africa

Case study 4: South-East Asia

In the jungles of Burma, American, British and other ALLIED troops found themselves fighting the Japanese.

SOURCE 12 A first-hand account of battles between British and Japanese soldiers around Rangoon in Burma in 1942

One tank was knocked out by a Jap mortar. The Japs were nowhere to be seen, yet the tanks were fired on from all directions. When the crews bailed out the Japanese were waiting for them with bayonets.

There were scores of Japs killed and many snipers hung dead in the palm tree tops where they had tied themselves. The Japs used snipers a lot. They were camouflaged and almost invisible. In the heavy forest they were difficult to detect. The snipers worked in pairs, one man to distract the enemy while his colleague was able to shoot undetected. Japanese infiltration parties would creep up to the tanks and lob in hand-grenades.

SOURCE 10

A shabby gritty landscape. The sweat oozes and trickles all day. Sweat and tiredness and no water till evening. The pain of muscles twisted from the weight of rifles, automatic guns and heavy equipment. The thud of feet on the sand 94 times every minute, 50 minutes an hour. And every night dig. Dig in case the bombs drop. Dig through sand. Dig through rock. Dig for bloody victory.

SOURCE 11

A tank had four petrol tanks, and each one filled with high octane. If any of these were hit, the whole machine would go up. At best you had 90 seconds to push the trap-door open. That would leave 40 seconds for three men to squeeze out. And what would happen if the trap-door was jammed? You'd die. It takes twenty minutes for a tank to incinerate; and the flames burn slowly, so figure it takes ten minutes for a man to die. You wouldn't even be able to struggle. You would sit and die like a dog.

1. What were the main dangers and hardships of serving as a soldier in the desert?
2. Which of the soldiers who wrote Sources 8, 10 and 11 disliked being in North Africa the most?

SOURCE 13 In 1942 the Japanese planned to invade India. To help transport their troops they built a railway linking Thailand with South Burma. It was 415 km long, through the roughest country. The work was done by prisoners of war. This account of the life of prisoners working on the railway was written in 1988, based on interviews with some of the prisoners

During the monsoons [rain storms] the men struggled back to their huts and often found them awash with human excrement. The sick suffered terribly. The Japanese cry of 'No work – No food' brought a shudder to those poor souls suffering from dysentery, malaria and tropical ulcers. The ravages of cholera were especially horrific.

Many of the jungle camps were of huts made of bamboo. They leaked. The dampness and the humidity of the jungle rotted clothes and encouraged vast swarms of malaria-carrying mosquitoes. Some men became blind through lack of vitamins. The prisoners often started sixteen hours of work with only a cupful of cold rice and a mug of cold tea with no sugar or milk to give them nourishment.

SOURCE 14 A photograph of prisoners of war in the medical section of a Japanese POW camp

Case study 5: China

China had been at war with Japan since 1937.

SOURCE 16 Chinese people fleeing Shanghai as Japanese forces invaded, February 1937

SOURCE 17 An account of life for Chinese villagers under Japanese rule, from a novel written in 1958. The author is Chinese and based the story on his experiences during the War

6 *Disaster was upon them, but disaster has never scared the Chinese people – every one of the villagers stood calm and firm, chests out, shoulder to shoulder. The Japanese soldiers looked like wild beasts sniffing and searching all around with their bloodshot, beady eyes, which they finally fixed on the totally unarmed villagers.*

A shout came from the crowd, 'Down with the Japanese invaders! Resist and fight to the end!'

Machine gun fire fanned out, mowing the angry people down. But they went on shouting to their last breath. 9

SOURCE 15
A photograph of British soldiers in Burma

1. Use Sources 12–15 to describe the hardships and dangers faced by soldiers fighting the Japanese.

1. Working in groups, consider all the evidence on the last four pages. Discuss who suffered more during the War: the soldiers or the civilians?

   It is best to start by making a list of all the points you can find about each group. Then on a large sheet of paper make a simple display putting forward your case.

2. On your own, write a short essay entitled 'Where I would least like to have been during the War'.

How did the Holocaust happen?

IN 1939 there were eight million Jews living in Europe. Between 1939 and 1945 six million Jewish men, women and children were murdered in the parts of Europe controlled by the Nazis. This attempt to wipe out the Jewish population is usually known as the Holocaust, although many Jews object to this term as it means 'sacrifice'. They prefer to use the word *Churban*, which means 'destruction'.

Hundreds of thousands of gypsies, homosexuals, Jehovah's Witnesses and mentally handicapped people and four million Russian prisoners of war were also victims of this mass murder.

Different methods of killing were used. Over a million people were killed in their own towns and villages or in GHETTOS, where they were deliberately starved of food or shot. The rest were transported by train across Europe to extermination camps.

The most notorious of these extermination camps was at Auschwitz in Poland. At least four million people were sent to Auschwitz. Only around 60,000 survived. The story of this mass murder, with the dreadful cruelty and suffering it involved, is extraordinary. How did it happen?

The background

For hundreds of years Christian Europe had regarded the Jews as the 'Christ-killers'. At one time or another Jews had been driven out of almost every European country. The way they were treated in England in the thirteenth century is a typical example. In 1275 they were made to wear a yellow badge and 269 of them were hanged in the Tower of London in 1287.

This deep prejudice against Jews was still strong in the twentieth century, especially in Germany and in Poland and the Ukraine in Eastern Europe, where the Jewish population was very large. It often caused outbursts of violence, which sometimes flared up of its own accord, but sometimes was deliberately encouraged by governments. After the First World War hundreds of Jews were murdered. In Germany, the Jews were blamed for the defeat in the War. Prejudice against the Jews grew during the economic depression which followed. Many Germans were poor and unemployed and wanted someone to blame. They turned on the Jews, many of whom were rich and successful in business.

During the 1920s a new, organised group in Germany began preaching hatred towards Jews. This was Hitler's Nazi Party. The party's private army, the Stormtroopers, beat up Jews in the streets. Julius Streicher, a Nazi, started a newspaper called *Der Sturmer*, which stirred up hatred towards the Jews.

SOURCE 1 A cartoon from *Der Sturmer*, 1932. The text reads, 'Father, why must we freeze at home when there is so much coal?' 'Because the hand of the Jew lies heavily on the people.'

Hitler was obsessed with the Jews. In his writings and speeches there was a mixture of racist hate and fear. He saw the Jews as a threat to the so-called superior 'Aryan' race, which was white and mainly German. He said there were many inferior races, such as Slavs (many of whom lived in the USSR) and Negroes, but the lowest of them all were the Jews.

SOURCE 2 Written by Lucy Dawidowicz in a recent book

The Jews inhabited Hitler's mind. He believed that they were the source of all evil, misfortune and tragedy. They were devils whom he had been given a divine mission to destroy.

SOURCE 3 Three extracts from *Mein Kampf*, written by Hitler in 1924

- *The black-haired Jewish youth lies in wait for hours on end, glaring and spying on the unsuspicious German girl whom he plans to seduce, corrupting her blood.*
- *As long as a people remain racially pure, they can never be overcome by the Jew.*
- *If during the [First World] War, twelve or fifteen thousand Jews had been held under poison gas, the sacrifice of millions at the front would not have been in vain.*

1. What does Source 1 suggest about the Jews?
2. From Sources 2 and 3, sum up in your own words Hitler's attitude towards Jews.
3. Is there any evidence so far of what Hitler wanted to do with the Jews?

In 1924 the views in Source 3 belonged to a not very well known extremist. But by 1930 unemployment and poverty had returned to Germany, and support for the Nazis grew. People voted for Hitler mainly because they thought he would solve Germany's economic problems, but Nazi views on the Jews were also well known. During the election campaigns of the early 1930s Hitler made speeches attacking the Jews, and his Stormtroopers publicly murdered and beat up Jews. Yet the Germans still voted for Hitler.

The concentration camps

In 1933 Hitler became Chancellor of Germany. One Jewish man remembered that when he and his friends heard the news, 'Everybody shook. As kids of ten we shook.'

It did not take long for Hitler to put his hatred into practice. During 1933, 36 Jews were murdered. Thousands were sent to concentration camps such as Dachau. Placards appeared outside shops and cafés and beside roads leading to towns and villages, reading 'Jews not wanted'. By the end of 1933 over 35,000 Jews had fled from Germany. Some went to Palestine, where the Jews wanted to set up a Jewish state, others to the USA and Britain.

SOURCE 5 This banner outside the German village of Rosenheim reads 'Jews are not welcome here'

SOURCE 6
A beer mat which says 'Whoever buys from a Jew is a traitor to his people'

SOURCE 4 Extracts from the Nuremberg Laws, passed by Hitler in 1935

■ *Marriages between Jews and citizens of German blood are forbidden.*
■ *Sexual relations between Jews and citizens of German blood are forbidden.*
■ *Jews are not permitted to employ female citizens of German blood under 45 years of age as domestic help.*
■ *No Jew can be a German citizen.*

1. Look at Sources 4–6. If people were continuously surrounded by PROPAGANDA like this, what do you think the effect would be?
2. Can you think of any recent examples when one race has been encouraged to hate people of another race?

187

HOW DID THE HOLOCAUST HAPPEN?

Jews were also being attacked, and similar laws were being made against them, in Poland, Rumania and Hungary during the 1930s.

Many Jews tried to flee to other parts of the world. Hitler encouraged this; some historians claim that he would have been satisfied if all the Jews had emigrated from Germany. Later, he even had a plan to set up a Jewish state in Madagascar! However, emigration was not an answer for most Jews because other countries, including Britain, were not keen to have them.

On 9 November 1938 the Nazis carried out what they called *Kristallnacht*, 'the night of the broken glass'. All over Germany Nazi Stormtroopers broke into and smashed up tens of thousands of Jewish shops, homes and synagogues. In many places ordinary Germans joined in and helped the Stormtroopers.

> **SOURCE 7** During *Kristallnacht* many more Jews were arrested and sent to concentration camps. One group was taken to the gates of the camp by German police. Martin Gilbert describes what happened in his book *The Holocaust*
>
> 66 *At the gates, the police were made to hand them over to an SS unit. The 62 Jews were then forced to run a gauntlet of spades, clubs and whips. The police, unable to bear their cries, turned their backs. As the Jews fell, they were beaten further. This 'orgy' of beating lasted half an hour. When it was over twelve were dead, their skulls smashed. The others were unconscious, some had their eyes knocked out, their faces flattened and shapeless.* 99

> **SOURCE 8** From a speech made by Hitler to the German Parliament in 1939
>
> 66 *Europe cannot find peace until the Jewish question has been solved.*
> *Today I will once more be a prophet: if the international Jewish financiers in and outside Europe should succeed in plunging the nations into a world war, then the result will be the destruction of the Jewish race in Europe.* 99

> 1. Describe how actions and attitudes towards the Jews in Germany gradually changed between 1919 and 1939. You might find it helpful to show the changes on a timeline.
> 2. Do you think Hitler changed his views at all?

The ghettos

After the German invasion of Poland and the outbreak of the Second World War even more Jews came under German control. The War made it impossible for Hitler to get rid of the Jews to other parts of the world. The Jews were trapped under Nazi rule.

SOURCE 9 A photograph of German soldiers kicking a Jew in Poland

Adolf Eichmann, a leading Nazi, was put in charge of 'Jewish resettlement'. Jews from Germany and Poland were rounded up and sent to an area which the Germans called a 'Jewish reservation' near Lublin in Poland.

In 1940 the Germans dropped the idea of a reservation and began instead to move Jews into a number of GHETTOS. The largest was in Warsaw. Walls were built to separate the ghetto district from the rest of the city. There were about seven people living in every room. They were given 300 calories of food a day – this amounted to 1.8 kg (two and a half loaves) of bread per person per month. Nearly all the flats were unheated. Many people caught typhus (a disease carried by lice). Anyone who left the ghetto was executed. Altogether over half a million Jews died in the ghetto.

SOURCE 10 A photograph of the Warsaw Ghetto wall

SOURCE 11 A description of life in the Warsaw Ghetto by a visitor

On the streets children are crying in vain, children who are dying of hunger. They howl, beg, sing, moan, shiver with cold, without underwear, without clothing, without shoes, in rags, sacks, flannel which are bound in strips around the emaciated skeletons, children swollen with hunger, half-conscious. Already completely grown up at the age of five, gloomy and weary of life. Every day and every night hundreds of these children die.

I no longer look at the people; when I hear groaning and sobbing I cross the road.

SOURCE 12 The Germans organised coach tours through the ghetto. This account was written by Albert Rosenberg, a leading Nazi, who went on one

Seeing this race which is decaying, decomposing, and rotten to the core will stop anyone having any sympathy for the Jews. It is the Reich [state] rubbish dump. Five to six thousand die each month. In answer to my question whether it was reckoned that in ten years' time the Jews would all have died, Dr Frank said he did not want to wait such a long time.

1. Compare the two descriptions of the Warsaw Ghetto in Sources 11 and 12. Do these two writers agree?

Gradually the Nazis achieved what they wanted. Forced to live in sub-human conditions, and becoming so weak and under-nourished, many Jews began to look like the sub-humans Nazi PROPAGANDA made them out to be. This made it easier for many people to take part in the dreadful treatment of the Jews. Some convinced themselves that they were not dealing with human beings.

The slaughter begins

In June 1941 the invasion of the USSR began. This brought even more Jews under Nazi rule. As the German army fought its way into the USSR, it was followed by the SS *Einsatzgruppe*. This was a special force, whose job was to murder all the Jews – men, women and children – it could find. Altogether, it murdered over two million people.

At first this policy of extermination was restricted to Russia, but soon it was used for all Jews under German control.

SOURCE 13 An eye-witness report of the activities of the *Einsatzgruppe* by a German builder

The people who had got off the lorries – men, women and children of all ages – had to undress on the orders of an SS man who was carrying a dog whip in his hand.

Without weeping or crying these people undressed and stood together in family groups, embracing each other and saying goodbye. I did not hear a single plea for mercy. I watched a family of about eight. An old woman with snow-white hair held a one-year-old child in her arms singing to it and tickling it. The child squeaked with delight. The father held a ten-year-old boy by the hand, speaking softly to him. The boy was struggling to hold back his tears. The father pointed a finger to the sky and stroked his head and seemed to be explaining something to him. The SS man counted off some twenty people.

I walked up to the huge grave. The bodies were lying so tightly packed that only their heads showed, from almost all of which blood ran down over their shoulders. Some were still moving. There were about 1000 bodies. An SS man sat, legs swinging, on the edge of the ditch. He had an automatic rifle, he was smoking a cigarette. The people, completely naked, climbed down steps, stumbled over the heads of those lying there and stopped at the spot indicated by the SS man. They lay down. Then I heard a series of rifle shots. I looked into the ditch and saw bodies contorting.

1. From the evidence in Source 13 what seems to be the attitude of a) the Jews who are going to be murdered, b) the SS men, c) the writer?

SOURCE 14 A photograph of Jewish women and children being led to the point where they will be killed

HOW DID THE HOLOCAUST HAPPEN?

The 'Final Solution'

On 20 January 1942 leading Nazis met at Wannsee to plan what they called a 'final solution' to the Jewish problem.

> **SOURCE 15** From the minutes of the meeting
>
> " *In the course of the Final Solution, the Jews will be brought to the East for labour. Large labour gangs will be formed, with the sexes separated, which will be used for road construction. No doubt a lot of them will drop out through natural wastage. The remainder who survive will have to be dealt with accordingly.* "

---

1. Source 15 does not actually mention death camps or extermination. How could you convince somebody that this is what it is really about?

The death camps

By the end of January 1942 the Germans were busy making all the arrangements for the extermination of the Jews. The death camps were built in remote areas of Eastern Europe. Railway trucks were prepared, timetables drawn up, and arrangements made for Jews to be rounded up all over Europe. Thousands of people helped to do all of this – administrators, police, soldiers and ordinary people, some of them not even German.

Jews were rounded up in Germany, in Eastern Europe, in France and every other part of Nazi-controlled Europe, and sent to the death camps.

SOURCE 16 A photograph of Jews being forced out of their homes, ready to be sent to a death camp

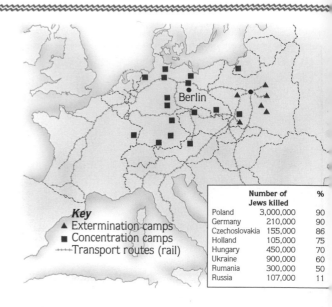

Key
▲ Extermination camps
■ Concentration camps
······ Transport routes (rail)

	Number of Jews killed	%
Poland	3,000,000	90
Germany	210,000	90
Czechoslovakia	155,000	86
Holland	105,000	75
Hungary	450,000	70
Ukraine	900,000	60
Rumania	300,000	50
Russia	107,000	11

SOURCE 17 The Holocaust in Europe, 1942–44

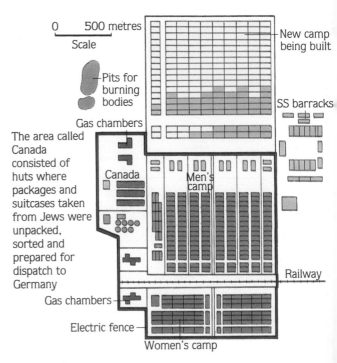

SOURCE 18 Plan of Birkenau death camp

Death camps such as Auschwitz were also slave labour camps. Many prisoners worked in the fields around Auschwitz or in one of the 40 branch camps. The guards were instructed to 'Work them to death'. Life expectancy was three months. Prisoners died through disease, exhaustion or lack of food. If they were too weak to work they were killed.

More than 150 German firms used Auschwitz prisoners as slave labour. They even competed for the contract to design the gas chambers where the prisoners were murdered (see Source 19).

SOURCE 19 From the memoirs of Rudolf Hoss, commandant of Auschwitz camp, written in 1946–47. Hoss was tried for war crimes and executed in April 1947

"The railway carriages were unloaded one after the other. After leaving their luggage the Jews had to pass individually in front of an SS doctor, who decided if they were fit enough for work. Those fit enough were taken off into the camp in small groups.

The remainder were taken to the crematoria, the men being separated from the women. In the undressing room Jewish prisoners would tell them in their own language that they were going to be bathed and deloused, that they must leave their clothes neatly together and remember where they had put them so they would be able to find them quickly, after delousing.

After undressing they went into the gas chambers, which were furnished with showers and water pipes and looked like a real bath house.

I had visited the Treblinka camp where the Commandant used monoxide gas and I did not think his methods were very efficient. So at Auschwitz I used Zyklon B [hydrogen cyanide gas]. Another improvement we made over Treblinka was that we built our gas chambers to accommodate 2000 people at one time.

The door would be quickly screwed up and the gas released through the vents in the ceilings of the gas chambers. The victims staggered about and began to scream for air. The screaming soon changed to death rattles and in a few minutes all lay still. It took from three to fifteen minutes to kill everybody.

We usually waited about half an hour before we opened the doors. Work then started on removing the gold from the teeth and cutting the hair from the women.

The bodies were taken up by lift and laid in front of the ovens which had been stoked up. Up to three corpses could be put into an oven at the same time. Sometimes the ovens broke down because of the huge number of corpses. Then we burnt the bodies in huge pits. Here the surplus fat had to be constantly drained off and the mountain of burning corpses turned over so that the draught might fan the flames."

SOURCE 20 Guards at Auschwitz selecting who would work and who would die

SOURCE 21 Prisoners putting a dead body into an oven

SOURCE 22 An eye-witness account of Treblinka camp explains that the women were shaved to the skin as soon as they arrived

"Because the little children at their mothers' breasts were a great nuisance during the shaving, the children were taken from their mothers as soon as they got off the train. The children were taken to an enormous ditch, they were shot and thrown into the fire. No one bothered to see if they were really dead. Sometimes one could hear infants wailing in the fire. If mothers managed to keep their babies with them a guard took the baby by its legs and smashed it against the wall until only a bloody mess remained in his hands. The mother then had to take this mass with her to the 'bath'."

1. What is Hoss' attitude to the exterminations? Is he sorry about what he did or proud?

HOW DID THE HOLOCAUST HAPPEN?

You probably find it hard to understand how anyone could behave like this to fellow human beings. Different explanations have been given:

- that the camp guards weren't human
- that they did not regard the Jews as humans
- that they hid from themselves what they were really doing
- that what they were doing was just another job and as soldiers they took pride in doing it well.

> 1. What evidence is there in Sources 23–26 to support each of these explanations?

SOURCE 23 Extracts from an interview with Franz Stangl, Commandant of Treblinka, when he was serving a life sentence in prison in 1971

❝ *Q: Did you think the Jews were human beings?*
A: Cargo. They were cargo.
Q: When did you begin to think of them as cargo?
A: I think it started the day I saw the death camp in Treblinka. I remember Wirth standing there, next to the pits full of blue-black corpses. It had nothing to do with humanity – it couldn't have; a mass of rotting flesh. Wirth said, 'What shall we do with this garbage?' I think that started me thinking of them as cargo. ❞

SOURCE 24 From the diary of an SS officer at Auschwitz. A special action was an arrival of victims for the gas chamber

❝ *6.9.1942 Sunday, an excellent lunch; tomato soup, half a chicken with potatoes and red cabbage, a marvellous vanilla ice cream. Left at eight in the evening for a special action.*
7.10.1942 Present at the ninth special action. Foreigners and women. ❞

SOURCE 25 Heinrich Himmler, head of the SS, was in overall charge of the 'Final Solution', yet he never actually killed anyone himself. In 1941 he visited Russia. This is an account by an SS general of what happened

❝ *Himmler had never seen dead people before and he stood right on the edge of this mass grave. While he was looking in, he had the bad luck to get a splash of brains on his coat, and he went very green and pale; he wasn't actually sick, but he was heaving and turned round and swayed and then I had to jump forward and hold him steady.* ❞

SOURCE 26 From a letter from a German police sergeant working in the USSR in 1942

❝ *Naturally, we are cleaning up considerably, especially among the Jews. But the population has to be kept firmly in check, too. We act fast. Well, we shall get home all the sooner.*
I have a cosy flat. Nothing is missing. Apart from my wife and children. My Dieter and my little Liese write often. Sometimes I could weep. It is not good to love one's children as much as I do. ❞

> 2. Look at Sources 25 and 26. Do you think that Himmler and the police sergeant were ordinary, decent people?
> 3. Discuss in class whether those involved in the extermination of Jews should still be hunted down and punished today.

Jewish resistance

The reactions of the Jews to this persecution varied widely. During the round-ups in Poland and Russia there were many occasions when Jews resisted. But they faced overwhelming odds and were often slaughtered. Those that did escape fled to the forests and formed resistance groups. Sometimes they were helped by the locals, sometimes they were betrayed. There are even a few examples of German soldiers helping them.

They blew up railway lines and attacked German soldiers, but the Germans took terrible revenge, often murdering innocent people. Jews were also active in the underground groups which disrupted German communications in France as the Allies were preparing to invade in 1944.

SOURCE 27 Jewish resistance fighters in the USSR

In some GHETTOS the Jewish leaders thought that by co-operating with the Nazis and producing goods for them in their workshops they were protecting their people. In other ghettos, such as Warsaw, there were many acts of resistance.

When German troops first entered the Warsaw Ghetto in April 1943 to destroy it, to their surprise they were beaten back, although the Jews were only lightly armed (see Source 28).

SOURCE 28 The strength of the two sides

	Germans	Jews
Numbers	2100	1200
Heavy machine guns	13	0
Hand-held machine guns	69	0
Sub-machine guns	135	2
Rifles	1358	17

However, the Germans then returned with mortars (heavy guns). They shelled the buildings and burnt the apartments down block by block.

SOURCE 29 Two diary entries by one of the Jews

■ *Our brave defenders are holding out at their posts. Germans have to fight for access to each house. Gates of houses are barricaded, each house is a defensive fortress – Jewish defenders are showering missiles from flat windows.*
■ *The Germans shelled every building to rubble and then moved in to kill off or round up any survivors. However, the Jews managed to keep fighting for another month. Seven thousand Jews were killed in the fighting and about 30,000 sent to the death camps.*

There was also resistance in the camps. In Treblinka in 1943 one of the prisoners managed to get into the arsenal (weapons store), from where he handed out grenades and guns. Petrol was then put into the camp disinfector, and so when the daily disinfection took place, petrol was sprayed all over the buildings. The camp was set on fire, the arsenal exploded, fifteen guards were killed and 150 prisoners escaped. But the Germans regained control and 550 other prisoners were killed.

Resistance in the camps could take many forms. Religion was banned in the camps, but the prisoners held services in secret. There were many escapes (three from Auschwitz between 1943 and 1944). Reports of what was happening in the camps were smuggled out, despite the threat of the death penalty. Many prisoners drew pictures, made carvings and wrote about their experiences.

SOURCE 30
A drawing by a prisoner, showing prisoners in their striped uniforms being made to do knee bends to see if they are fit enough to carry on working. If not, they will be sent to the gas chambers

SOURCE 31 Watch towers and defences on the perimeter fence at Auschwitz. The fence was electrified

1. List all the different ways the Jews resisted the Nazis.
2. Why do you think some Jews decided not to resist?

Activity

Work in groups.

Using the evidence in Sources 1–31, write a dialogue between prisoners discussing whether or how they should oppose the Nazis. Consider four possible courses of action; escaping and fleeing, escaping and joining the resistance, leading an uprising in the camp or not resisting. Your teacher will help you.

Should Dresden have been bombed?

TERRIBLE things happen in wars, but it is usually understood that there are some things which are not allowed – even in war. At the end of the Second World War a number of Nazis were put on trial at Nuremberg for WAR CRIMES, including the massacre of the Jews and the U-boat campaign in the Atlantic.

Some historians have argued that the Allies also committed 'war crimes'. One example often given is the bombing of the city of Dresden, in eastern Germany, in 1945. After you have considered the evidence which follows, you will be asked whether you think this was a war crime.

Changing ideas about bombing

The Second World War was not the first war in which bombs were dropped on civilians. In 1914, during the First World War, German warships shelled the town of Scarborough and killed civilians. Later in the War the Germans used Zeppelin airships to drop bombs on Britain. Altogether, 498 civilians were killed.

Between the two world wars bombing became more deadly. During the Italian invasion of Abyssinia in 1935, Italian aircraft dropped gas bombs on unarmed tribesmen. An Italian general even claimed that airforces could win wars by themselves by dropping so many bombs on enemy cities that they would have to surrender. The British government was so worried about bombing that in the late 1930s it made plans to build a million coffins.

The first time mass bombing of a civilian target took place was in 1937, during the Spanish Civil War. German planes destroyed the town of Guernica, killing hundreds of people (see Source 2).

As you have already seen on pages 164–167, during the Second World War German planes bombed British cities. This was partly to destroy British industry, but also to frighten the British into giving in. Winston Churchill, the British Prime Minister, hit back by ordering bombing raids on German cities.

By the end of the War the bombers were powerful planes which could fly long distances with heavy loads (see Source 3).

SOURCE 3
British Stirling bombers over Lubeck in Germany. A poster produced by the British government in 1942

Heavy "Stirling" bombers raid the Nazi Baltic port of Lübeck and leave the docks ablaze

BACK THEM UP!

---

1. Use Sources 1–3 and the information above to explain how bombing changed between 1914 and 1944.

REMEMBER SCARBOROUGH!

The Germans who brag of their "CULTURE" have shown what it is made of by murdering defenceless women and children at SCARBOROUGH.

But this only strengthens

GREAT BRITAIN'S
resolve to crush the

GERMAN BARBARIANS

ENLIST NOW!

SOURCE 1
A British government poster reacting to the bombing of Scarborough in 1914

SOURCE 2 The Spanish artist Pablo Picasso painted this picture after the bombing of Guernica

British bombing tactics

> **SOURCE 4** Written by a modern historian
>
> *In 1940 Churchill believed that 'The bombers alone provide the means of victory.' He was convinced that raids of sufficient intensity could destroy Germany's morale. He planned a campaign that abandoned the accepted practice of attacking an enemy's armed forces and instead, made civilians the main target. Night after night, RAF bombers in ever-increasing numbers struck throughout Germany, usually at working-class housing because it was more densely packed.*

> **SOURCE 5** An account by an official historian appointed by the British government
>
> *Both the British and the Germans were engaged in destroying cathedrals and hospitals and killing civilians of all ages. Some of these attacks were meant for industrial and military areas. However, they also thought built-up areas were military targets and that any course of action which shortened the War was justified.*

SOURCE 6 Statistics about the bombing of Germany by the Allies

Type of target	Tons of bombs dropped during the War
Oil depots	224,000
Transport (road and rail)	319,000
Aircraft industry	57,000
German cities	674,000

Early British efforts to bomb Germany were unsuccessful. A survey made in August 1941, but not published at the time, showed that in daylight bombing more British soldiers were killed than German civilians, while night-time bombing was inaccurate: one third of the RAF bombers failed to drop their bombs, and only a third of the rest dropped them within five miles of the target.

1. What evidence is there in Sources 4–6 that civilians were the target of the British bombers?
2. What evidence is there that industry was the main target?
3. How successful does the bombing seem to have been?

Reactions to the bombing

People in Britain who had suffered most from German raids were the ones who were most opposed to raids on Germany. Not only did they not want other people to suffer as they had suffered, but they also thought that terror raids on Germany would lead to more terror raids on Britain.

SOURCE 7 A German government poster, 1942. The words read 'Blackout! The enemy sees your lights.' Goebbels, the propaganda minister, used British bombing raids to his own advantage, as a way of keeping up the Germans' hatred of the enemy

1. How does Source 7 present the British?

Bomber Harris

The failure of British bombing was reversed soon after the appointment of Sir Arthur Harris to Bomber Command in 1942. Harris believed in an all-out assault on both industrial and residential areas of German cities. Harris said at the time 'You destroy a factory and they rebuild it. I kill all their workmen and it takes 21 years to provide new ones.'

SHOULD DRESDEN HAVE BEEN BOMBED?

The bombing of Dresden

On 13–14 February 1945, when the Germans were retreating on all fronts, 805 RAF bombers dropped 2600 tons of bombs on the centre of Dresden. The weather was perfect for bombing and there was no resistance from German fighter planes or anti-aircraft guns. The bombs caused an enormous firestorm. Temperatures in places rose to about 1000°C. Between 35,000 and 150,000 people were killed, and 70 per cent of the city was destroyed.

SOURCE 8 A photograph of Dresden after the bombing

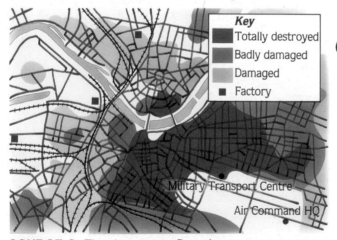

SOURCE 9 The damage to Dresden

Key
- Totally destroyed
- Badly damaged
- Damaged
- Factory

Military Transport Centre
Air Command HQ

SOURCE 10 An eye-witness account of the effects of the bombing, by a woman interviewed in 1985

I saw people clinging to the railings, burnt to cinders. I kicked what I thought was a big tree stump – but it was a person, burnt to death. There was a big heap of arms, legs, bodies, everything – I tried to piece together a leg, arm, fingers, body – to recognise one of my family – but I passed out.

Was the bombing justified?

Hitler did not surrender after the bombing. The War continued. When news of the bombing was made public there was criticism from around the world.

SOURCE 11 From a letter written by Winston Churchill to his army commanders in March 1945

It seems to me that the moment has come when the question of bombing German cities simply for the sake of increasing the terror, though under other pretexts, should be reviewed. Otherwise we shall come into control of an utterly ruined land. I feel the need for more concentration upon military targets such as oil and communications, rather than on mere acts of horror and destruction.

1. What evidence is there in Sources 8–11 about the purpose and target of the raids?

Sources 12–17 should help you decide for yourself whether the bombing of Dresden was either necessary to achieve Britain's war aims, or morally justifiable.

SOURCE 12 Written by a historian, Dr Noble Frankland, in 1985

The attack on Dresden was the product of a carefully laid plan. To understand that plan you have to look at it in the context of the War.

Every day that the War went on cost the lives of countless more Jews, Slavs and Poles. So the numbers killed at Dresden, dreadful as they were, were nothing like so dreadful as the numbers of people Hitler was killing.

The Germans already had rocket-propelled fighters and Schnorkel submarines. What other weapons might they not produce? A decisive blow was needed to end the War quickly.

SOURCE 13 From a radio broadcast by the official German foreign information services

The Americans have proved that they can hit precise targets whenever they please. It would therefore have been possible to have spared the residential districts of Dresden, and the historic town centre. The use of incendiaries [fire bombs] proves that residential districts were being deliberately attacked. It is pointless to drop incendiaries on railways.

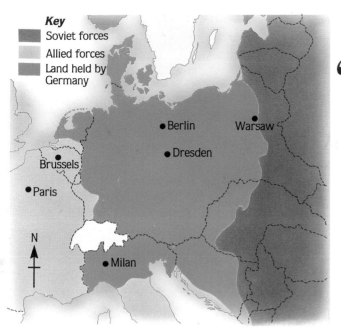

Key
- Soviet forces
- Allied forces
- Land held by Germany

Cities shown: Paris, Brussels, Berlin, Warsaw, Dresden, Milan

SOURCE 14 The state of the War just before the Dresden raids. British officials claimed that the bombing was necessary to halt German troops who were passing through Dresden on their way to fight the advancing Soviet army

SOURCE 15 From the German newspaper *Suddeutsche Zeitung*, 1953

The explanation of the Americans that Dresden was bombed, on Soviet instructions, to hinder the movement of troop reinforcements through Dresden, is a clear contradiction of the facts. It would have been simple for the RAF to have destroyed the railway between Dresden and the Czech frontier.

SOURCE 16 A statement made by a clergyman in a television programme in 1985

The raid on Dresden was a grossly immoral act. The city at the time was full of refugees. It had no military, strategic or industrial importance. It was simply bombing civilians as civilians, and that was wrong.

The government said that the military targets were being bombed. This was done in part to reassure church leaders that nothing immoral was happening. In fact, they knew civilians were being bombed.

Dresden remains as a reminder to us that in warfare we have to think very carefully about targeting. Simply to massacre is always a gross violation of the 'just war' tradition.

SOURCE 17 Written by a British historian, David Irving, in *The Destruction of Dresden*, 1963

By 12 February, with the arrival of the refugees from the East [Germans escaping from the advancing Russian army], the city was nearing its maximum population. The refugee columns poured into Dresden on foot and in horse-drawn carts.

The idea of Dresden as a target for attack came as a surprise to the RAF Command's Intelligence Staff. There was very little to show that Dresden was of much industrial importance, or that it was being used for large-scale troop movements. RAF commanders, including Harris, queried the decision. It was understood that the attack was part of a programme in which Churchill was personally interested, and that the Russians had asked for the attack. The Russians deny this.

2. Sources 12–17 provide both facts and opinions about the bombing of Dresden. Draw up two lists, one of facts, and one of opinions.
3. Is there any reason to doubt the reliability of any of these sources?

1. Work in pairs. Some pairs should collect together all the evidence from pages 196–197 that suggests Dresden was a military target. Other pairs should collect together all the evidence that suggests Dresden was not a military target.

   Which evidence is the strongest?
2. Still in pairs, prepare arguments for or against this statement: 'The Dresden raid was a criminal act of war.' Think about these points:
   ■ By the time of the Dresden raids the British knew about Hitler's slaughter of Jews, Russians and gypsies. Should German civilians have been killed in retaliation?
   ■ In a modern war should everyone who can help the enemy war effort be treated as a fair target?
   ■ Most people in Britain believed that the Second World War was 'a just war' – a war to defeat something that was evil. If the War was just, does that mean the British cannot be blamed for deaths they caused in fighting that war?
   ■ Some historians claim that as the War was nearly over and the Germans were already retreating the bombing was unnecessary.

Was the dropping of the atomic bombs justified?

Victory in Europe

ON 6 June 1944, 4000 landing craft and 600 warships carried 176,000 British, Commonwealth and North American soldiers across the English Channel. They landed at several places along the coast of Normandy. By nightfall 120,000 men were ashore. The battle to take back Europe from the Nazis had begun. By the end of July there were more than a million Allied soldiers on French soil. The Germans were fighting on two fronts, with the Soviet army advancing from the East.

By April 1945 British and American troops were within 50 miles of Berlin and Soviet troops were in the city's eastern suburbs. On 30 April, with the sound of fighting in the background, Hitler committed suicide. On 8 May Germany surrendered.

Victory in Japan

On 6 August 1945 an American bomber called the *Enola Gay* dropped the world's first atomic bomb on the Japanese city of Hiroshima. A Japanese journalist described a glaring pinkish light in the sky, which burned people's eyes out. Anyone within a kilometre of the explosion became a bundle of smoking black charcoal within seconds. Within minutes about 70,000 people were dead. Those who were still alive writhed in agony from their burns. Then there was the blast wave, which destroyed 70,000 of the city's 78,000 buildings.

Three days later the USA dropped another bomb on Nagasaki. About 36,000 people were killed. On 14 August Japan surrendered and the Second World War was finally over.

SOURCE 1 From J. Hersey's account of the effects of the bomb, published in 1946

" *Father Kleinsorge found about twenty men in the bushes. They were all in the same nightmarish state; their faces were wholly burned, their eye sockets hollow, the fluid from their melted eyes had run down their cheeks. Their mouths were mere swollen, pus-covered wounds, which they could not bear to stretch enough to admit the spout of a teapot. So Father Kleinsorge got a large piece of grass and drew out the stem so as to make a straw, and gave them all the water to drink that way.* "

SOURCE 2 A photograph of Hiroshima after the bomb

SOURCE 3 A photograph of some of the victims of the bomb

The Americans denied that radiation sickness existed and they banned other journalists from Hiroshima. However, by 1950, the number of people who had died from the Hiroshima bomb had gone up to 200,000.

---

1. Why do you think the Americans:
a) stopped letting journalists visit Hiroshima
b) denied that there was such a thing as radiation sickness?
2. Compare the effects of the atomic bombs with those of ordinary bombing (see pages 164–165 and 196–197).

SOURCE 4 An eye-witness account by a girl who was five years old at the time

The skin was burned off some of them and was hanging from their hands and from their chins.

SOURCE 5 Three weeks later a British journalist managed to get to Hiroshima. He wrote the first public account of radiation sickness. It appeared in the *Daily Express*

In Hiroshima, 30 days later, people who were not injured in the bombing are still dying mysteriously and horribly from an unknown something which I can only describe as the atomic plague.

SOURCE 6 A Japanese eye-witness account of radiation sickness

Survivors began to notice in themselves a strange form of illness. It consisted of vomiting, loss of appetite, diarrhoea with large amounts of blood, purple spots on the skin, bleeding from the mouth, loss of hair and usually death.

Why did they drop the bombs?

When Harry Truman, the American President, heard of the bombing, he said, 'This is the greatest thing in history.' Yet over 40 years later people are still dying from the effects. The results of the atomic bomb explosions were so terrible that we have to ask why the bombs were dropped when the War was almost won.

The Americans had gradually pushed the Japanese out of nearly all the land they had occupied in the Pacific region. In Europe Hitler was defeated.

So why did the Americans want to drop the bomb? Several reasons have been suggested:
■ The Americans believed that the Japanese would never surrender. If the atomic bombs had not been used hundreds of thousands of Americans could have been killed in an invasion of Japan.
■ The bomb had cost a lot of money to develop and the Americans therefore wanted to use it.
■ The bomb was used to show USA's military superiority to the USSR.
■ The Japanese had been particularly cruel to prisoners of war. Some Americans thought that the Japanese deserved to be taught a lesson.

---

1. For each of the reasons above, briefly explain whether you think that the reason justifies dropping the bombs.

WAS THE DROPPING OF THE ATOMIC BOMBS JUSTIFIED?

Look back at your answer to question 1 on the previous page. You probably decided that some of the reasons would have justified dropping the bombs, while others would not. What we can now do is look at a wide range of evidence, such as Sources 7–20, to examine these reasons in more detail.

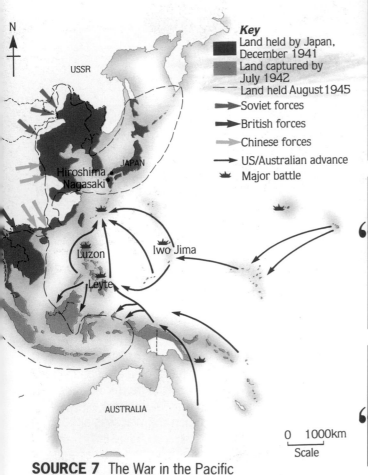

SOURCE 7 The War in the Pacific

SOURCE 8 An American report about the defences of Kyushu, a part of Japan which the Americans were planning to invade

Top priority has been given to defence. There is considerable activity in the construction of heavy artillery positions. It is probable minefields have been laid along the beaches. At the back of the beaches are hills which are heavily fortified.

SOURCE 9 From the memoirs of Harry Truman, who became American President in 1945, published in 1958

All of us realised that the fighting would be fierce and the losses heavy. General Marshall told me it might cost half a million American lives.

SOURCE 10 Extracts from a document sent by the military chiefs of the USA to the President

We should attack Kyushu on 1 November. By that time:
- *air action will have smashed every industrial target, as well as destroying huge areas in the Japanese cities*
- *the Japanese navy will be completely powerless. Casualties: These should not exceed the price we have paid for Luzon – see below.*

Battle	US casualties	Japanese casualties
Leyte	17,000	78,000
Luzon	31,000	156,000
Iwo Jima	20,000	22,000

SOURCE 11 From an interview with the secretary to the Japanese War Minister in 1963

We thought we would be able to defeat the Americans on their first landing attack. But if the Americans launched a second or third attack, first our food supply would run out, then our weapons. The Americans could have won without using atomic bombs.

SOURCE 12 From the memoirs of Admiral D. Leahy, President Truman's adviser, published in 1950

The use of this barbarous weapon was of no assistance to our war against Japan. The Japanese were already defeated.

SOURCE 13 From a speech by Japanese Prime Minister Suzuki

I expect the 100 million people of the glorious Empire [Japan] to join themselves in a shield to protect the Emperor and the Imperial land from the invader.

SOURCE 14 From an article written by Henry Stimson, the American Secretary for War, in 1947

There was no weakening in the Japanese determination to fight. The total strength of the Japanese army was about five million men. The Allies would be faced with the enormous task of destroying a force of five million men and 5000 suicide aircraft, belonging to a race which would fight to the death.

SOURCE 15 Written by Henry Stimson in 1946

A demonstration in an uninhabited area was not regarded as likely to make Japan surrender. There was the danger of the test being a dud. Also, we had no bombs to waste.

SOURCE 16 From a booklet published by the Campaign for Nuclear Disarmament in 1985

General Groves, the engineer director of the Manhatten Project, was desperate to see the fruits of his labours before the end of the War. The bomb had been developed at a cost of $2000 million. It would have been difficult to justify not using it after such a vast financial investment. Two types of bomb had been developed. Nagasaki was simply an experiment to try out the second type.

SOURCE 17 Robert Oppenheimer, director of the project which developed the atomic bomb, being questioned by the American Senate in 1954

Q: Wasn't there a particular effort to produce a bomb before the Potsdam Conference [a meeting of the Allies in July 1945]?
A: It was the intention of the President to say something about this to the Russians. The President said no more than that we had a new weapon which we planned to use in Japan, and it was very powerful. We were under incredible pressure to get it done before the conference.

SOURCE 18 A note from American nuclear scientists to the government in June 1945

A demonstration of the bomb might best be made on the desert or on a barren island. Japan could then be asked to surrender.

SOURCE 19 From an interview with James Byrnes, American Secretary of State, twenty years later

We were talking about the people who hadn't hesitated at Pearl Harbor to make a sneak attack, destroying not only ships but the lives of many American sailors.

JAPAN WAS SEEKING PEACE BEFORE THE FIRST ATOM BOMB WAS DROPPED ON HIROSHIMA, ACCORDING TO DOCUMENTS JUST LEAKED TO THE U.S. PRESS.

"DON'T YOU SEE, THEY HAD TO FIND OUT IF IT WORKED..."

SOURCE 20 A British cartoon published in 1945

Activity

You have been asked to prepare evidence for an investigation into the bombing of Hiroshima and Nagasaki, and whether it was justified. You have been given Sources 7–20.

1. What evidence do they provide for or against the view that:
   - American casualties would be heavy if the USA did not drop the bomb
   - the USA wanted to test its expensive new weapon
   - the USA wanted the USSR to see how powerful it was
   - the USA wanted to teach the Japanese a lesson?

   You might find it helpful to divide your page into four columns – one column for each reason – and list the evidence for and against in each column.

2. Looking at the evidence you have compiled, which now seems to be the main reason why the Americans used the bomb?

3. Have you changed your mind about which reasons, if any, justified the dropping of the bomb?

Churchill and Hitler as war leaders

CHURCHILL and Hitler are both famous as wartime leaders of their countries. We are going to compare them to see what makes someone a good war leader. But first let's think about the general qualities people look for in the leader of a country.

> 1. Make a list of some famous leaders today.
> 2. List words that describe a good leader.
> 3. What do you think are the two most important qualities of a good leader? Give reasons.
> 4. Do you think that wartime leaders need the qualities you have chosen or different qualities?

Churchill: the public image

Churchill was one of the fiercest opponents of Chamberlain's policy of Appeasement. When this policy failed and war broke out it was clear Britain needed a new leader. In May 1940 Churchill became Prime Minister.

Sources 1–5 show how the government wanted Churchill to be seen by the British people.

SOURCE 3 A photograph of Churchill visiting people in Manchester whose homes have been bombed

SOURCE 4
A cartoon from *Punch*, October 1941. Churchill is dressed as an air raid warden

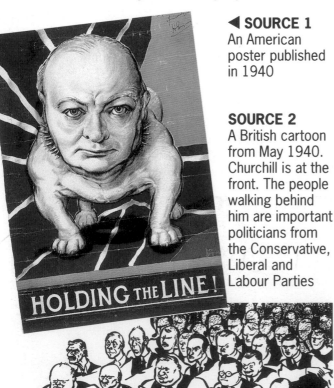

◀ **SOURCE 1**
An American poster published in 1940

SOURCE 2
A British cartoon from May 1940. Churchill is at the front. The people walking behind him are important politicians from the Conservative, Liberal and Labour Parties

HOLDING THE LINE!

"LET US GO FORWARD TOGETHER"

SOURCE 5 A government poster from 1942

> 1. Study Source 1. What were the people who saw this poster meant to feel about Churchill?
> 2. Why might Churchill have felt that Source 3 was good propaganda for him?

Hitler: the public image

The German Minister of PROPAGANDA was Goebbels. Germany's early victories in the War made it easy for him to show Hitler as a great war leader in posters and newspaper reports. But by the end of 1941, when the German army was bogged down in the USSR, Hitler was making fewer speeches and public appearances. By 1944 the German people hardly ever saw him.

SOURCE 9
A photograph of Hitler and his generals in Paris just after it had been conquered in 1940. The generals had been doubtful about Hitler's *Blitzkrieg* tactics, but he was proved right

SOURCE 6
A poster of Hitler published just before the War started

SOURCE 7
A German poster of 1939. The words say 'One people, one Empire, one leader'

Ein Volk, ein Reich, ein Führer!

SOURCE 8
A photograph taken by Goebbels' Propaganda Ministry. It shows Hitler with the paratroopers who daringly landed gliders on the roof of Fort Eben-Emael, in France, and captured it. Hitler had planned the raid

3. Study Source 6. What were people who saw this poster meant to feel about Hitler?
4. Why might Hitler have felt that the photographs in Sources 8 and 9 were good propaganda for him?

5. What overall impression do Sources 1–9 give you of a) Churchill, and b) Hitler? Choose any of the following phrases or write ones of your own:
   ■ A strong warrior
   ■ A man who is trusted by the ordinary people
   ■ A man who works well with others
   ■ An ordinary person like everyone else
   ■ A clever general

Activity

It is the winter of 1940. The Blitz has started. Britain has no allies. Some people want to give in.

Your group is in charge of British propaganda. You are artists and writers. Your job is to organise a new poster campaign with the aim of getting people to support the war effort.

1. Discuss each of the pictures of Churchill in Sources 1–5. Produce a report explaining whether each picture should be used in the campaign.
2. Write a set of instructions for your war artists, explaining what makes a good propaganda poster.
3. Produce three posters which follow the instructions. You can include Churchill if you want to.
4. Compare the different posters. Explain which one you will use.

CHURCHILL AND HITLER AS WAR LEADERS

Churchill and Hitler: the reality

Many people at the time, and more recently, have questioned the public images of these two men. Sources 10–22 give many different judgements of their strengths and weaknesses. Read them and then decide for yourself what kind of men they really were.

SOURCE 10 An account by Marion Holmes, Churchill's secretary

When Churchill took over as Prime Minister the whole place exploded. It was as if a current of electricity was let loose, not only in Number 10 itself but throughout Whitehall. We heard that elderly civil servants were seen running along the corridors.

He introduced stickers saying 'Action This Day'. I never remember being released to get to bed before 1.00 a.m. and it was more often 2.00 or 3.00 a.m.

SOURCE 11 From the diary of Robert Menzies, Australian Prime Minister. He visited Britain in 1941 and attended the War Cabinet

■ *Winston is acting as the master planner of the War without forceful Chiefs of the Armed Forces to guide him.*
■ *There is no War Cabinet, since Winston deals with the conduct of the War himself.*
■ *Winston should be at the helm, instead of touring the bombed areas, as he has been doing most of the week.*
■ *Winston is not interested in finance and agriculture. He loves war and spends hours with maps and charts. There is no proper policy for growing food.*

SOURCE 12 From a history book published in 1987

Churchill ignored the advice of the generals, and this did lead to some military disasters. He was restless for action, whatever the state of the British forces. He was incapable of seeing a whole strategical problem. His gaze always settled upon just some part of it.

But no one doubted that he was a great leader. He was a powerhouse of a man. For a while with him Britain pursued visions of glory. In Britain's desperate need he renewed her youth and strengthened her spirit.

SOURCE 13 Written by a historian, A.J.P. Taylor, to celebrate the 100th anniversary of Churchill's birth. Taylor knew Churchill after the War

Churchill often talked as if Britain might overthrow Hitler all on her own. This was a fantasy, though it was what the British people wanted.

SOURCE 14 Written by Dr Anthony Storr, a psychiatrist

When you are up against the threat of defeat, as we were, and when we were standing alone, then you have to have somebody like Churchill who isn't rational, who isn't weighing up chances soberly, but who is describing his fantasy life in his speeches and who rallies everyone round, so that people become heroes and work twice as hard.

GENTLEMEN, THE NEW CHAIRMAN, THE AMPHIBIAN SUPERMAN, FLYING-ADMIRAL-GENERAL CHURCHILL

CHIEFS OF STAFF COMMITTEE

THE HEAD MAN

SOURCE 15 A British cartoon of May 1942. The Chiefs of Staff were the heads of the armed forces

SOURCE 16 A German cartoon of September 1940 showing Churchill broadcasting confidence during the Blitz. The words read 'Everything is going well'

SOURCE 17 From *Explaining Hitler's Germany* by J. Harden and J. Farquharson, published in 1988

It is hard to find another area of German life in which Hitler took as little notice of the experts [as in military affairs]. As Goering testified at the Nuremberg War Trials, Hitler regarded both defence and foreign policy as his special field.

The belief in his own ability prevented him from taking advice from those he dismissed as 'mere experts'. Historians agree that Hitler was responsible for many of the failures of the German Army.

SOURCE 18 From a biography of Hitler by W. Carr, published in 1978

Hitler was a jack-in-the-box, who did whatever suited him, whether he was being consistent or not. This points to a great struggle taking place in Hitler's mind. His head told him Germany was bound to lose the War. His heart told him that he was a man with a mission, and that fate would protect him.

SOURCE 19 Written by a historian, Hugh Trevor-Roper, in 1961

Hitler could not face facts. He could not face the reality of the way the War was going. This is a dangerous sign at any time in a leader, but especially in time of war.

SOURCE 20
This Soviet cartoon shows Goebbels painting a picture of Hitler

SOURCE 21
This American cartoon comments on Hitler's bad judgement when he attacked the USSR. The figures represent Hitler's allies

WHO'S FOR IT THIS TIME!

SOURCE 22 A British cartoon of April 1942, after the German defeats in the USSR. It refers to Hitler's habit of always blaming someone else

1. What were Churchill's strengths and weaknesses as a war leader?
2. Taking into account Sources 17–22 and what you have learned about Hitler up to now, do you think Hitler shared the same strengths and weaknesses?
3. Do Sources 10–22 give a different impression of the men from that in Sources 1–9?

Activity
Produce a short magazine feature comparing Hitler and Churchill as leaders. You can only write 100 words on each man, and you can choose one picture for each.

Stalin and Roosevelt: friends or enemies?

THE two most powerful men in the world before, during and after the War were the leaders of the USSR and the USA, the two 'super-powers'. What kind of men were they?

Joseph Stalin (1879–1953)

Stalin was born into a poor family in Georgia, a remote region of the Russian Empire. His father was the village shoemaker and an alcoholic, who deserted the family. So Stalin's mother had to bring him up by herself. She took in washing and baked bread to earn enough money.

SOURCE 1 Stalin's family lived in huts like these

During his childhood Stalin suffered from smallpox and other diseases, which left his face pock-marked and his left arm useless.

He attended school and a training college for priests. Here he got involved in SOCIALIST activities and was thrown out. He became an outlaw, organised bank raids and spent much time in prison.

He did not play a leading part in the Communist Revolution of 1917. He was not a good public speaker and was not well known by the public. However, as General Secretary of the Communist Party he schemed and plotted his way to power. By 1928 he was DICTATOR of the USSR. He ruled by fear and terror. He had opponents and critics murdered and hundreds of thousands of people sent to labour camps.

When Stalin came to power the USSR was still a backward country. Through his 'Five Year Plans' (targets for what industry should be producing at the end of every five years) he greatly expanded the USSR's industries. He also forced peasants off their own farms to work together on collective farms. As many as ten million peasants were forced to move, and many starved or froze to death.

He wanted to spread Communism to other countries, and he particularly hated Fascism. Even so, in 1939 he signed a pact with Hitler.

But in 1941 the USSR was invaded by Germany, and was in danger of being defeated. Stalin had to organise and inspire his people to defend their country. The capital, Moscow, was almost captured by the Germans, but Stalin refused to run away and stayed in the city throughout the War. For three years the USSR had to stand up to German power almost single-handed. The Soviet people suffered terribly, but they stood firm.

SOURCE 2 From a speech by Stalin to the Soviet people in July 1942

Not a single step backward. You have to fight to your last drop of blood to defend every position, every foot of Soviet territory.

SOURCE 3 An American historian's view of Stalin's wartime leadership

Stalin did not leave Moscow. His nerve did not break. Despite appeals from generals he held back enough of his troops to mount a counter-attack. Stalin himself never went to the front. He exercised control by appointing and moving generals, and he supervised all major operations.

What can we say of Stalin as a war leader? He held firmly the reins of military leadership. He encouraged a revival of nationalism among the Russian people and held fast to his basic idea, which was to grind the Germans down – despite millions of Russians dying in the process.

SOURCE 4 Stalin in one of his favourite poses

Franklin D. Roosevelt (1882–1945)

Roosevelt came from a rich New York family. He went to a private school and to university and then became a successful lawyer.

In 1910 he entered politics as a Senator (government representative) for New York. In 1921 he was paralysed by polio. He fought back bravely against the illness and perhaps because of it became more understanding of the sufferings of other people.

In 1933 he became President. The USA was in an economic crisis, with much unemployment and poverty. Roosevelt was an excellent public speaker. His optimism and high spirits gave hope to people. He believed in the 'American dream' – that anyone who worked hard enough could become rich. Even more importantly, his POLICIES rescued America. He brought in unemployment benefits and paid unemployed men to work on big STATE building projects, such as roads and dams. He became very popular and he was re-elected as President three times.

When the War started the American people did not want to get involved, but Roosevelt was determined that Fascism had to be defeated. He placed trade SANCTIONS on Japan and supplied Britain with weapons and food. He was afraid of Communism, but respected the suffering and efforts of the Soviet people during the War. In 1941 he sent weapons and food to the USSR.

SOURCE 7 A photograph of Roosevelt in about 1938

SOURCE 8 An American historian's view of Roosevelt

66 *Russia urged the Allies to take pressure off Russia by attacking the Germans in Western Europe. Roosevelt wanted to do this, but was persuaded by Churchill that the Allies were not ready. This amount of give and take, this high degree of co-operation was essential to the final victory.*

Roosevelt put General Eisenhower in command of American troops in Europe. Eisenhower was a first-rate military planner. He got on well with all kinds of people. 99

1. Compare the personal backgrounds of Stalin and Roosevelt. What were the main differences and the main similarities?
2. Find one similarity and one difference between their styles of leadership.
3. Although the beliefs of CAPITALIST and Communist countries are opposed to one another, Roosevelt and Stalin got on well together when they met at the Yalta conference in January 1945. Why do you think this was?

SOURCE 5 From a speech by Roosevelt in January 1939, before the war in Europe had started

66 *There comes a time in the affairs of men when they must be prepared to defend not only their homes alone but the principles of faith and humanity on which their civilisations are founded.* 99

SOURCE 6 From a speech by Roosevelt about Lend–Lease in 1940

66 *Our country is going to be the arsenal [weapons store] of democracy.* 99

1. We have studied the roles of four wartime leaders: Hitler, Churchill, Stalin and Roosevelt. Think back over the events of the Second World War. It may help if you look at the timeline on pages 150–151. For each leader choose two events which he might think of as his greatest and worst moments of the War.

A better world?

The Allies fall out

The Allies had been united while they faced a single enemy. But would they remain allies after the War? Remember that Britain and the USA were DEMOCRATIC countries, whereas the USSR was a COMMUNIST country. Both sides were supicious of each other. As you can see from Source 1, problems began even before the War was over.

Agreement at Yalta

On Germany

■ The Allies' agreed aim was 'to ensure Germany will never again be able to destroy the peace of the world'.

■ Germany would be disarmed and divided into four sectors. These would be run by Britain, France, the USSR and the USA. Berlin would also be divided into four zones, although it would be inside the USSR's part of Germany.

■ Germany would have to pay compensation for all the damage done during the War. Much of this compensation would go to the USSR.

On Eastern Europe

■ The countries of Eastern Europe which had been conquered by Germany and were now under Soviet control should be free to elect governments of their own choice.

■ The USSR was given some land from Poland, and Poland was given some land from Germany. Any German-speaking people in these areas would be moved into the new Germany.

The United Nations

■ An international organisation to keep the peace would be set up.

SOURCE 1 The Allies fall out

1 1941-44 The Soviet people suffer terrible losses fighting against the German invasion. Stalin asks the USA and Britain to help by invading France so that the Germans have to fight on two fronts. They refuse. They delay the invasion until June 1944. Until then the USSR takes on Germany alone.

We've been starving for over two years. Why won't the British and the USA help us?

2 February 1945. Germany is invaded from east and west. Churchill is worried that if the Soviet army gets to Berlin first the USSR will be in a strong position in the peace talks. He wants to race the Soviet army to Berlin but the Americans refuse.

BERLIN
GERMANY
FRANCE

3 February 1945 Roosevelt, Stalin and Churchill meet at Yalta. The three leaders have worked closely together throughout the War and get on well. There is much agreement.

4 March 1945 Roosevelt dies. The new President, Truman, is much more suspicious of Stalin.

The Communists will take over the whole of Eastern Europe if we let them!

USSR
POLAND
CZECHOSLOVAKIA
GERMANY
BERLIN

5 July 1945. Stalin, Truman and a new British Prime Minister, Atlee, meet at Potsdam. They have not worked together before. There is much suspicion. They disagree over Eastern Europe, especially Poland, where the Communists are still in power.

Disagreement at Potsdam

The Western Allies (Britain, France and the USA) did not think that the Yalta agreement on Eastern Europe had been put into action.

■ Free elections had not been held in Poland. A Communist government had been set up.

■ It was clear that the countries in Eastern Europe would be under Soviet control, and run by Communists.

■ Many of the German-speaking peoples of Eastern Europe were fleeing from Soviet rule. The USSR did not want them, and so the Western Allies had to agree to them coming to Germany.

6 August 1945. America drops an atomic bomb on Japan. Some people think this is done to show off American strength to the USSR. The USSR begin to develop an atom bomb.

7 1947. Truman is worried that Greece and Turkey are falling under Communist influence. He sends aid to support the non-Communist governments.

MARSHALL AID

8 1947. The USA gives aid (Marshall Aid) to European countries to help them rebuild. When the government of Czechoslovakia accepts American help the Communists seize power and the country comes under Soviet influence.

> We wanted that money to protect Czechoslovakia from Communism!

9 1948. The Western Allies plan to combine their three 'sectors' to create a new West German state. The USSR is furious. Stalin closes the roads and railways that link West Berlin with Western Germany. The Americans and British have to fly all supplies into West Berlin for 318 days before the USSR stops the blockade.

BERLIN

EAST GERMANY

WEST GERMANY

1. Look at the events in the cartoon strip. Choose three which you think harmed the relationship between Britain, America and the USSR.
2. Explain how each one made relations worse.

A BETTER WORLD?

Now let's look more closely at these events and try to see them through the eyes of the two sides.

Soviet attitudes

> **SOURCE 2** From a speech by Stalin in March 1946
>
> *The following should not be forgotten. The Germans made their invasion of the USSR through Poland, Rumania, Bulgaria and Hungary. They were able to do this because these countries had governments hostile to the Soviet Union. The Soviet Union's loss of life in the War has been several times greater than that of Britain and the USA put together. The Soviet Union, anxious for its future safety, is trying to see that these countries have governments friendly to the Soviet Union. How can anyone, who is not mad, describe these peaceful hopes as a desire to expand our power?*

Do not sow seed. I will sell you maize.

Do not build new shipyards. I will sell you old ones cheaply.

Why do you want to strengthen your currency? Why don't you try mine?

Is it difficult to carry out your policy? Carry out ours!

SOURCE 3 A cartoon showing the Soviet view of American foreign policy and the Marshall Plan in particular

---

1. Why do you think there was so much disagreement between the USSR and the West? Use Sources 1–6 to support your answer.

Western attitudes

> **SOURCE 4** From a speech by President Truman after the conference at Potsdam, 1945
>
> *Force is the only thing the Russians understand. Stalin is planning world conquest.*

> **SOURCE 5** From a speech by Winston Churchill in March 1946
>
> *An iron curtain has descended across Europe. Behind that line all the countries and peoples of Central and Eastern Europe lie under Soviet control.*
>
> *In a great number of countries throughout the world, Communist supporters work in obedience to the directions they received from Moscow. What Russia desires is the expansion of her power.*

" WHO'S NEXT TO BE LIBERATED FROM FREEDOM, COMRADE ?"

SOURCE 6 A cartoon showing the Western view of Soviet foreign policy

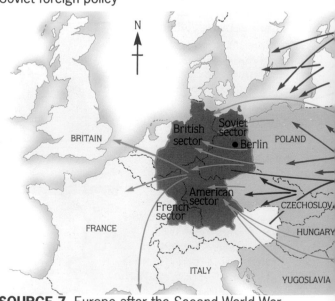

SOURCE 7 Europe after the Second World War, showing movements of refugees

The refugees

After the Second World War, unlike after the First World War, no new countries were created, and no countries disappeared. The main changes of borders were in Poland (see Source 7). However, beneath the surface there were enormous changes. People were moved instead of frontiers.

As the Soviet armies moved westwards towards Germany in 1945, they took their revenge on the many Germans living in Eastern Europe. Many were killed, many fled. When new governments were set up, such as the Communist government in Poland, they began to persecute and expel Germans. The result was that between 1945 and 1947 sixteen million Germans either fled to Germany of their own accord or were forced to go. But they were going to a Germany which was in ruins, with no food, no jobs and no industry. (The Soviet army was busy dismantling German factories and machines in the Soviet sector and carrying them off to the USSR.) About two million of these REFUGEES died.

SOURCE 8
A photograph of German refugees from Eastern Europe

SOURCE 9 An account of the refugees written by a British journalist in November 1945

Millions of Germans are now on the move. Groups of 1000 to 5000 will take to the road, trek hundreds of miles, and lose half their numbers by death through disease or exhaustion. The roadsides are dotted with graves. Children have arrived in Berlin looking like creatures from the concentration camps.

One train from Danzig [in Poland] started with 325 patients and orphans. They were packed into five cattle trucks, with nothing to cover the floors. There were no doctors or nurses. About 50 died during the journey. The bodies were simply thrown out of the train. When the train arrived in Berlin, 65 of them had to be removed to hospital, nine of them died.

Another group had been travelling in open cattle trucks for eighteen days – 2400 set out, 1050 died on the way.

Other groups of refugees included the Jews who had been freed from the extermination camps, but who had no homes or families. Many of them wanted to emigrate to Palestine, the area of the world where Jews originally came from. But Britain, which was in charge of Palestine at the time, tried to prevent this. In 1947 the ship *Exodus*, carrying 4500 Jews from the extermination camps, was rammed by a British warship as it tried to get to Palestine. The passengers were returned to refugee camps in Germany. But in 1948 Jews in Palestine set up the Jewish state of Israel. This made it much easier for Jews to go and live there. In 1949 a quarter of a million Jews emigrated there.

There were also the Cossacks

from the south of the USSR, who so hated Communism that they had fought on the German side. The British captured many of them and agreed to return them to the Soviets, who massacred many of them and sent the rest to labour camps.

1. Why were the Germans living in the USSR and Eastern Europe so afraid of the Soviet armies?
2. What is your opinion of British POLICY towards Jewish refugees trying to reach Palestine after the War?
3. Do you think people should be allowed to live in any country they like?

Key

Countries which became Communist 1945–48
German refugees
Baltic refugees
Russians
Polish refugees
Czechs
Prisoners of war

USSR

A BETTER WORLD?

The United Nations

In 1945 representatives from 50 countries met in San Francisco to set up the United Nations (the UN). This was designed to replace the League of Nations. The League had failed. Could the United Nations be more successful?

SOURCE 10 An extract from the UN Charter

> *We, the peoples of the United Nations, determined to save succeeding generations from the scourge of war, which twice in our lifetime has brought untold sorrow to mankind...*

The Charter also said that the UN would only use force for the common good, and that it would not interfere in the internal affairs of any of its members.

HISTORY DOESN'T REPEAT ITSELF

SOURCE 12 A British cartoon comparing the League of Nations and the United Nations

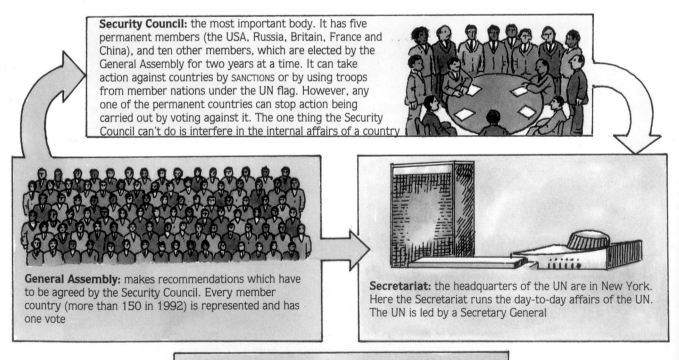

Security Council: the most important body. It has five permanent members (the USA, Russia, Britain, France and China), and ten other members, which are elected by the General Assembly for two years at a time. It can take action against countries by SANCTIONS or by using troops from member nations under the UN flag. However, any one of the permanent countries can stop action being carried out by voting against it. The one thing the Security Council can't do is interfere in the internal affairs of a country

General Assembly: makes recommendations which have to be agreed by the Security Council. Every member country (more than 150 in 1992) is represented and has one vote

Secretariat: the headquarters of the UN are in New York. Here the Secretariat runs the day-to-day affairs of the UN. The UN is led by a Secretary General

Other bodies: the United Nations Educational, Scientific and Cultural Organisation (UNESCO), and the United Nations International Children's Emergency Fund (UNICEF) were set up to help provide education around the world and to help refugees.

SOURCE 11 The organisation of the United Nations

SOURCE 13
Two British cartoons about the membership of the Security Council, both published in 1945

A

B

1. Look at Source 13. These cartoons were drawn by the same person. Do the two cartoons agree in their view of the United Nations?

SOURCE 14 Extracts from UN's Universal Declaration of Human Rights. All countries joining the United Nations have to sign this declaration

❝
■ *All human beings are born free and equal in rights. They should act towards one another in a spirit of brotherhood.*
■ *Everyone has the right to life, liberty and freedom from fear and violence.*
■ *Everyone has the right to protection of the law without discrimination.*
■ *No one shall be subjected to arbitrary arrest and everyone has the right to a fair trial.*
■ *No one shall be held in slavery.*
■ *No one shall be subjected to torture or to cruel, inhuman or degrading punishment.*
■ *Everyone has the right to seek and to enjoy in other countries asylum [shelter] from persecution.*
■ *Adult men and women have the right to marry, regardless of their race and religion.*
❞

Since it was set up the UN has been involved in many disputes. Troops are sometimes sent to a country to fight under the UN flag; for example in 1950 UN troops fought successfully against the invasion of South Korea by North Korea. At other times UN troops have been used to try and keep the peace by keeping the two sides apart, but not doing any actual fighting. In 1992 peace-keeping forces were sent to the disintegrating Yugoslavia to fulfil this role and to help provide food and medicine for the civilians.

2. Do you think that some of the rights in Source 14 are more important than others?

Activity 2
Choose one of the following tasks.
A. You can probably see how the experiences of many people during the Second World War helped shape the Declaration of Human Rights.
Turn back to pages 122–123 on life in Nazi Germany. It is 1938. You have been sent to make a report on whether the German government allows people in Germany their basic human rights. You might want to use some of the points in Source 14 as headings for your report.
B. Look at events which have been happening around the world recently. Can you find any examples of these promises being broken? Can you find any examples of the UN enforcing any of the rights?

Activity 1
You are representing your country at the meeting in San Francisco in 1945. You are holding a press conference. What would be your answers to these questions:
■ Why has the UN been set up?
■ Why will the UN be more successful than the League of Nations?

Glossary

abolitionist   person who campaigned for the abolition of slavery

Allies   usually used in Britain to mean Britain and its allies. In the First World War these were France, Russia (until 1917) and the USA (from 1917). In the Second World War they were France (until 1940), the USSR and the USA (both from 1941)

apprentice   a young person who is learning a trade by working alongside an expert, usually for a set period of time at low wages

capitalist   with an economic system based on individual **investors** making profits

census   an official count of the population, carried out every ten years. It includes details on every member of a household, e.g. name, age, occupation and place of birth

Chartists   a group who demanded reform of the voting system between 1837 and 1848. They were called Chartists after their six-point charter, or list of demands

colony   a country which is run by the government of another country. Officials and many inhabitants often come from the 'mother country'

Communist   part of a political system where all property is owned by the **state** and people are paid by the state according to their needs

conscription   a law that forces all men (and sometimes women) to join the armed forces if and when they are needed

controversial   something which people do not agree about, which causes a lot of debate or argument

democracy   a system of government where the whole population has the right to vote for government representatives from several political parties

dictatorship   a system of government where one person or political party runs the country without holding free elections, and where no opposition is allowed

Domestic System   the main system of making goods before the **Industrial Revolution**, where people worked in their homes or in small workshops rather than in factories. They might be employed by a large company which used many home workers scattered around the countryside

enclosure   the process of dividing up open or common land, farmed in strips, into small **enclosed** fields owned by individuals

enlightened   someone who is well informed, without prejudices

evacuate   to move people out of a danger area

Fascist   a person or political party with extreme right-wing views, often including racism, nationalism and complete obedience to authority

ghetto   an enclosed part of a city where Jews had to live

industrialist   a factory owner or other business person

Industrial Revolution   the name given to the rapid development of Britain's industries in the late eighteenth and early nineteenth centuries

inflation   a rise in prices

internment   imprisoning people who come from an enemy country, without trial, to stop them spying, etc.

invest   to pay money for the development of a project, or into a company, e.g. to buy machinery or supplies. The **investor** will then receive a share of any profits made

isolationist   deliberately keeping out of the affairs or disputes of other countries to avoid trouble

joint-stock company   a company owned by a number of people, who have all **invested** money in it, e.g. by buying **shares**, and who all receive a share of any profits

Lend–Lease   an arrangement by which the USA 'loaned' weapons and supplies to Britain and the USSR, in return for the use of British air bases. In practice, the loan became a gift

manufacturer   a factory owner, somebody who produces goods

Marshall Plan   the scheme by which the USA gave money (Marshall Aid) to European countries to help them rebuild after the Second World War

policy   a course of action deliberately followed by a government. Economic policy is the way a government manages the country's money

propaganda   information which is spread by a government to influence people's opinions

rationing   giving every person a fixed official amount of certain sorts of food, fuel or clothing, when they are in short supply

raw materials   usually natural materials, e.g. coal, iron ore, cotton, which have to be turned into finished goods in a factory

rearmament   building up a new store of weapons, or replacing old weapons with better ones

refugee   a person who has to leave their home because of war or persecution and tries to find shelter in another country

reparations   money that Germany was ordered to pay as compensation to the Allies by the Treaty of Versailles in 1919

return   the share of profits received by an investor in return for money put into a company. 'A good return on an investment' would be a large amount of money received as profit in relation to the size of the investment

rotten borough   a borough (town) which had the right to elect an MP to Parliament, but which by 1832 had very few or no voters

sanctions   a punishment given to a country for breaking an international agreement. Economic sanctions usually involve other countries refusing to export or import certain goods to or from the country being punished

shares   if the owners of a company want to raise money, they can sell shares in the company to members of the public (**investors**). These investors then own the company between them, which in practice means that they receive a share of the profits

socialist   a person who believes that the community as a whole should own businesses, rather than individuals

Soviet   belonging to the USSR (the Union of Soviet Socialist Republics)

state   a country, or the government of a country. A state school, for example, is one that is run by the government

Tories   the party in Parliament in the eighteenth and nineteenth centuries which supported the established religious and political system

Triple Alliance   the alliance between Germany, Italy and Austria–Hungary, made in 1852 and lasting until the end of the First World War. They promised to help each other if any of them was attacked

Triple Entente   the alliance between Britain, France and Russia between 1907 and 1917. They promised to help each other if any of them was attacked

turnpike trust   a group of business people who **invested** money to build roads called turnpikes. They built gates on the roads where travellers had to pay a toll in order to use the road

war crimes   actions taken during a war which are considered unnecessarily cruel or violent in relation to the military benefits gained, if any. Often war crimes are committed against civilians or prisoners of war

Whigs   the party in Parliament in the eighteenth and nineteenth centuries which in general was more in favour of reform

Index

M

Mahomed, Sake Deen 60–1
Manchester 34–9
Manchuria 146–7
match workers 98–9, 100
medicine 2, 4, 6
Merthyr Tydfil 56–9
Mussolini, Benito 119, 143–5

N

Nagasaki 198–9
Nazi Party *see* Germany; Hitler
Nazi–Soviet Pact 130, 138–9
New Lanark 16, 20–1
Newport 95
Norfolk 29
North Africa 183–4

O

overcrowding *see* living conditions
Owen, Robert 20–1

P

Parliament 86–7
   reform 88–91, 92–5, 100–1
Pearl Harbor 180–1
pilots 162–3
Poland 125, 130–1
political reform 86–95, 100–1
politics 3, 5, 7, 86–7
Poor Law (1834) 53, 76, 93, 96
popular culture 62–3, 102–3
popular protest movements 100–1
   Captain Swing 53
   Chartists 92–5
   dockers 99
   match workers 98–9
   Rebecca Riots 96–7
   trade unions 21
population 2, 4, 6, 46

R

racism 60, 74–5
railways 5, 6–7, 36–9, 41, 62–3
rationing 170–1, 174
raw materials 30–1, 46
Rebecca Riots 96–7, 100
reform
   factories 80–1
   political 86–95, 100–1

Reform Act (1832) 90–1
refugees 211
   see also civilians
Rhineland 125, 127, 144
roads 3, 5, 32–3, 40
   see also turnpike trusts
Roosevelt, Franklin D. 207
   see also USA
Russia 110–13, 115, 118
   see also USSR

S

sailors 177–9
schools 3, 5, 7, 54
Scotland 16, 20–1
Second World War 150–1
   causes 124–49
   battles 158–63, 172–81
   aftermath 208–13
Shaftesbury, Lord 80–1
Sharp, Granville 82
slavery 42–4, 70–4
   abolition 82–5
Soho Works 22–5
soldiers
   in First World War 114–5
   in Second World War 158–61,
   172–3, 183–5
spinning *see* textiles
Stalin, Joseph 118–9, 206
   see also USSR
steam power 2, 4, 6, 22–5, 38–9
Stephenson, George 36–9
Sudetenland 125, 129

T

textiles 12–15, 48–9
   working conditions 16–21
Townshend, Lord 28
trade 42–5, 47
trade unions 21, 100–1
transport 3, 5, 6, 47
   canals 34–5, 36, 40
   railways 36–9, 41, 62–3
   rivers and sea 32, 40
   roads 32–3, 40
Treaty of Versailles 116–7, 136–7
Tull, Jethro 28
turnpike trusts 3, 5, 33, 96–7

U

Union of Soviet Socialist Republics *see*
   USSR
United Nations 212–3
United States of America *see* USA
universities 3, 5, 7
USA 115, 147, 208–11
   Treaty of Versailles 116
   isolationism 140–1
   attack on Pearl Harbor 180–1
   treatment of Japanese Americans
   182
   atomic bomb 198–201
   see also Roosevelt, Franklin D.
USSR 125
   rise of dictatorship 118–9
   pact with Germany 130, 138–9
   invasion by Germany 172–5, 183
   after Second World War 208–11
   see also Russia; Stalin, Joseph

V

values 64–9
Versailles, Treaty of 116–7, 136–7
Victorian values *see* values

W

Wales 56–9, 96–7
Watt, James 22–5
weaving *see* textiles
Wedgwood, Josiah 9, 83
Wilberforce, William 82–3
women
   in the Industrial Revolution 80–1,
   98–9
   in World War II 168–9
workhouses 76–9
working conditions
   agriculture 52–5
   coal mines 80–1
   Domestic System 16, 48–9
   iron industry 57
   match factories 98–9
   textile mills 16–21
World War I *see* First World War
World War II *see* Second World War

Acknowledgements

Every effort has been made to trace copyright holders; if any remain unacknowledged, the publishers will be pleased to rectify this.

Illustrations by David Anstey; Art Construction; Peter Bull Art Studio; Sean Humphries; Steve Smith.

Photographs reproduced by kind permission of:
Cover: *left* Hulton Deutsch Collection; *right* Popperfoto. **p.1** Hulton Deutsch Collection. **p.2** *top* Leeds Central Library; *centre* Bridgeman Art Library/British Library; *bottom* Hulton Deutsch Collection. **p.3** *top and centre* Bridgeman Art Library/Guidhall Library, Corporation of London; *bottom* Tate Gallery, London. **p.4** *top and bottom right* Mansell Collection; *bottom left* Hulton Deutsch Collection. **p.5** *top* Borough of Darlington Art Collections; *bottom left and right* Mansell Collection. **p.6** *centre right* Leeds Central Library; *centre left* University of Reading, Rural History Centre; *bottom* The Furness Museum, Barrow-in-Furness. **p.7** *top* Hulton Deutsch Collection; *bottom left* Mansell Collection; *bottom right* Bridgeman Art Library/Guildhall Library, Corporation of London. **p.8** *top and centre* Hulton Deutsch Collection; *bottom* Mansell Collection. **p.9** *centre left* By Courtesy of the Trustees of the Wedgwood Museum, Stoke-on-Trent; *bottom* Bridgeman Art Library/Private Collection; *centre right* E. T. Archive. **p.11** *both* Ironbridge Gorge Museum Trust. **p.12** *top* Bridgeman Art Library/Philip Mould Historical Portraits Ltd, London. **p.13** *bottom* Mary Evans Picture Library. **p.14** *top* Private Collection; *bottom* Andy Reid. **p.17** *top* Manchester Central Library; *centre left* Mary Evans Picture Library; *centre right and bottom* Mansell Collection. **p.18** Mansell Collection. **p.20** *all* Mansell Collection. **p.22** *both* Birmingham Museums and Art Gallery (with thanks to Rita Maclean). **p.28** *top* Mansell Collection; *bottom* University of Reading, Rural History Centre. **p.29** University of Reading, Rural History Centre. **p.31** *top left* Ironbridge Gorge Museum Trust; *top right* E. T. Archive; *centre* Bridgeman Art Library/Guildhall Library, Corporation of London; *bottom left* Bridgeman Art Library/Science Museum, London; *bottom right* By Courtesy of the Post Office. **p.32** *all* Mansell Collection. **p.35** *top* Mansell Collection. **p.38** Hulton Deutsch Collection. **p.39** *top* Mansell Collection; *bottom* Hulton Deutsch Collection. **p.41** Bridgeman Art Library/Royal Holloway and Bedford New College, Surrey. **p.45** Guildhall Library, Corporation of London. **p.48** *top* Peter Newark's Historical Pictures; *bottom left* Mansell Collection; *bottom right* B. T. Batsford. **p.49** *top* National Museums and Galleries on Merseyside, Walker Art Gallery; *centre* Mansell Collection; *bottom* The Salvation Army. **p.51** *all* Mrs P.M. Reid. **p.52** *centre and bottom* Mary Evans Picture Library. **p.53** Mansell Collection. **p.55** *bottom left* University of Reading, Rural History Centre; *bottom right* Hulton Deutsch Collection. **p.56** Cyfartha Castle Museum and Art Gallery, Merthyr Tydfil. **p.57** *left* Glamorgan Record Office; *right* Welsh Industrial and Maritime Museum. **p.58** *both* Welsh Folk Museum. **p.59** *top left and bottom* Welsh Folk Museum; *top right* Fotomas Index. **p.60** *top* Mary Evans Picture Library; *bottom left and right* East Sussex County Library. **p.61** *top and bottom left* East Sussex County Library; *right* Mary Evans Picture Library. **p.62** *top* Hulton Deutsch Collection; *centre top and centre bottom* East Sussex County Library; *bottom* Mansell Collection. **p.63** *top* Mary Evans Picture Library; *centre left* Bridgeman Art Library/Birmingham City Museums and Art Gallery; *centre right* East Sussex County Library; *bottom* Punch Library. **p.64** *top* Network Photographers/John Sturrock; *bottom* Bridgeman Art Library/Harrogate Museums and Art Gallery, N. Yorkshire. **p.65** Manchester Art Gallery. **p.66** *bottom* Tate Gallery, London. **p.67** Norfolk Museums Service. **p.68** Bridgeman Art Library/Guildhall Library, Corporation of London. **p.69** *all* E. T. Archive. **p.70** *top and bottom* Mansell Collection; *centre* Fotomas Index. **p.72** *top* Wilberforce House Museum, Hull City Museums and Art Gallery; *bottom* Mansell Collection. **p.73** *top* Fotomas Index; *centre* Mansell Collection; *bottom* Bridgeman Art Library/British Library. **p.74** *both* Bridgeman Art Library/British Library. **p.75** *top* Mary Evans Picture Library; *bottom* The Bodleian Library, University of Oxford. **p.77** *top* Mansell Collection. **p.78** *top left* Mansell Collection. **p.80** Mansell Collection. **p.83** *top left* By Courtesy of the Trustees of the Wedgwood Museum, Stoke-on-Trent; *top right and bottom* Fotomas Index; *centre* Mary Evans Picture Library. **p.84** Bridgeman Art Library/Royal Albert Memorial Museum, Exeter. **p.86** *top* Rex Features; *bottom* Frank Spooner Pictures. **p.87** *top* Bridgeman Art Library/Sir John Soane Museum, London; *bottom* Mansell Collection. **p.89** *top and bottom* Fotomas Index; *centre* E.T. Archive. **p.90** *top* Mansell Collection; *bottom* Bristol Museums and Art Gallery. **p.91** Mansell Collection. **p.92** *top* Communist Party Picture Library; *bottom* Mansell Collection. **p.93** *top* Mary Evans Picture Library; *centre* Mansell Collection; *bottom* The Royal Archives © 1993 Her Majesty the Queen. **p.94** British Library. **p.95** *top* Hulton Deutsch Collection; *bottom* Mansell Collection. **p.96** *top* Mansell Collection; *bottom right* National Library of Wales. **p.98** *top* Mary Evans Picture Library; *centre* Hackney Archives; *bottom* Mansell Collection. **p.99** Mansell Collection. **p.101** *top and bottom* Mansell Collection; *centre* Bridgeman Art Library/Trades Union Congress. **p.102** *top* Museum of London; *centre* Greater London Photograph Library. **p.103** *top left* Bridgeman Art Library/Museum of London; *top right* Mary Evans Picture Library; *bottom left* Greater London Photograph Library; *bottom right* E.T. Archive. **p.104** Mansell Collection. **p.106** *top left* Bridgeman Art Library/ Wallington Hall, Northumberland; *top right and top centre* Mansell Collection; *bottom centre* Bridgeman Art Library/By Courtesy of the Trustees of the V&A; *bottom left* Bridgeman Art Library/Guildhall Library, Corporation of London; *bottom* Ironbridge Gorge Museum Trust. **p.107** *top left* Public Record Office; *top right* Columbia Pictures; *centre right* Ronald Grant Archive; *bottom* John Townson. **p.109** Popperfoto. **p.111** *bottom* Imperial War Museum, London. **pp.114–5** Imperial War Museum, London. **p.116** Imperial War Museum, London. **p.119** *top* Novosti (London); *bottom right* Mary Evans Picture Library. **p.120** Hulton Deutsch Collection; *bottom* Suddeutscher Verlag. **p.121** Suddeutscher Verlag. **p.122** *top* Ullstein; *centre* British Library of Political and Economic Science; *bottom* Bundesarchiv, Koblenz. **p.123** *top left* Bildarchiv Preussischer Kulturbesitz; *top right* Ullstein; *bottom* Wiener Library, London. **p.124** Popperfoto. **p.126** *left* Wiener Library, London; *right* Bildarchiv Preussischer Kulturbesitz. **p.127** *left* Los Angeles Times; *right* E.T. Archive. **p.128** *top left* Hulton Deutsch Collection; *top right* Simplicissimus; *bottom* Mansell Collection. **p.129** *top left* News of the World/News Group Newspapers; *right* Völkischer Beobachter. **p.130** *top* Ullstein; *bottom left* Evening Standard/Solo. **p.131** Daily Express/Express Newspapers plc. **p.133** *top* Mansell Collection; *bottom* Evening Standard/Solo. **p.134** Hulton Deutsch Collection. **p.135** *top* Daily Worker; *centre* Evening Standard/Solo; *bottom* Hulton Deutsch Collection. **p.136** *top* Mary Evans Picture Library; *bottom* Simplicissimus. **p.137** *top* Daily Herald/News Group Newspapers; *bottom* Daily Express/Express Newspapers plc. **p.138** Evening Standard/Solo. **p.139** *bottom* Evening Standard/Solo. **p.140** Chicago Tribune. **p.141** Mansell Collection. **p.142** *left* Hulton Deutsch Collection. **p.144** *both* Associated Press, London. **p.145** *left* Simplicissimus; *right* Evening Standard/Solo. **p.147** Associated Press, London; *bottom left* Simplicissimus; *bottom right* Evening Standard/Solo. **p.152** *top* Topham; *bottom left and right* Imperial War Museum, London. **pp.154-5** *all* Hulton Deutsch Collection. **p.156** Topham. **p.157** *left* Giles/Express Newspapers plc; *right* Imperial War Museum, London. **pp.158-9** *top and bottom* Imperial War Museum, London. **p.160** Evening Standard/Solo. **p.163** *top* Hulton Deutsch Collection; *bottom* Topham. **p.165** Hulton Deutsch Collection. **p.166** *top left* Topham; *top right* Popperfoto; *centre and bottom right* Hulton Deutsch Collection; *bottom left* Centre for the Study of Cartoons and Caricature/Express Newspapers plc. **p.167** Imperial War Museum, London; *centre* Popperfoto; *bottom right* Noreen Branson. **p.168** *top* Mary Evans Picture Library; *centre* Public Record Office; *bottom right* Popperfoto. **p.169** *left* Popperfoto; *right* E.T. Archive. **p.170** Giles/Express Newspapers plc. **p.171** *left* Daily Mail/John Frost Historical Newspapers; *right* Imperial War Museum, London. **p.173** *top* David King Collection; *centre* Evening Standard/Solo; *bottom* St Louis Post-Dispatch; **pp.174-5** *bottom* Itar-Tass News Agency. **p.175** *top* David King Collection; *centre* Evening Standard/Solo. **p.179** *left* US Coast Guard. **p.177** *bottom* and **p.178** Ullstein. **p.179** *left* Imperial War Museum, London; *right* John Hamilton/Imperial War Museum, London. **p.181** *top* E.T. Archive; *bottom* National Maritime Museum, Greenwich. **p.182** Photri. **p.183** Novosti Photo Library. **p.184** E. T. Archive. **p.185** *top left* Camera Press; *top right* Topham; *bottom* Imperial War Museum, London. **p.186** Bayerischen Staatsbibliotek, Munich. **p.187** *top* Imperial War Museum, London; *bottom* Wiener Library. **p.188** *top* Wiener Library/The Beate Klarsfeld Foundation, New York; *bottom* Wiener Library/William Collins and Sons Ltd. **p.189** Yad Vashem, Jerusalem. **p.190** Hulton Deutsch Collection. **p.191** *top* Wiener Library; *bottom* Popperfoto. **p.192** Yad Vashem, Jerusalem. **p.193** *top* Wiener Library; *bottom* Camera Press. **p.194** *top* Public Record Office; *centre* Imperial War Museum, London; *bottom* Bridgeman Art Library/Prado, Madrid/Pablo Picasso *Guernica* 1937 © DACS 1993. **p.195** Imperial War Museum, London. **p.196** *top* Bildarchiv Preussischer Kulturbesitz. **p.198** E.T. Archive. **p.199** Hulton Deutsch Collection. **p.201** Centre for the Study of Cartoons and Caricature/Vicky, Evening Standard/Solo. **p.202** *top, centre left, bottom right* Imperial War Museum, London; *centre right* Punch Library; *bottom left* Evening Standard/Solo. **p.203** *top left* Ullstein; *top right and bottom* Hulton Deutsch Collection; *centre* Bildarchiv Presussischer Kulturbesitz. **p.204** *top* Evening Standard/Solo; *bottom* Imperial War Museum, London. **p.205** *top* Saul Steinberg; *centre* Evening Standard/Solo. **p.206** *top* Novosti Photo Library; *bottom* Mansell Collection. **p.207** Peter Newark's American Pictures. **p.208** E.T. Archive. **p.210** *left* School of Slavonic and Eastern European Studies; *right* Centre for the Study of Cartoons and Caricature/ Evening Standard/Solo. **p.211** Popperfoto. **p.212** *top* Centre for the Study of Cartoons and Caricature/Evening Standard/Solo. **p.213** *top* Evening Standard/Solo; *bottom* Centre for the Study of Cartoons and Caricature/ Evening Standard/Solo.